AN INTRODUCTION TO
HUMAN-COMPUTER INTERACTION

AN INTRODUCTION TO
HUMAN-COMPUTER INTERACTION

Paul A. Booth

Department of Computing,
Manchester Polytechnic, U.K.

LEA LAWRENCE ERLBAUM ASSOCIATES, PUBLISHERS LEA
Hove and London (UK)   Hillsdale (USA)

Reprinted 1990, 1991, 1992, 1995

Lawrence Erlbaum Associates Ltd., Publishers
27 Palmeira Mansions
Church Road
Hove
East Sussex, BN3 2FA
UK

British Library Cataloguing in Publication Data

Booth, Paul A.
An introduction to human-computer interaction
1. Man. Interactions with computer systems
I. Title
004'.01'9

ISBN 0-86377-123-8

Printed and bound in the UK by BPC Wheatons Ltd, Exeter

DEDICATION

To my parents, Gordon and Joan,
and my wife, Gill,
for their love and support

Contents

Acknowledgements

I began writing this book as a set of notes for students during the summer of 1987. Phil Scown suggested that a book might be a good idea, and I am grateful for this prompting. It was Phil Marsden who encouraged me to send these notes, in the form of a couple of draft chapters, to a publisher. Consequently, Michael Forster, Patricia Simpson, Rohays Perry and Melanie Tarrant at Lawrence Erlbaum became involved. I would like to thank Phil Marsden for his enthusiasm and encouragement, and for his comments on various sections of the book, and Michael, Patricia, Melanie and Rohays for their help and commitment.

Several people have contributed comments, criticisms, ideas and suggestions. These include: John Bastow, Niels Bjørn-Andersen, Gill Brown, Adrian Castell, Simon Davis, Dan Diaper, Ken Eason, Chris Fowler, Thomas Green, Lars Ginnerup, Adrian Jackson, Mark Kirby, Linda Macaulay, Gilbert Mansell, Nick McMillan, Andrew Monk, Mike Sharples, Deborah Twigger, David Woods and several anonymous reviewers. In addition, Amanda Prail and Brendan McManus were influential in the development of a number of the ideas in Chapter Five. I am especially grateful to Chris Marshall and Peggy Newton, who commented in detail on all of the chapters in the book, and to Jon Gomersall, who not only provided comments, but also helped me with several of the more complex figures used in some of the chapters.

Gill Brown co-authored two chapters, while Chris Marshall and Phil Marsden co-authored one chapter each. Their salutary and patient approach was very much appreciated, particularly when I misinterpreted and distorted their contributions. I have been saved from a number of embarrassing mistakes, and this book is undoubtedly much improved as a result of the help I received from all who read the earlier drafts. It goes without saying, that any inaccuracies or deficiencies that remain are entirely the responsibility of the author, although I will, no doubt, find some excuse or scapegoat when any mistakes that have slipped through the net are discovered.

I must also thank various friends for their interest and support during the arduous task of producing this book. I would particularly like to thank Pete Kennedy and Lian Trowers for providing a happy and untroubled refuge from the writing process, and Graham Wheatly for his welcome distractions and interruptions. I am deeply indebted to John Perkins, for although he was unaware of this project, he has imparted a positive outlook which has guided much of what I have done.

I would also like to thank both the Booth (Gordon, Joan, Susan and Sally) and the Brown (Gordon, Barbara, Michael, Alison and David) families for their encouragement and support. Most of all, however, I am indebted to my wife, who has been a constant source of inspiration, and suffered many hours of my self-enforced isolation. Finally, I would like to thank George, Katie, Ben and Sam (the cat and the dogs) for providing endless amusement and entertainment.

Preface

Within academia, industry and government there is a growing awareness of the importance of human-computer interaction, both in research and in commercial terms. Every year, as the proportion of the population that use computers increases, then so the number of people who experience difficulties in understanding and using these machines also grows. Moreover, many businesses, both large and small, are discovering that the computer systems in which they have invested large resources have become the foci for conflict within their organizations, or remain idle because they do not properly support users in their everyday tasks.

The purpose of this book is to explain the underlying causes of these cognitive, social and organizational problems. In essence, the aim is to provide a comprehensive and readable introduction to the burgeoning discipline of human-computer interaction. The book is intended for readers with almost any background and assumes as little as possible.

Each chapter is preceded by an overview which outlines the major topic areas, while the main body of the text deals with the ideas and themes within these areas. Towards the end of each chapter a summary of the principal points of interest is provided, together with a selective annotated bibliography. This bibliography is intended as a guide to the literature, to allow readers to pursue their own particular interests once they have become familiar with the overall field of knowledge dealt with in the chapter.

The book begins with a definition of human-computer interaction and a discussion of the various disciplines that contribute towards the field. Human-computer interaction is characterized as consisting of five major areas of study; research into interactional hardware and software, research into matching models, research at the task level, research into design, and research into organizational impact.

At the interactional level, input and output devices are discussed, as well as the principles behind speech generation and recognition. The process of communication that occurs via these input and output devices can be thought of as a form of dialogue. Indeed, the similarities and differences between this human-computer dialogue and normal human dialogue are discussed at some length.

However, the concept of dialogue at the interface is inadequate to capture all aspects of the communicative process that occurs between user and computer. Consequently, the discussion moves away from considering the observable processes that occur at the interface, and the notion of the user's cognitive model of the task and computer system is introduced. Moreover, some of the cognitive modelling techniques for predicting the user's behaviour are described and discussed

Although this theoretically orientated cognitive approach provides a basis for understanding human-computer interaction, it has been the human factors or ergonomic approach that has concentrated upon the practicalities of measuring and improving the usability of computer systems. Therefore, the question of how to define the usability of a computer system is addressed, as well as the problem of how to measure a system against this sometimes vague concept.

The notion of evaluating the usability of a computer system is also introduced as part of the discussion on the design process and the move towards iterative design and evaluation. However, not all of the research within the design field has centred around a human factors approach. Consequently, the mathematical approach to specifying systems, as well as the cognitive approach to modelling the user are discussed with respect to the design process.

Following this discussion, some of the methodologies that are intended to encourage socio-technical design are outlined. Socio-technical design is where both the technical and the social implications of a design are considered as part of the design process. Indeed, the impact that computer systems can have on users and the organizations in which they work is considerable. This influence, and the general organizational aspects of computer systems, are discussed at some length, from the impact that a system has on the user's role, to the changes it evokes in the organization's structure and functioning.

However, the picture of human-computer interaction portrayed in this book can only be considered as a snapshot of an ever-changing field. Therefore, some of the trends in human-computer interaction are addressed, from developments in interactional hardware and software, to the impact of intelligent systems on dialogue, and the move towards new ideas such as organizational interfaces. Finally, the relationship between theory and practice within human-computer interaction is discussed, as well as the role of cognitive science and cognitive engineering within the area.

The field of human-computer interaction cannot accurately be described as unified. It often appears as a disorganized collection of research areas that are only gradually building into a coherent and well-structured field. However, this process of development requires time, and presently the area can often appear confusing and difficult to those who are new to the subject. The aim of this book is to present human-computer interaction in terms that are as clear and as concise as possible, while at the same time, attempting to avoid oversimplifying important issues and ideas. As a result, it is hoped that readers will feel confident to explore this interesting and exciting field further.

1 Introducing Human-Computer Interaction

OVERVIEW

Firstly, some of the reasons why we need research into human-computer interaction are discussed, and an explanation as to why human-computer interaction has become such an important issue in recent years is offered. Following this, the question *what is human-computer interaction* is addressed and a series of definitions is offered. Finally, the roles of the disciplines that contribute towards human-computer interaction are examined.

INTRODUCTION

Throughout academia, industry and government there is an increasing awareness of the importance of human-computer interaction. Evidence of this development can be seen not only in the interest shown by the general computing press, but also in the growing number of articles and books devoted to human-computer interaction (HCI).

The computing industry has been encouraged to increase its expenditure on HCI by large research programmes. These programmes have often funded joint collaborative projects between computer companies and academic institutions. Consequently, the strengthened links between academia and industry, together with the expansion in the numbers of researchers concerned with HCI, have led to a considerable growth in the numbers of HCI conferences, seminars and workshops.

1

The past 10 years have witnessed large-scale development and progress in HCI and today HCI continues to expand, both in financial terms and in terms of the areas and disciplines it embraces. The disciplines involved in HCI will be discussed later in this chapter, but first it may be useful to consider why it is developing in this way.

Why Do We Need Research Into HCI?

In the opinion of many researchers in the HCI field, although computer technology has made great advances over the past 30 years, the designer's knowledge and understanding of the user has not significantly changed. It is now the communication with the user that is seen as the greatest obstacle to the efficient functioning of many systems.

Unfortunately, angry and frustrated users are the norm rather than the exception, as many researchers in the field have noted, including Bertino: "Users of advanced hardware machines are often disappointed by the cumbersome data entry procedures, obscure error messages, intolerant error handling and confusing sequences of cluttered screens. In particular, novice users feel frustrated, insecure and even frightened when they have to deal with a system whose behaviour is incomprehensible, mysterious and intimidating." (Bertino, 1985).

The importance of this problem has been highlighted by Baker (1977), who estimated that *people costs* exceed *machine costs* in HCI for 95% of the time. Many systems have been developed that are considered to be functionally excellent, but perform badly in the real world. The poor performance of these systems has been linked to the human-computer interface (Eason, Damodaran, & Stewart, 1975) and it is now generally accepted that poor interfaces can lead to stressed users, lower work rates, decreased job satisfaction and even higher absenteeism. These undesirable effects can be produced in a number of ways. Some of the following examples provide a flavour of what sometimes creates difficulties:

Designers do not properly understand the user, the user's needs and the user's working environment.

Computer systems require users to remember too much information.

Computer systems are intolerant of minor errors.

Interactional techniques are sometimes used for inappropriate tasks (e.g. command language may be unsuited for use in a task requiring the production of graphics/pictures).

As a result a variety of undesirable effects are produced:

Computer systems often do not provide the information that is needed, or produce information in a form which is undesirable as far as the user is concerned. Alternatively, systems may provide information that is not required.

Computer systems can seem confusing to new users.

Computer systems sometimes do not provide all of the functions the user requires, and more often provide functions that the user does not need.

Computer systems force users to perform tasks in undesirable ways.

Computer systems can cause unacceptable changes in the structure and practices of organizations, creating dissatisfaction and conflict.

While these illustrations may underline the need for research into HCI, a question that they raise is, if computer systems have been in serious commercial use for the past 25 years why has HCI only become an important issue in the last 10 to 15 years?

The Growth of HCI

In previous decades the majority of computer users were themselves programmers and designers of computer systems. Consequently, a person using a computer system was likely to have been immersed in the same conventions and culture as the individual who designed it. In recent years, however, there has been a substantial growth in the number of users who are not computer experts. This change has focused attention upon the needs of what Eason (1976) has termed the *naive user* and the lack of understanding of the naive user on the part of many designers. Shackel summarizes the situation in the following way: "The users [of computer systems] are no longer mainly computer professionals, but are mostly *discretionary* users. As a result, the designers are no longer typical of or equivalent to users; but the designers may not realize just how unique and therefore how unrepresentative they are." (Shackel, 1985).

As designers are no longer typical of most users, we need tools, techniques, design practices and methodologies that will inform design and development teams of how users behave at an interface, and what users require from a system. It is a widely held view that this will require a multi-disciplinary approach. Branscomb, a Vice President and Chief Scientist of IBM, clearly adopts this view: "No longer the exclusive tool of specialists, computers have become both commonplace and indispensable. Yet they remain harder to use than they should be. It should be no more necessary to read a 300 page book of instructions before using a computer than before driving an unfamiliar automobile. But much research in both cognitive and computer science will be required to learn how to build computers that are easy to use." (Branscomb, 1983, cited in Shackel, 1984).

WHAT IS HCI?

We have examined the question of the need for research into HCI. We now need to consider the question, *what is HCI*?

The term *"human-computer interaction"* is commonly used interchangeably with terms such as "man-machine interaction" (MMI), "computer and human interaction" (CHI) and "human-machine interaction" (HMI). Terms which use "machine" may be taken to have a wider remit than terms where the term "computer" is used. However, these terms are often taken to mean the same thing, although researchers may argue over which is the most appropriate term. Here, and throughout following chapters, the term *"human-computer interaction"* will be used, not because it is in any way *better* than other terms, but because it is the most common in the literature.

Having decided that *"human-computer interaction"* (HCI) is the term we prefer to use, we now need to define it. An oversimplified definition of HCI might say that *it is the study of the interaction between humans and computers*. This may be acceptable as a general definition of HCI, but alone it does not do justice to the true complexity and multi-disciplinary nature of the subject. Therefore, rather than suggest an extended alternative, five further definitions will be offered, each of which covers one aspect of HCI. These definitions reflect the different areas of study within HCI (see Fig. 1.1) and their purpose is to supplement rather than replace the general definition just given. It should also be mentioned that the terms and concepts used in these definitions will be discussed in greater detail in later chapters.

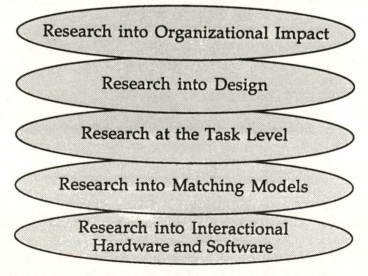

FIG.1.1.   A representation of the different areas of study within HCI.

Research Into Interactional Hardware and Software

First, and possibly most obviously, HCI is concerned with both the software and hardware of interactional techniques and technologies. While in the past the most common form of input has been in a command language dialogue style via a keyboard, many more methods are becoming available (the term *command language* simply means that the user types in commands in a particular format to the computer). For example, many systems are being developed that present the user with menus of alternative commands. These new techniques, however, present not only new possibilities, but sometimes new problems. The problems of interactional techniques, and how they affect communication between the user and the system, is one of the central issues of HCI. Subsequently, *HCI is concerned not only with how present input and output technologies affect interaction, but also with the consequences of new techniques such as speech recognition and generation (input and output). The aim of HCI is to both develop interactional techniques and to suggest where and in what situations these technologies and techniques might be put to best use.*

Research Into Matching Models

Second, HCI is the study of *how* users interact with computer systems. The central issue here, and throughout the whole of HCI, is how to match the computer system's model of the task to that of the user. If models are to match then both parties to the communicative process must have a shared understanding of the task at hand. That is to say, that communication requires *mutual knowledge* (Habermas, 1981). Consequently, the knowledge users need to operate a system, and *how* users apply their knowledge, has been the focus of much research aimed at providing tools to predict and describe user behaviour at the human-computer interface. In short, *HCI is concerned with providing theories and tools for modelling the knowledge a user possesses and brings to bear on a task. Its purpose is to enable designers to build more usable systems by making explicit the user's model of the task and system.*

Research at the Task Level

Third, successful HCI depends upon systems fulfilling users' information needs and allowing them the freedom to perform tasks in the way that they wish. The *task fit*—the extent to which a system provides the information and the facilities a user needs—is a major determinant of the success or failure of most computer systems (Eason, 1976). Therefore, good design requires the elicitation of the user's functional and information needs, and this is often more complicated than it first seems. For example, the user's needs may not be fixed and constant, but may vary. This, in turn, may determine whether a task needs to be structured or unstructured.

This discussion of the task may appear similar to the discussion associated with the last definition. The crucial difference, however, is that the last definition concentrated upon *how* users perform tasks whereas here we are concerned with the overall nature of tasks and the users' information needs, although these areas clearly overlap to some extent. Consequently, *at a task level our concerns are with the means by which the user's needs and a system's functions and information provision might be matched. The purpose of HCI is to develop methods for determining users' needs, thus ensuring that systems provide users with the functions they need and the information they require (in the form they desire) without excessive effort on their part.*

Research Into Design and Development

Fourth, HCI is the study of both the individuals involved in design, and the design and development process itself. If any of the methods and findings produced by research into HCI are to influence the design of systems then they must be compatible with the process of design. Therefore, a consideration of the design and development process is, by necessity, an integral part of HCI.

The design stage in the life-cycle of many software products suffers from both inadequate *specification*, and a lack of communication between members of the design team. *Specification* is the process where the requirements and function of the system are agreed, or more often passed to the designers in the form of a document. A further compounding problem in design is that many designers pay more attention to the technical elegance of a system than they do to the more practical consideration of *is it usable?* This *technological determinism* (Bjørn-Andersen, Eason, & Robey, 1986) is one of the major obstacles to good systems design. Consequently, it can be concluded that *HCI is the study of the design process. The aim of HCI is to suggest how design might be improved by taking more account of the user. In short, this means engineering a shift from system-centred to user-centred design.*

Research Into Organizational Impact

Finally, HCI is the study of the impact that new systems have on organizations, as well as the impact they have on individuals and groups within these companies or corporations. When a system is installed within an organization the duties and responsibilities of many employees change. Groups of workers may find their status and influence within the new system has either increased or decreased. This includes secondary users as well as primary users (where primary users are those who interact directly with the new technology and secondary users are those who do not interact directly, but either provide input to the system, receive output or are affected by the system in some other way).

Understandably, change within any organization can generate difficulties, firstly for those who are introducing the new system and secondly, for the organization as a whole. Research in HCI is directed towards the *examination of the impact a new system has upon the roles of individual users and user groups within an organization. The objective of such research is to suggest both design and implementation techniques that might prevent problems such as job deskilling and conflict between groups.*

None of the definitions given above accurately characterizes HCI when taken alone. HCI has been artificially divided into these five supplementary definitions, and while this partitioning might prove to be a useful way of considering some of the different problem areas, in reality these areas are not easily distinguished. The true picture is of a multi-disciplinary approach to a whole series of different but related problems. The question that this introduces is, *which disciplines contribute towards HCI research?*

ROLES VARIOUS DISCIPLINES PLAY WITHIN HCI

There may be general agreement on the need for a multi-disciplinary approach, but what exactly are the roles that the various disciplines within HCI fulfill? Here, it is suggested that there are 10 major disciplines that

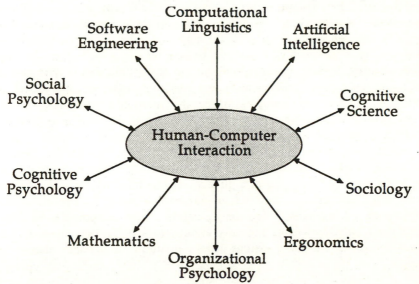

FIG. 1.2.   An overall view of the disciplines which contribute towards HCI.

contribute to research into HCI (see Fig. 1.2). This list is very much a personal view. It may be argued that other areas of study have a role to play, such as systems theory, neuroscience, anthropology or physiology and anthropometry. As part of the perspective presented here, and mainly for reasons of brevity, their contribution is considered to be subsumed within either one or several of these 10 contributing disciplines.

Ergonomics

Some researchers in HCI regard ergonomics (also sometimes known as human factors) as the study and design of the physical characteristics of computer workstations. It is certainly true that the discipline of ergonomics has a great deal of experience of the design of automobiles and aircraft, for example, that can be applied in HCI (Shneiderman, 1987). Ergonomists however, would strongly disagree with such a limited definition. They would argue that ergonomics is as much about the cognitive, social and organizational aspects of HCI as it is about the physical design of hardware.

The differences in the use of the term *ergonomics* can be traced to the origins of the discipline. Ergonomics grew out of the experiences of the Second World War, when there was found to be a need to design machines to suit their human operators. Ergonomics began at this physical level and this tradition has remained. However, many ergonomists quickly realized that considering only the physical requirements of humans was not enough. As a result, the discipline broadened to include cognitive, social and organizational aspects of human behaviour, yet the image of ergonomics as a discipline concerned only with the physical aspects of machinery has remained in some quarters. Consequently, the term *ergonomics* can be used in two senses; first, to mean the study of the physical design of hardware in HCI, and second, to mean almost any research regarding any aspect of human interaction with complex machinery (including computers). In this book the terms *ergonomics* and *human factors* will be used mainly in the second, broader sense.

Whether ergonomics is considered in the narrow or broad sense, there is little doubt that it possesses a great deal of knowledge that can be applied to HCI For over 40 years the discipline of ergonomics has been concerned with fitting machines to the needs of human operators. As a result of this experience, a large body of knowledge, together with an approach, has been developed This knowledge not only applies to specific human needs, but more importantly, to the questions of how to study and accommodate these needs.

Software Engineering

Software engineering may be viewed as the "odd one out". It is an area of engineering, as the name implies, while the other areas are all *pure* disciplines. Nevertheless, because of its role in the control and management of the design and development process, software engineering appears to have an important role to play, regardless of whether it is a *pure* or engineering discipline.

Software engineering arose, as a discipline, out of the software crisis that developed during the late-1960s to mid-1970s, although its origins can be traced to two conferences that occurred earlier. Before this period little attention had been paid to the needs of developing software. The major thrust of the computer advance had concentrated upon hardware development. However, the demands placed upon those who wrote software grew. More complex programs were needed, and this complexity meant that teams of programmers were needed rather than individuals. Projects required careful planning to ensure that the different pieces of a program fitted together. These projects also needed careful management to ensure that the software was developed within certain cost constraints. Furthermore, management skills were required, not only the skills to plan the technical aspects of these projects, but also the skills to manage the people within them. People with the skills and knowledge to do this did not exist, and consequently the *software crisis* arose, although others have termed this problem the *complexity barrier* (Steward, 1987) as the problems that arose were entirely due to the size and complexity of the software that was being written.

The software crisis of the mid-1970s has given shape to the discipline of software engineering. It is not simply about writing computer programs, but is concerned with using formal methods to check the logical consistency of programs, planning complex technical projects, managing personnel, managing costs and producing competitive and usable software (Conte, Dunsmore, & Shen, 1986).

Moreover, software engineering is concerned with the development of new methods for producing software. The purpose of new languages and programming techniques is not only that they should be more cost effective, but that they should produce more usable and hence more saleable computer systems. However, the role of software engineering with respect to HCI is not only to provide new tools to improve the interaction between human and computer, but also to manage and control the design process. Consequently, the interests of HCI and software engineering are inextricably bound together.

Mathematics

The discipline of mathematics it not something that is easily defined if true justice is to be done to its vast array of areas and applications. The role of mathematics within HCI, however, can be more easily stated.

Mathematical formalisms have been used for some time to verify the structure and logic of computer programs. Some researchers are now applying these formalisms (or grammars) to the human-computer interface as a means by which logical inconsistencies can be exposed. Furthermore, these formal grammars (or analytic techniques) are being used as a form of task analysis to assess the cognitive complexity of a task or interface.

Consequently, the mathematical approach to HCI can help us to expose the logical relationships between various system elements. A mathematical approach, via formal specifications and descriptions of interfaces, allows us to show systems in new and revealing lights.

Cognitive Psychology

In the last century James (1890) described psychology as *the science of mental life*. However, the early part of the 20th century saw psychology in the USA dominated by the behaviourist paradigm. Within Germany, however, an interest in cognition continued with the Gestalt psychologists (as well as people such as Piaget in Switzerland, and Bartlett in the UK). The Gestalt school of psychological thought, built on the tradition established by Wundt (1907), laid the groundwork for the research into some of the most significant areas of cognitive research, such as the cognitive aspects of perception and attention.

It was not until the late 1950s that interest in human cognition redeveloped in the USA and in the UK (see Scane, 1987). Curiously enough, it was the invention of the computer that provided a focus for the re-emergence of the study of mental life. The computer provided a new paradigm for psychology; that of the human as an *information processor*. It was this new paradigm that became cognitive psychology. A formal definition of cognitive psychology has been provided by Mayer, who states that: "Cognitive psychology is the scientific analysis of human mental processes and structures with the aim of understanding human behaviour." (Mayer, 1981).

Over the last 30 years cognitive psychology has developed a large body of knowledge about human cognitive processes and structures. Much of what cognitive psychology knows of human information processing and behaviour is of use within HCI (i.e. the constraints of the human mind, the errors we make, etc.), and of particular use are the investigative methods and techniques that an empirical approach to the study of human behaviour has to offer. Many of the pitfalls of studying human behaviour have already been encountered within cognitive psychology, and knowledge of these problems, particularly knowledge of how to avoid these problems, is likely to be of great use in the study of HCI.

Artificial Intelligence

Artificial intelligence is generally considered to have begun with Alan Turing's paper in 1950. Here Turing addressed the question: "Can machines think?". Turing suggested that this question was absurd and proposed an imitation game as an alternative. The Turing Test, as it has become known, is based on the idea of a game where an interrogator can ask either a person or a computer a set of questions. Following these questions the interrogator must correctly identify whether it was a machine or a human that has been replying to the questions. Turing believed that by the year 2000 machines of such sophistication would exist that an interrogator would only have a 70% chance of providing the right answer. While the confidence that Alan Turing displayed in setting a date is no longer universally shared within the artificial intelligence (AI) community generally, there is a widely held view that significant advances have been made since Turing's pioneering paper.

One definition of artificial intelligence has been provided by Charniak and McDermott who state that: "Artificial intelligence is the study of mental faculties through the use of computational models." (Charniak & McDermott, 1985). This approach to understanding cognition has provided many workable and interesting methods for representing cognitive processes and structures. As it is, artificial intelligence offers the study of HCI two things: first, it offers a variety of cognitive models for representing the user, as well as the means to test these models. Second, it offers the possibility of intelligent systems for use in HCI. That is to say, intelligent systems that might adapt to the needs of the user, systems that might intelligently help the user understand the system, and systems that might tutor the user in an educational setting.

Computational Linguistics

Computational linguistics has been defined by Grishman as: "...the study of computer systems for understanding and generating natural language." (Grishman, 1986). In many ways computational linguistics might be seen as the link between artificial intelligence and linguistics generally. It has its origins in the work of Chomsky (1957), who believed that the structure of sentences reflects deeper representations of meaning which are common to all languages. Chomsky proposed a transformational grammar to represent the relationship between the surface structure of sentences and their deeper meanings within human memory. Later, other theories were proposed and the computer provided a convenient means for testing these complex grammars.

The work within computational linguistics has expanded to cover not only the syntactic structure and semantics (the meanings) of language, but also the *pragmatics* of human dialogue. Pragmatics is concerned, not only with the meanings of the natural language sentences, but also their meanings within the context of a conversation or dialogue.

Computational linguistics, as a discipline, has two potential contributions to the study of HCI. The first is a better understanding of the dialogue that occurs at the human-computer interface. The second is the possibility of natural language systems. Such systems would be able to converse with the user in much the same way as humans speak to one another and are seen in some quarters as vital components for some of the computer systems of the future.

Cognitive Science

Cognitive science has its origins in the early- to mid-1970s. It developed, not out of any one discipline, but out of the realization that a multi-disciplinary approach is required if we are to understand higher mental processes and structures. The rigid experimental approach was viewed as inadequate as a means of investigating these higher cognitive processes. This does not mean that empiricism was rejected, only that there was seen to be a need to acquire evidence about the nature of cognition from a variety of sources, rather than just one or two. Gardner (1985) lists the major disciplines within cognitive science which might contribute towards our understanding of cognition: philosophy, psychology, linguistics, anthropology, neuroscience and artificial intelligence. Gardner's view of cognitive science, however, excludes some of the more socially orientated areas of study, as well as considerations of issues such as *emotion*. Others, such as Norman (1981b; 1981c) see cognitive science as having a wider remit, and it is this wider interpretation of the term *cognitive science* which is adopted here (see Leventhal & Scherer, 1987, for a discussion of emotion and cognition).

There are several definitions of cognitive science (e.g. Miller, 1979; Norman, 1981b; 1981c), and while few agree on all of the details of what cognitive science is, most agree on its essence, which is that of *a collection of interwoven disciplines whose overall aim is to understand and explain the higher cognitive processes, such as understanding, thought and creativity. In other words, cognitive science is an approach to cognition that is more global than any of its constituent elements, such as cognitive psychology or artificial intelligence.* Bearing this in mind, the question that now arises is, what does cognitive science offer to the study of HCI?

In attempting to predict and understand users' behaviour at the human-computer interface, it has become apparent that we need to understand users from a cognitive point of view. In other words, we need to understand what users understand and *how* they understand it. It is at this point that the larger global theories of cognitive science are of relevance, for in applying the findings from artificial intelligence and cognitive psychology we are, in effect, applying cognitive science (Norman, 1986 and 1987, calls this application *cognitive engineering*). Much of the research within cognitive science has been outside of the confines of rigid empiricism (some of the work within artificial intelligence for example) and consequently cognitive science has a great deal to offer within those areas which require a degree of interpretation, such as issues associated with *understanding* and *meaning*. For example, how users understand complex systems is of great importance in HCI, and the mental models that users construct have been the focus of much research. (Mental models will be considered in detail in Chapter Four; for the moment they can be considered as knowledge structures that users construct within their own memory to enable them to understand and predict a computer system or any other complex device.) In short, what cognitive science offers to HCI is *a more interpretative approach to examining the role of knowledge, meaning and understanding within human-computer interaction.*

Social Psychology

As a discipline, social psychology has grown throughout the 20th century. Yet most research into social psychology has occurred only within the last 30 years (Shaver, 1977). Gergen and Gergen define social psychology as: "...the systematic study of human interaction and its psychological basis." (Gergen & Gergen, 1981). Social psychology is concerned with the individual actor, and how individuals act with respect to other actors, but what relevance has this to HCI?

Within HCI it is generally accepted that we need a better understanding of the social aspects of both system design and implementation. As has been mentioned in the section on software engineering, systems are rarely designed by individuals, but by teams of people. How these individuals interact may have important consequences for many of the design decisions that are taken. Another area of interest that concerns social psychology is system implementation. During the implementation of systems there is often resistance to change, as has been mentioned earlier. These difficulties are sometimes so great that it is possible that systems, which are technically excellent and potentially usable, could be rendered unusable if proper account is not taken of the interests various individuals and groups have, in both the existing system and the system which is being implemented (Bjørn-Andersen et al., 1986).

Organizational Psychology

An organization has been defined as: "...a collection of interacting and interdependent individuals who work toward common goals and whose relationships are determined according to a certain structure." (Duncan, 1978). Organizational psychology, according to Duncan, is concerned with aspects of individual behaviour such as learning, perception, and decision making as a practical application of problem-solving. However, organizational psychology is also concerned with the relationships between groups of individuals within a business or institution. Indeed, Schein (1970) suggests that organizational psychology has developed from its individually orientated industrial psychology standpoint, to the systems approach that is presently employed. From this viewpoint an organization is considered in terms of its individuals, how these individuals interact, and the effect that this interaction has upon the organization.

Organizational psychology offers HCI a knowledge of businesses and institutions that can be used to understand the impact of computer systems upon these organizations. It can provide techniques for the study of these organizations, and can help to direct research aimed at identifying problems that are created when computer systems are introduced into everyday work environments.

Sociology

Goldthorpe (1974) defines sociology as: "...the scientific study of human social behaviour", while Burke defines it as: "...the study of human society, with the emphasis on generalizing about its structure." (Burke, 1980). Like most of the social sciences, sociology has a strong philosophical background, and can trace its origins from the Greek philosophers to Durkheim and Weber. Although the sociological aspects of political theory formed much of the early subject matter for the discipline, it has since broadened to include many more modern issues; from the sociology of the family to social mobility.

While much of the work on political and historical sociology may not be pertinent to the design of efficient human-computer systems, the same cannot be said of other areas of sociology. The sociological approach to bureaucracy and social role appears particularly relevant to the processes of system design and implementation. Moreover, sociology lends itself to the study of issues such as the influence of the user's social class, gender and education in determining the acceptance of the user within a system. It seems likely that a sociological perspective on these areas of HCI concern would complement the study of the same areas from a social psychology standpoint. This is because social psychology considers the individual within a social setting while sociological study adopts a more holistic view.

The Neglected Disciplines

While there may be general agreement that HCI is a multi-disciplinary venture, not all of the disciplines we have just examined are represented equally. Some disciplines potentially contribute towards several of the five areas of HCI research identified earlier (see Fig. 1.3). Moreover, some disciplines appear to have been almost totally neglected with respect to HCI. Therefore, it may be useful to understand a little of the coverage the different disciplines receive within the HCI literature.

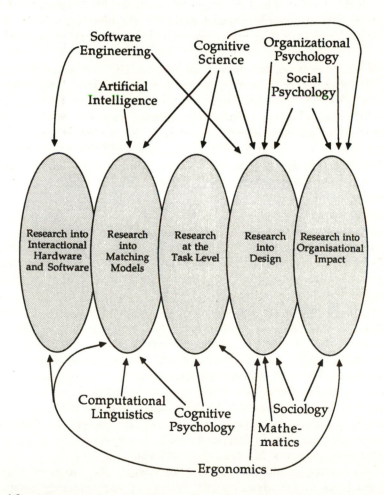

FIG. 1.3.   A representation of the different areas of study within HCI, which shows how the 10 disciplines feed into these areas.

Ergonomics is probably the discipline which has been associated with the study of HCI for the longest period of time, stretching back even to the mid-1960s. Cognitive psychology is equally well established, and its presence was confirmed in *"The Psychology of Human-Computer Interaction"* by Card, Moran, and Newell (1983).

The roles of artificial intelligence and cognitive science developed once a need was perceived for a modelling approach within HCI, such as that of Card et al. Recently, these two subjects have come to be accepted as integral parts of HCI. The position of computational linguistics within HCI has developed gradually over the past 10 years. First, its relevance arose out of the perceived need for natural language interfaces. More recently, as the true complexity of human-computer dialogue has been recognized, then computational linguistics has become more acceptable as part of mainstream study.

Curiously, there is not the interaction between HCI and software engineering which might be expected, given their shared goals and common subject area. While software engineering may not be totally neglected within HCI, and although software engineering may continue to thrive independently of *human-computer interaction*, the two areas are certainly not integrated to the extent that many researchers believe would be most profitable. In other words, although software engineering is not neglected within HCI, it does not appear to be integrated into HCI in the same way that other disciplines are.

Social psychology and sociology have been classed as the *neglected disciplines* as they have not been given the representation and coverage they deserve within the literature, given the importance of the problems that they might address. This may be because most studies of HCI have tended to concentrate upon one user and one system. The questions regarding several users working together, either at or through a system, are only beginning to be addressed. Consequently, the importance of social psychology and sociology has only, more recently, become apparent. While there is some work from a social psychology perspective (e.g. Bannon, 1986a), and although it has been significant and useful, the volume of this work has not been great. Worse still is the representation of sociology within HCI research. There has been HCI work from a sociological viewpoint, for example there is a section on the "Sociological implications of office automation" in the proceedings of the "Human Factors in Computer Systems" conference, held in Maryland (1982). The volume of sociologically orientated work, however, has been pitifully small.

The contribution sociology might make towards the study of HCI is within the areas of the organizational impact of implementing computer systems, the values that people place upon new technology, and the ways in which technology might discriminate against groups or individuals.

Research within this area, from an organizational perspective, is well established (e.g. Bjørn-Andersen et al., 1986), but it is also recognized as one of the least understood areas of HCI interest. Whether the representation of social psychology and sociology within HCI increases in the coming years may depend, not only upon the organizations that fund research, but also upon researchers from those areas taking on the HCI challenge.

In summary, software engineering, mathematics, ergonomics, cognitive psychology, cognitive science, artificial intelligence, computational linguistics, social psychology, organizational psychology and sociology have knowledge of human behaviour and research techniques to offer HCI. Applying the knowledge from these disciplines to HCI is sometimes known as *human factors* or *ergonomics*. There is nothing wrong with this, but it is important for anyone new to the field to recognize that this term is sometimes used in this way.

The view of HCI presented in this chapter is of a multi-disciplinary venture with boundaries which are easily traversed. The blend of disciplines within HCI is an undoubted strength and will, it is hoped, one day lead to a cohesive and unified theory of *human-computer interaction*.

SUMMARY

The past 10 years has witnessed large-scale development and progress in *human-computer interaction* and today HCI continues to expand, both in financial terms and in terms of the areas and disciplines it embraces. Terms such as "man-machine interaction" (MMI), "computer and human interaction" (CHI) and "human-machine interaction" (HMI) are commonly used interchangeably with *"human-computer interaction"* and these terms are often taken to mean the same thing. We need research into HCI because the poor performance in the real world of many systems, that were considered to be functionally excellent, has been linked to failures at the human-computer interface.

HCI is the study and theory of the interaction between humans and complex technology (usually computers). HCI is concerned with how current input and output technologies affect interaction and in what situations these technologies and techniques might be put to best use. It is also concerned with modelling the knowledge a user possesses and brings to bear on a task. HCI's interests at a task level are in the means by which the user's information needs and a system's information provision might be matched. In terms of design, HCI is the study of the design process, and its overall aim is to engineer a shift from system-centred to user-centred design. At an organizational level, the objective of HCI research is to suggest both design and implementation techniques that might prevent problems such as job deskilling and conflict between groups.

HCI is a multi-disciplinary venture involving not only ergonomics and software engineering, but also cognitive psychology, cognitive science, social psychology, mathematics, organizational psychology, artificial intelligence, computational linguistics and sociology. The term *ergonomics* or *human factors* in HCI is sometimes used to refer to the application of any or all of these disciplines.

A SELECTIVE ANNOTATED BIBLIOGRAPHY

Allen, R. B. (1982). Cognitive factors in human interaction with computers. In A. N. Badre & B. Shneiderman (Eds.), *Directions in human-computer interaction.* Norwood, New Jersey: Ablex Publishing Corporation. *The paper is concerned with the user's cognitive processes at the interface. It is a wide-ranging review of some of the literature and introduces many of the ideas and concepts of cognitive psychology that are likely to be of relevance to HCI including sections on short-term memory, long-term memory and problem-solving. The paper goes on to consider the nature of the dialogue between the user and the computer. After an examination of some of the literature regarding both visual displays and non-visual modes of interaction, some of the research issues are addressed.*

Baecker, R. M. & Buxton, W. A. S. (Eds.) (1987). *Readings in human-computer interaction: A multidisciplinary approach.* Los Altos, California: Morgan Kaufmann. *This extensive book is a collection of over fifty of some of the most interesting and important papers in the recent HCI literature. The commentaries provided by the editors are easy to read and particularly informative. This book is highly recommended for anyone who wishes to gain a greater understanding of the different areas of HCI.*

Bertino, E. (1985). Design issues in interactive user interfaces. *Interfaces in Computing, 3,* 37–53. *This is a well-written review and introduction to HCI. Besides an examination of command languages, input/output devices, evaluation methods and the issues associated with information display, the user's requirements of a system and the user's model of a task and system are also considered. The section on the user's conceptual model is well worth reading.*

Eason, K. D. (1976). Understanding the naive computer user. *The Computer Journal, 19 (1),* 3–7. *This paper outlines the attributes of the "naive user" and has become something of a classic within HCI. The author explains why users differ from designers and relates these differences to the information needs of the user as well as differences in preferred task structure. The paper goes on to consider the roles of users within organizations, particularly the extent to which a user's role directly involves contact with the computer system. Finally, an outline for future work is presented based upon the six factors discussed (information needs, task structure, frequency of use, relationship between job and system, status and the technical language of the system).*

Gaines, B. R. & Shaw, M. L. G. (1986a). From timesharing to the sixth generation: The development of human computer. Part 1, *International Journal of Man-*

Machine Studies, 24, 1–27. See below.

Gaines, B. R. & Shaw, M. L. G. (1986b). Foundations of dialogue engineering: The development of human computer. Part 2. *International Journal of Man-Machine Studies, 24,* 101–123. *In these two articles the authors chart the progress of HCI and compare it with other subject areas. They argue that HCI has already passed through the "breakthrough", "replication" and "empirical" periods and that it is currently in the "theoretical" period, with the "automation" and "maturity" periods still to come. These two articles are recommended for HCI.*

Scane, R. (1987). A historical perspective. In M. M. Gardiner & B. Christie (Eds.), *Applying cognitive psychology to user-interface design.* Chichester: Wiley & Sons. *The author provides an interesting and readable history of cognitive psychology. Themes dating back to the greek philosophers are identified and the development of cognitive psychology is charted; from Wundt's thought experiments, through the "dark ages" of behaviourism up to the information-processing paradigm.*

Shackel, B. (1984). Information technology–a challenge to ergonomics and design! *Behaviour & Information Technology, 3 (4),* 263–275. *This begins by describing the extent to which information technology has grown before offering a definition. Following this, the author outlines the research needs, the design procedures, an ergonomics design procedure and the industrial design aspects associated with information technology. The longer term questions of "will we become a paperless society?", "will handwriting fade away?", "will we move towards speech input and output?", "will we all be connected to electronic mail systems?", are then considered. This article provides a readable overview of the development, not only of ergonomics in information technology, but also of information technology itself.*

Shneiderman, B. (1987). *Designing the user interface: Strategies for effective human–computer interaction.* Reading, Massachusetts: Addison-Wesley. *This comprehensive book reviews the techniques, methods and ideas that designers might need if they are to introduce human factors (ergonomics) into the design process. While not all issues are covered in great depth, this book provides a worthwhile account of almost every aspect of HCI today.*

Storrs, G., Rivers, R., & Canter, D. (1984). The future of man-machine interface research: a discussion and a framework for research. *Applied Ergonomics, 15 (1),* 61–63. *The authors chart the different areas of HCI research and suggest which disciplines might be of use, and in what way. This is an interesting perspective on the future of HCI that is still relevant despite its age.*

Suchman, L.A. (1988). *Plans and situated actions: The problem of human–machine communication.* Cambridge: Cambridge University Press. *This book is derived from Lucy Suchman's Ph.D. thesis. Unlike most Ph.D. theses, which are usually destined for dusty shelves in obscure corners of libraries, this is a major work in the field of HCI. The author's central concern is the role of knowledge and actions within their social and cognitive context. The book is an excellent example of how anthropological and sociological theory and technique can be applied within HCI. This book can only be described as essential reading.*

2

Interactional Devices
and Technologies

OVERVIEW

The chapter is divided into three sections. The first is concerned with devices and technologies that enable users to input information into a computer system, from keyboards to both direct and indirect pointing devices. In the second section the processes of speech recognition and generation are considered, as well as the question of the usefulness of speech. The third section deals with devices and technologies that are employed to present information to the user.

INTRODUCTION

The subject matter of this chapter fits into the first area of HCI research, described in Chapter One. In other words, it is concerned with the *hardware and software of human-computer interaction*. To some, this may appear to be the most important area of HCI development. The number of inter-actional devices, techniques and technologies is continuing to expand, and many of these new devices are finding important niches within different types of task. Some devices are so successful that their users now argue that they could not manage without them. For example, many experienced users of the Apple Macintosh personal computer find it difficult to imagine using the system without a mouse (a mouse is a hand-held pointing device which will be explained later in this chapter).

21

Not all devices are this successful, however, and there are undoubtedly tasks where the choice of interactional device is unlikely to make a significant impact upon human performance. It is this that leads some within the HCI field to err towards the view that the physical interface does not deserve such a prominent position within HCI research. Neither this view, nor the view that interactional devices should be the major focus of HCI research, appear to be justified. It is important to recognize that new interactional devices enable novel and potentially profitable forms of interaction. Consequently, research into the hardware and software of interaction has a major role to play within HCI. Nevertheless, new interactional devices and technologies do not constitute a general panacea for the many problems that are associated with human interaction with computers. For these reasons interactional devices and technologies have been given the same prominence within this book as the other areas of research within HCI.

INPUT DEVICES AND TECHNOLOGIES

An input device might be simply thought of as *any instrument, apparatus or mechanism that can be used to enter information into a computer.* As stated earlier, the development and refinement of input devices forms a significant part of HCI research. *The purpose of this development is to create input devices that maximize the advantages of human physical and cognitive characteristics, and so promote efficient, reliable and even pleasurable input to a system.*

The Keyboard

The keyboard is one of the oldest forms of input device, and for many tasks it is still the most efficient. Indeed, our stereotyped image of a computer is not complete without a keyboard sitting in front of a visual display unit (VDU).

The traditional layout of letters on the keyboard was proposed by Christopher Sholes during the middle of the last century, when there was a great deal of effort directed towards the development of reliable typewriters. The keyboard that Sholes developed slowed typists down. Consequently, the mechanism of these typewriters did not become jammed. As a result the keyboard that Sholes developed became the standard for all typewriters. This layout has been termed the QWERTY keyboard (see Fig. 2.1), but has the disadvantage that it is slow compared to other layouts such as the Dvorak keyboard (see Fig. 2.1). This is because the distance between the most frequently used keys is greater on the QWERTY keyboard than it is on the Dvorak keyboard (Shneiderman, 1987). Furthermore, the workload distribution between the hands appears to be more evenly balanced using the Dvorak keyboard. These two factors may account for why typists using

The QWERTY Keyboard

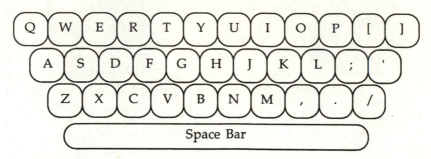

The Dvorak Keyboard

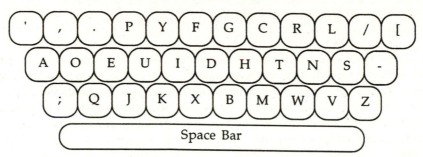

FIG. 2.1.   The QWERTY keyboard and the Dvorak keyboard layout.

the Dvorak keyboard make fewer errors than with the QWERTY keyboard (Martin, 1972; Kroemer, 1972). It appears unlikely, however, that the QWERTY keyboard will quickly go out of fashion, despite its evident disadvantages. Millions of typists around the world have learnt to use this less efficient type of keyboard and would be reluctant to relearn their skills.

Although the research into different keyboards has not led to generally accepted changes in layout, the research into the ergonomics of keyboards has produced more tangible effects upon design. It has been found that keyboards should gently slope towards the user (Emmons & Hirsch, 1982), and that keyboards should not be directly attached to the VDU, other than by a flexible lead (see Fig. 2.2) or infra-red link. A sloping keyboard appears to be more comfortable for users, while having the keyboard separate from the VDU allows users to sit with the keyboard just in front of them, while the screen (VDU) can be kept at any suitable distance. Furthermore, thinner keyboards and desks allow more room for users to fit their legs under the desk and obtain a comfortable posture.

FIG. 2.2. An older type of terminal (on the left) where the keyboard and the VDU were part of one unit, and a more modern type of terminal (on the right) where the keyboard can be adjusted for slope and is separate from the VDU.

These findings have had a significant effect upon hardware design, as can be seen in Fig. 2.2. The left-hand figure shows an old terminal where the keyboard is an integral part of the visual display unit. Towards the right of the figure a more modern terminal is shown, where the keyboard is separate from the VDU and can be adjusted to sit either flat or at an angle to suit the user. These changes have been motivated by the desire to enable users to adopt ergonomic postures while at the same time allowing them more flexibility in the way that they might arrange their equipment.

Drawing, Positioning and Pointing Devices

Generally, a drawing or pointing device is used by the user to select an item or command displayed on a VDU. In recent years there has been a considerable increase in the number of different pointing and drawing devices available. However, the first type of positioning device, and possibly still one of the most common, is the cursor key.

Cursor Keys. A cursor is a shape (often flashing) that indicates where text will be entered on the screen. Cursor keys are a natural extension of the keyboard. Usually they consist of four extra keys; one for upward, one for downward, and one each for sideways movement, left and right. These keys move a cursor or pointer around the screen. The pointer or cursor is moved over a command or item and usually the RETURN or ENTER key is then pressed to select the item or command.

Unfortunately, cursor keys have the disadvantage that they tend not to be particularly useful for moving the pointer across the screen rapidly.

However, if a system is arranged so that cursor keys can be used to move rapidly, then accuracy seems to suffer. An answer might be to have a two-mode cursor key operation; one where the cursor moves in large jumps for each key press and another where the cursor moves in small movements for precision. However, a simpler answer is often to employ a more suitable pointing device; one which can be used to position pointers both quickly and accurately, such as a mouse.

The Mouse. A mouse is a hand-held device that rests upon the desktop next to the computer. As the mouse is moved about the desktop, then a corresponding pointer displayed on the VDU also moves. As the mouse is moved away from the user, then the pointer moves up the screen. If the mouse is moved towards the user then the pointer on the screen moves downwards. Likewise, the pointer moves left when the mouse is moved left and right when the mouse is moved to the right.

In addition to its movement of a pointer on the screen, the mouse can also be used to select items or commands over which the pointer rests. This can be done by pressing buttons positioned on top of the mouse. The number of buttons will depend upon the mouse, but will usually be between one and three. Different functions are often performed by pressing the different buttons on the mouse. Where only one button exists, then different functions are often performed by pressing the button twice or three times in quick succession. Price and Cordova (1983), however, have found that users tend to be both faster and more accurate when they use a mouse with two or three buttons, rather than a mouse with only one button that requires several presses.

The advantage of using a mouse is that it is not only relatively accurate as a pointing device, but also that it can be used to move the cursor or pointer quickly across the screen. Furthermore, as with other indirect pointing devices such as the graphics tablet, it allows the user a feeling of directly manipulating the objects on the screen. Its disadvantage is that it requires desk space to move around.

The Tracker Ball. A device that is very similar in operation to a mouse is a tracker ball. This device rests on the desktop, usually next to the computer, and the user rotates the ball on the top of the device. As the top of the ball moves left, then so the pointer on the screen moves left. If the tracker ball is rotated right, then the pointer moves right. To move the pointer to the top of the screen the tracker ball is rotated so that the top of the ball moves away from the user. To move the pointer downwards, the tracker ball is rotated in the opposite direction.

As stated earlier, the tracker ball is similar, as a device, to the mouse. The tracker ball has the same advantages of being able to move the cursor quickly across the screen, while at the same time its accuracy when positioning the cursor is good. However, the tracker ball has the further advantage that, unlike the mouse, it does not require a significant area of the desk space.

The Joystick. Curiously enough, the joystick is probably the input device that almost everyone has come across. It can be seen most often in fairgrounds and amusement arcades where it is used as the input device for video games. The joystick works in a very similar fashion to the mouse or the tracker ball. If pressure is applied to the stick towards the left, then the pointer on the screen moves left. If the stick is pushed forwards, away from the user, then the pointer moves up the screen. The joystick has the advantages that it requires little desk space and can even be built into the keyboard, as well as being an accurate, self-centring pointing device. It has the disadvantage, however, that it cannot usually be used to move the pointer or cursor rapidly across the screen. This advantage does not necessarily apply to pressure-sensitive joysticks, however, where the degree of pressure exerted by the user determines how fast the pointer moves.

With the exception of games, flight simulators and the like, joysticks are not widely used for input to a wide range of tasks. It has become, like so many input devices, a tool that is used only for a certain range of tasks. This trend, of different input devices being suited to only certain tasks, will become evident as more input devices are considered.

The Graphics Tablet. As the user holds the stylus for the graphics tablet, and moves this about the tablet, then a corresponding pointer moves about on the screen. Some graphics tablets do not require a stylus, but can be operated using the finger or a pencil. The very term "graphics tablet" suggests an input device for a specific range of tasks. As we might expect, the graphics tablet is particularly well suited to drawing tasks, and can be used to trace over existing drawings. Its disadvantage is that it takes up desktop space.

The Lightpen. All of the pointing devices we have so far considered, such as mice, tracker-balls, etc., have been indirect pointing devices. That is to say, that they are not used to directly point at the screen, but have a pointer on the screen which they manipulate. Lightpens and touchscreens are referred to as direct pointing devices as items are selected by directly pointing at the screen. They have the advantage that they do not require the same degree of hand-eye co-ordination that mice or tracker-balls demand. Lightpens can be used for drawing, in much the same way as graphics tablets can. Their advantage is that the user can change what is on the screen in a very direct way. Furthermore, they are useful as a pointing and positioning device. Their disadvantage is that, in using the lightpen, part of the screen is obscured by the user's hand. Added to this is the problem of fatigue; holding a light pen to a screen for any length of time can become tiring, unless the screen is set at an angle of 30° or more from vertical.

The Touchscreen. The idea of being able to touch the computer screen and that this should alter what the system displays seems intuitively attractive. The advantage of touchscreens is that they do not take up any significant proportion of the desktop area. They are useful for tasks where the user needs to choose commands or select items. They work quite simply by the user touching the screen with a finger or pen. Furthermore, their use appears intuitive, and as touchscreens do not require a separate pointing device they may be less susceptible to the problems of theft and abuse.

Some touchscreens have a transparent plastic membrane over them. This membrane senses when and where the screen has been touched. Other touchscreens use infra-red light (see Fig. 2.3). In this second sort of screen beams of light are shone across the screen. When the user's finger breaks two of the beams of light then the corresponding operation is begun or an item is selected.

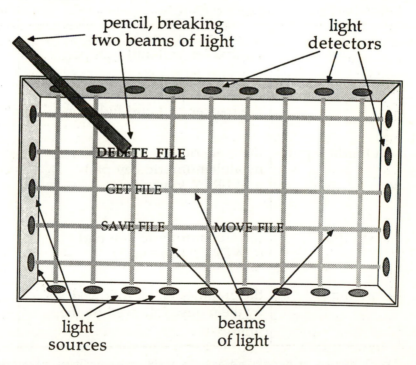

FIG. 2.3. A diagram of a touchscreen mechanism. In this diagram a pencil touches the command "delete file". In doing so it breaks two beams of light. The two light detectors that do not receive any light will provide the coordinates, from which the command can be calculated.

Both of these types of screen have the same problem. Users' fingers tend to be too large to select items accurately and consequently, selection can be a rather clumsy process. Moreover, using touchscreens creates dirty screens, causes tiredness in the arm, and has the added problem that large parts of the screen are obscured by the user's hand while an item or operation is being selected.

The Best Device.   There have been numerous experiments to discover which are the *better* input devices (cf., Card, English, & Burr, 1978; Ewing et al., 1986; Albert, 1982; see Shneiderman, 1987, for a discussion). Researchers have looked at measures of speed and accuracy, and although the results of these studies have been useful, the major conclusion that can be deduced from these studies is that *the best device for any particular task will depend upon the nature and characteristics of the task in question.* Reid (1985) however, has summarized Newman and Sproull's (1979) recommendations regarding input activity and choice of device. These recommendations are summarized in Fig. 2.4.

ACTIVITY	BEST DEVICE
Picking	mouse and joystick, followed by the tracker ball and lightpen
Positioning	mouse and joystick, followed by the tracker ball and lightpen
Numeric input	the numeric key pad, followed by alphanumeric key pad (QWERTY keyboard)
Text input	the alphanumeric key pad (QWERTY keyboard)
Drawing	the graphics tablet followed by the mouse followed by the lightpen

FIG. 2.4.   A summary of Newman and Sproull's (1979) recommendations, taken from Reid (1985).

Novel Approaches to Input

At the beginning of this section on input devices and technologies it was stated that *the purpose of the research and development of input devices is to create input devices and technologies that maximize the advantages of human physical and cognitive characteristics, and so promote efficient, reliable and even pleasurable input to a system.* It appears as though we have some way to go, however, for as Buxton (1986b) points out, human physical characteristics are still not properly exploited. In the vast majority of computer systems, the user's feet are not involved in the interaction. Furthermore, with the exception of the keyboard, input to a system is usually achieved using only one hand at a time.

To emphasize the extent to which present input to computer systems is restricted we will consider the activity of driving a car for a moment. For much of the time both of our hands are on the steering wheel. However, either hand can be taken off the steering wheel to use the indicators, the windscreen wipers, adjust the heating, turn the stereo on, or more often, just to change gear. The throttle (or accelerator), the brake and the clutch are all controlled by the feet. The brake is arguably more important than the steering wheel, yet we trust ourselves to operate it with our feet. Furthermore, the brake, the throttle and sometimes the clutch, all require delicate adjustment, which demonstrates that the feet can be used for sensitive manipulation. What is more, not only can we use two hands and both feet for driving, but because we know the task so well, we can carry on a conversation with our passengers at the same time.

This *driving-the-car* example demonstrates that we can use more than one hand to perform a task. Moreover, studies of HCI have shown that people sometimes prefer to perform a task using two hands. Buxton & Myers (1986) gave subjects a task where they could use either one or two hands. They found that, without prompting, novice subjects began performing the two experimental sub-tasks simultaneously, using both hands. Furthermore, in a second experiment they found that subjects who used two hands were significantly faster than subjects who were only allowed to use one hand. There are, however, few commercially available input devices that allow users to interact with computers using two hands, except, of course, for the keyboard. Moreover, the number of systems that support dual input is fewer still.

Input to Pictorial Systems.   Nevertheless, there has been some research into new methods and techniques that might make input easier for the user. Some researchers have looked at input techniques for pictorial systems. (These are systems that use graphics/pictures.) An example of this sort of research can be seen in the work of Barker & Najah (1985) and Barker, Najah, and Manji (1987), who have looked at the selection of items on a screen by operations such as *pecking, stroking, touching* or *ringing*. Barker et al. have used a combination of a graphics tablet, a bar-code reader (like the kind you see in supermarkets and libraries), and a selection of keyboards. Users have been introduced to the idea that they can *peck* an item (touch it lightly with a stylus or pen), they can *stroke* an item (draw a stylus across the item), *touch* the item with their finger, or *ring* the item with a finger or a pen. Using different combinations of *pecking, stroking, touching* and *ringing* operations Barker and his colleagues have attempted to show that this is a potentially viable form of input for certain types of task.

Input Using the Feet. The *driving-the-car* example demonstrates that our feet are a potentially useful, but neglected, source of input. Consequently, there has been research into using the feet for input to computer systems. Some of the tasks for which the feet might be used can be quite easily identified. For example, text editing systems often require both hands to be placed on the keyboard. Cursor movement and positioning using cursor keys can be slow and inefficient. Using a mouse or tracker ball is faster than using cursor keys, but entails users removing their hands from the keyboard. A more efficient solution might be to use the feet to position the cursor and to select commands from menus.

Pearson and Weiser (1986) discuss a variety of foot input devices. They have called these devices moles because they are *underfoot*, although they are also sometimes called *footmice*. These devices include apparatus that swings backwards and forwards, or from side to side. Some devices have no moving parts, but rely upon users positioning their feet on planar or cylindrical surfaces.

The examples given above are only a flavour of some of the research that is currently underway. Nickerson (1986) for example, mentions an input device that uses light reflected off the user's eyeball to judge what a user is looking at on a screen (*Computer-Disability News*, 1984). As stated earlier, the objective of this area of research is to optimize human physical and cognitive characteristics to enable efficient and pleasurable input to computer systems. Many of the devices which are developed will hopefully attain this goal, but whether each new input device is a success may ultimately depend upon whether suitable tasks exist where the device might be of benefit.

SPEECH AS AN INTERACTIONAL MEDIUM

The idea of speaking to a computer and the computer system speaking back seems particularly appealing. Indeed, many science fiction films and television series include speaking computers, but in reality *why are we inter-*

ested in speech as an interactional medium? Our interest in speech may stem from a wish to communicate with computers as easily and quickly as we communicate with other people. Looking at the issue from a practical standpoint, however, there are certain identifiable advantages to using speech.

Speech is a skill that is practised every day and most people can speak faster than even the most skilled typists can type. The cognitive processes involved in speech are so well automated that we can speak while we carry out other tasks using our hands, eyes and feet (e.g. the *driving-the-car* example). Moreover, because speech is such a well developed skill, and because many people do not possess the typing skills that are often required to use many of our current computer systems, speech input and output has the potential to allow a whole new group of people to use computer systems.

However, as a communication medium, speech is likely to be suited only to particular tasks, in the same way that many input devices are only suitable for certain types of task. These tasks appear to fall into two categories. The first, is where the telephone may be the most suitable form of communication. Many users do not have access to the appropriate technology to link up with computers which are not close at hand. In these cases speech may be the most appropriate form of communication. For example, imagine a system that could provide general members of the public with information regarding train or flight timetables.

The second category of task where speech may be the most useful form of communication, is where the user's hands and eyes need to be left free. Some quality inspection tasks on production lines, for example, have been automated using speech input and output. In these tasks the inspector often wears a headset which includes a microphone. The user (inspector) can then speak his instructions, such as *pass* or *fail*, to the computer system. This sort of system leaves the inspector's hands and eyes free for the task in question.

Automatic Speech Recognition

Many inspection tasks and the like may be suitable for speech input and output. But how do speech systems work? The answer is that systems rely upon either identifying (automatic speech recognition, ASR) or producing (generation) *phonemes*. Bailey defines phonemes in terms of "...the minimal sound change that will change meaning." (Bailey, 1985).

These phonemes roughly correspond to letters of the alphabet. For example, the word *cat* consists of three letters and three phonemes: *c a t*. The word *school* however, consists of six letters, but only four phonemes:

s ch oo l. The English language has approximately 40–60 phonemes (Michaelis & Wiggins, 1982), while other languages have as few as 15 (Bailey, 1985).

In recent years there has been a considerable amount of work directed towards developing machines that can recognize human speech, based on the principle of recognizing phonemes. There are commercial systems available that are claimed to be able to recognize several thousand words. Many systems, however, can only recognize words that are spoken individually, or spoken as part of a sentence but with pauses between each word. Unfortunately, human speech rarely consists of discrete words. Our words are spoken one after another, usually without pause. Detecting the end of one word and the beginning of another is often difficult. Nevertheless, there are now commercially available machines that can recognize continuous speech, albeit with smaller vocabularies and in a limited way.

Almost all of the systems developed to date, however, require trained speakers; people who speak to the machine carefully. Unfortunately, the way we speak does not remain constant. Although researchers have found that there are no significant differences between the young and old in the way that they speak (Ogozalek & Praag, 1986), our speech is quite different in noisy environments when compared with quiet environments (Rollins, 1985). Moreover, our tone of voice and word pronunciation can alter in stressful situations and present systems are not robust enough to cope with these changes. Overall, despite these present disadvantages, speech input to computer systems is a potentially useful means of communication, if used in a correct situation with an appropriate task.

Speech Generation

There are two basic methods for generating speech, *concatenation* and *synthesis-by-rule*. Concatenation is usually taken to mean the process where segments of human speech are recorded digitally and later played back to produce words and sentences. In other words, the computer has recordings of all of the basic phonemes and can manipulate and broadcast these recordings to produce the desired sounds. Alternatively, the recordings may even be of whole words or phrases. This second approach tends to limit the scope of the sentences that can be produced to those words and phrases that have been recorded.

The first approach to concatenation, of taking recordings of the more basic elements of speech (i.e. phonemes), has the disadvantage that the speech that it produces can sound unnatural. This is because speech does not simply consist of basic phonemes, but also of the various intonations that are associated with these basic sounds. (*Intonation* refers to the accents that are placed on words and parts of words depending upon the context of the sentence.) As a result, several different recordings of speech elements have to be used to enable natural sounding speech to be produced. An example of speech generation using concatenation can be found in some speaking clocks, where a few phrases are used to produce many time statements.

Synthesis-by-rule on the other hand, does not use recorded human speech. The synthesis of words and sentences is dictated by rules that relate, not only to the basic speech sounds (phonemes), but also to the context of the sentence or phrase. In other words, phonemes are not simply generated one after another, but in more advanced systems some of the *prosodic* information is also taken into account. Prosodic information is extra-linguistic information, and is also sometimes called *supra-segmental* information (see Bailey, 1985). This extra-linguistic information is communicated by changes in pitch, volume and rhythm, and is used to provide emphasis and emotion, as well as helping to indicate when a speaker has finished speaking.

Synthesis-by-rule has the advantage that the variety of words and sentences that can be produced is much greater than can normally be produced using concatenation. The disadvantage of the synthesis-by-rule approach is that the speech that is produced tends to sound less natural than speech produced using concatenation. The intelligibility of artificial speech has sometimes been a problem, and slowing down the delivery of such speech does not necessarily increase the ease with which it can be understood (Waterworth & Lo, 1985).

Curiously, however, artificial voices have the advantage that they attract attention. Shneiderman (1987) provides the example of a *robot-like* voice providing passenger directions in a subway to an airport. Apparently, more people paid attention to the robot-like voice than they did to a human voice giving the same directions. This suggests that the tone of generated speech might also be used to communicate information. Rosson and Cecala (1986), for example, found that voices with different qualities may suit different types of task, some tones being better suited for urgent messages, etc.

However, there is little doubt that speech output will not suit all tasks. Michaelis and Wiggins (1982) have suggested a list of criteria for judging when speech output is likely to be most appropriate. They suggest that speech output may be preferable when:

1. The message is simple.
2. The message is short.
3. The message will not be referred to later.

4. The message deals with events in time.
5. The message requires an immediate response.
6. The visual channels of communication are overloaded.
7. The environment may be too brightly lit, too poorly lit (possibly to preserve dark adaptation), subject to severe vibration, or otherwise unsuitable for transmission of visual information.
8. The user must be free to move around.
9. The user may be subjected to high G forces or anoxia (lack of oxygen, typically at high altitudes). The magnitude of the G forces or anoxia at which eyesight begins to be impaired is well below that needed to affect hearing.

Michaelis & Wiggins suggest that display of information on a VDU or a hard copy (printed on paper) might be better than speech when:

1. The message is complex, contains technical or scientific terms, or uses terms with which the user might not be familiar.
2. The message is long.
3. The message needs to be referred to later. (In this case, the hard-copy printer would be better than the CRT [VDU].)
4. The message deals with spatial orientation or the location of points in space. (Such information is usually best presented graphically. For this sort of application, an alphanumeric display would have no advantage over speech output.)
5. There is no urgency in the message.
6. The auditory channels are overloaded with messages, signals, or sounds to which the user must pay attention.
7. The auditory environment is too noisy or otherwise unsuitable for the reception of aural messages.
8. The user may remain in a position where he or she can easily see the displayed messages.
9. The system output consists of many different kinds of information which must be displayed simultaneously and which must be monitored and acted upon by the user.

These criteria are intended to be of practical use in the design of systems. However, by describing those situations where speech output might not be appropriate, they also serve to demonstrate that speech is not a general panacea for the problems of HCI. Some companies, with interests in marketing speech recognition and generation devices, suggest that speech will revolutionize HCI. It may be more precise to state that speech is a form of input and output that may be particularly useful for some tasks in specific situations.

OUTPUT DEVICES AND TECHNOLOGIES

One output technology, that of speech, has just been considered in the previous section. In this section other forms of output will be considered. These are visual display units (VDUs) and printers. First, however, *what is an output device?*

An output device might be simply thought of as *any instrument, apparatus or mechanism that can be used to present information to the user.* In the same way that input devices and technologies are a concern of HCI research, then so *the development and refinement of output devices also forms a significant part of HCI investigation.* As before, *the purpose of this development is to create output devices that maximize the advantages of human physical and cognitive characteristics, and so promote efficient, reliable and even pleasurable interaction between humans and computers.*

Visual Display Units

Presenting information visually is probably the most common form of output from computer systems. Many of the problems associated with using VDUs relates to physical issues such as screen flicker, poor lighting, difficulties with heating and ventilation, inadequate screen resolution, and poor character shape and spacing (Stewart, 1976). These issues will not be considered in any detail here, but it is important to recognize the substantial effects that these problems can have upon user performance and satisfaction. However, for a discussion of some of the ergonomic factors associated with the design and use of VDUs see Waern and Rollenhagen (1983).

Within HCI, research has been focused upon the ways in which visual information is presented to the user. Reid (1985) has used this research to formulate recommendations for designing visual display layouts. A summary of Reid's recommendations is as follows:

1. Avoid overfilling the screen with information. If a large amount of data is displayed then this will reduce the user's ability to locate and recognize information.
2. Use the upper right-hand quadrant of the screen for important messages. Danchak (1977) reports that users are generally more sensitive to changes in this portion of the screen.
3. Use different letter typefaces and colour to distinguish different parts of the display. Use mixed case text rather than text that consists of capital letters only, as mixed case is often easier to read. Try to use command names that fit with the user's expectations.
4. Design the layout so that the user's eyes fall naturally onto the next item of importance, although some experimentation may be needed to determine how best this might be achieved.

5. Use blinking to attract attention. A flashing message is usually more noticeable. However, these should be used sparingly, as they can be distracting and sometimes irritating for users.

These recommendations, like all guidelines, are approximations of good design. They should not be applied rigorously, but should be used to guide rather than dictate design.

Graphics

Graphics (the use of drawings and pictures for information presentation) are increasingly being used in many computer applications and for many different tasks (see Fig. 2.5). In a recent survey of commercial organizations, 85% of respondents reported that they used graphics to present information at management meetings (Nickerson, 1986).

Knapp, Moses, and Gellman (1982) have considered information presentation in graphical displays and suggested that *coding* and *sequencing* can be used to highlight information. *Coding* is where symbols are displayed so as to maximize symbol differentiation. Symbols can be coded using colour, alphanumerics (text), shape, intensity, flashing (blinking), and orientation. *Sequencing* is where segments of an entire display area are shown over time, so reducing the total number of symbols that are present on the screen

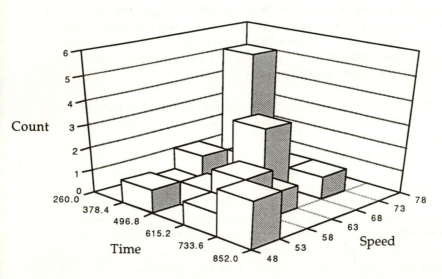

FIG. 2.5.   A 3-D histogram produced using a typical graphics package.

at any one time. In other words, only part of a display, part of a map for example, is shown. However, this relies on the user being able to relate one display to the next. The purpose of coding and sequencing in graphical displays is to allow users to pick out the information they require. In essence, the object of these sorts of techniques is to reduce clutter on the screen, *but what is clutter*?

If users are to be able to identify and select information then they need to be able to conceptually organize and distinguish information (Badre, 1982). The idea of clutter on a screen is one that, at first, appears intuitively obvious. Sometimes, however, screens that appear cluttered from a distance seem straightforward and well organized when we come to view them at close range. The difference between a cluttered and an uncluttered screen does not necessarily depend upon the number of items that are displayed. An uncluttered screen is often one where the user has a principle or concept around which the items on the screen can be organized.

For example, the concept of *windows* is often used to organize the presentation of large amounts of data on a screen (see Fig. 2.6). Windows are portions of a screen. These portions are usually rectangular, often

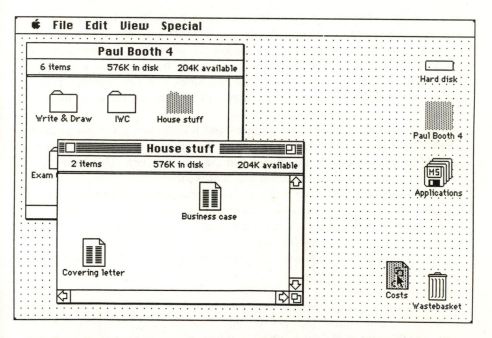

FIG. 2.6. Windows on an Apple Macintosh. The active window is shown by the dark lines towards its top. The role of metaphors in HCI will be dealt with in Chapter Four. By permission of Apple Ltd.

overlap and can usually be adjusted for size. Often the user selects the window that is required and this window is displayed over the other windows. Screens containing windows may, at first glance, appear cluttered. However, the windows organize the information into manageable *chunks*, and so what first appeared cluttered is in reality, quite usable. Evidence of the usefulness of an organizing concept such as windowing can be seen in both the commercial success of systems that use windows, such as the Apple Macintosh, and in experimental comparisons with other forms of display (i.e. Bury, Boyle, Evey, & Neal, 1982).

The ideas that have just been expressed will be properly dealt with in Chapter Four (as part of mental models and metaphors), but for the moment this argument should serve to emphasize the relative dangers of rigorously applying guidelines. Guidelines are useful pointers for design, but ultimately the intelligibility of a display relies upon whether it can be conceptually organized and understood, not upon whether it is "25%" full, or upon any other physical measurement or approximation.

Printers and Plotters

Although there has been a good deal of research into how best to present information to users on VDUs, displaying information on a screen is still considered to be inferior in several ways, to presenting information on paper. The notion of a paperless society, envisaged by some, still appears to be a distant ideal. It seems likely that machines that can produce paper copies of computer-held text and pictures will be required for some time to come.

If we think of computer-held pictures and text as being *soft copy*, then printers and plotters produce *hard copy*. In other words, they produce something we can actually touch, not just view on a screen. This hard copy can be produced by several different kinds of device.

Plotters operate by moving a pen about on the paper. Some plotters can use several different pens to produce text and drawings (graphics) in different colours. Dot matrix, impact line and daisy wheel printers all work by striking an ink ribbon against the paper. Daisy wheel printers operate in a very similar way to typewriters, where the letter is selected and then stamped onto the page.

Impact line printers print a whole line at a time, unlike daisy wheel and dot matrix printers, and can produce up to 1200 lines per minute (Shneiderman, 1987). Dot matrix printers on the other hand, cannot produce the letter-quality print of the daisy wheel, but have the advantage of being more versatile, producing graphs and drawings (graphics), as well as text. Dot matrix printers have the further advantage that they can be used to produce print in different colours.

Inkjet printers can also be used to produce print in different colours, but offer higher quality output than dot matrix printers, as well as being considerably quieter. Laser printers also offer high quality output. They are quiet, but also expensive by comparison to other types of printer. Thermal printers use specially treated paper which changes colour when heated. While the quality of the output does not match that of other types of printing, thermal printers have the advantage of being quiet and economical.

Shneiderman (1987) has produced a list of criteria against which different types of printer might be considered:

- Speed
- Print quality
- Cost
- Compactness
- Quiet operation
- Use of ordinary paper (fanfolded or single sheet)
- Character set
- Variety of fonts and font sizes
- Highlighting techniques (boldface, underscore, etc.)
- Support for special forms (printed forms, different lengths, etc.)
- Reliability.

Three further criteria that we might add to this list are, the ability of the printer to produce diagrams and pictures (graphics), the usability of the printer, and the ease with which it can be maintained.

These criteria should be considered in the context of the place of work. In other words, if the work environment is particularly noisy then *quiet operation* may not be an important consideration. In a quiet environment, however, such as a library, a dot matrix or daisy wheel printer might be disturbing and prove unsuitable.

COMMENTARY

Almost throughout the history of computing there has been an emphasis within some quarters on developing new interactional devices and technologies. This is to be expected given the initial limited range of tools that could be used for input and output. Indeed, there still appears to be a need for a greater variety of devices and technologies for interaction. If we consider the range of input devices for other types of technology then this illustrates the limitations of our present options. For example, imagine the wheels and levers that are used to operate a steam engine. Then imagine having to adapt these same controls (or input devices) to allow us to operate a sewing machine or fly an aircraft. This, in effect, is what we attempt to do when we develop graphics software where our drawings are produced using cursor keys. We clearly need to increase the range of interactional media if we are to adequately fulfill the needs of users who often wish to perform very different tasks on the same technology.

As other forms of technology have emerged then specific devices have been developed for the control and operation of each technology. A similar trend can be identified within information technology, as interactional devices and technologies become more task specific, as well as reflecting the general movement towards particular forms of interaction, such as direct manipulation (direct manipulation is where users move objects on the screen in such a way that it provides a sensation of *directness* for these users, as well as allowing users to *feel* in control, see Shneiderman, 1974; 1982).

One area of interactional technology that receives considerable attention is that of speech recognition and generation. However, with respect to the trend towards task-specific devices, there is no reason to believe that speech as an interactional medium is any different from any other interactional technology. That is to say, that speech is likely to be used only for a limited range of tasks. The attraction of speech, and the possible reason why it is sometimes mistaken for a general panacea for the problems of HCI, appears to lie in its implied promise. For example, if we are asked "wouldn't it be nice to be able to speak to the computer?", then this also seems to imply that the computer has some human-like qualities, such as intelligence, besides the ability to recognize and generate speech. In reality, the research into speech is only likely to produce systems that generate or recognize speech (a considerable achievement in itself), not systems that can intelligently converse and interpret instructions. Nevertheless, this is what the notion of speech with computers appears to imply, even if speech researchers are quite clear about what can be achieved. This may be one reason why those who are less well informed believe speech input and output to have greater potential than is justified.

Although research into speech generation and recognition may be perceived as an exciting and worthwhile area of HCI interest, the same cannot always be said of research into other interactional devices. There is a tendency to view this area as being dull and unimportant. Whether the area is dull is a matter of opinion, although many, including myself, believe that it is particularly challenging and interesting. What appears clear is that this area is far from unimportant. Besides the question of developing devices that make best use of the user's physical abilities, there is also the issue of how we choose an interactional device for any particular device. At present the choice of any particular device tends to be based on intuitive judgement rather than any theory, framework or technique. This appears to be one of HCI's present needs; *a means by which the requirements of a task can be matched to the optimum physical actions the user might perform and, eventually, to a device that might best suit these physical actions.*

At present, however, this area of HCI, like several others, appears to rely upon guidelines instead of theory and proven techniques. While guidelines may be useful, they are, nevertheless, a second-best answer. Guidelines require interpretation and, consequently, are subject to bias. Furthermore, they are frequently ignored or used in too superficial a manner.

Overall, I would suggest that there needs to be more research into this sometimes neglected area of interest as our physical abilities remain underutilized. If we are to enable efficient interaction then we require a greater variety of interactional devices and technologies. Furthermore, we require a framework and techniques that will show us how to match the media of interaction to tasks in an optimum fashion.

SUMMARY

An input device might be simply thought of as any instrument, apparatus or mechanism that can be used to enter information into a computer. The development and refinement of input devices forms a significant part of HCI research. The purpose of this development is to create input devices that maximize the advantages of human physical and cognitive characteristics, and so promote efficient, reliable and even pleasurable input to a system.

Common input devices include alphanumeric keyboards, cursor keys, mice, tracker balls, joysticks, graphics tablets, lightpens, and touch screens. Less common (more experimental) forms of input include moles or footmice and even devices that detect eye movement.

Speech is perceived as a useful interactional medium because it is a skill that is practised every day, and most people can speak faster than even skilled typists can type. The cognitive processes involved in speech are well automated and we can speak while we carry out other tasks using our hands, eyes and feet. Speech input and output has the potential to allow a new group of people, who lack typing skills, to use computer systems. However, as a communication medium, speech is likely to be suited only to particular tasks and situations.

Speech can be broken down into phonemes, which are the basic units of sound in speech. Automatic speech recognition (ASR) systems are based on the principle of recognizing these basic sounds. Current systems, however, require trained users and few can recognize continuous speech. Moreover, these systems are not always robust enough to cope with changes in the voice, such as those where the speaker is in a noisy environment and has to shout, or where the speaker is under stress.

Speech generation is achieved using one of two methods; concatenation or synthesis-by-rule. Synthesis-by-rule has the advantage that the variety of words and sentences that can be produced is much greater than can normally be produced using concatenation. The disadvantage of the synthesis-by-rule approach is that the speech that is produced tends to sound less natural than speech produced using concatenation.

An output device might be simply thought of as any instrument, apparatus or mechanism that can be used to present information to the user. The development and refinement of output devices also forms a significant part of HCI investigation. The purpose of this development is to create output devices that maximize the advantages of human physical and cognitive characteristics, and so promote efficient, reliable and even pleasurable interaction between humans and computers.

The most common output devices are visual display units (VDUs) and printers. If users are to be able to identify and select information on VDUs then they need a principle or concept around which the items on the screen can be organized. Guidelines are useful pointers for design, but ultimately the intelligibility of a display relies upon whether it can be conceptually organized and understood.

Among the devices that produce hard copy are plotters, dot matrix printers, inkjet printers, laser printers, daisy wheel printers, thermal printers and impact line printers. The criteria against which printers can be judged are; speed, print quality, cost, compactness, quiet operation, use of ordinary paper (fanfolded or single sheet), character set, variety of fonts and font sizes, highlighting techniques (boldface, underscore, etc.), support for special forms (printed forms, different lengths, etc.), reliability, the ability of the device to produce diagrams and pictures (graphics) the usability of the printer and the ease with which it can be maintained.

A SELECTIVE ANNOTATED BIBLIOGRAPHY

Bailey, P. (1985). Speech communication: The problem and some solutions. In A. F. Monk (Ed.), *Fundamentals of human-computer interaction*. London: Academic Press. *This article considers human speech and explains some of the basic concepts that underpin automatic speech recognition and generation, such as phonemes and prosody (or supra-segmentation). Although this is a technical and theoretical paper, it is nevertheless interesting and readable.*

Barker, P. G., Najah, M., & Manji, K. (1987). Pictorial communication with computers. In H. J. Bullinger & B. Shackel (Eds.), *Human-computer interaction– Interact '87: Proceedings of the second IFIP conference on human-computer interaction, Stuttgart*. Amsterdam: North-Holland. *The authors suggest new techniques for input into computer systems. This paper serves as an example of the kind of research and development of interactional devices and technologies that is currently being undertaken.*

Brauninger, U. & Grandjean E. (1983). Lighting characteristics of visual display terminals from an ergonomic point of view. In A. Janda (Ed.), *Human factors in computer systems: Proceedings of the CHI'83 conference,* Boston. Amsterdam, Netherlands: North-Holland. *The authors discuss character presentation on VDU screens. This includes the sharpness, the contrast and stability of characters, as well as reflection off the screen surface and lighting ratios for areas around the VDU workstation. The paper finishes by providing seven useful guidelines about lighting at visual display units. This is a concise and helpful introduction to some of the physical ergonomic issues associated with reading information from VDUs.*

Buxton, W. (1986b). There's more to interaction that meets the eye: Some issues in manual input. In D. A. Norman & S. W. Draper (Eds.), *User centred system design: New perspectives on human-computer interaction.* Hillsdale, New Jersey: Lawrence Erlbaum Associates Inc. *The author suggests that current interactional devices do not adequately exploit human physical and cognitive characteristics. Various input devices are discussed, as well as many of the important issues associated with manual input. This is an essential paper for anyone interested in the problems of manual input.*

Card, S. K. (1982). User perceptual mechanisms in the search of computer command-menus. In *Human factors in computer systems, conference proceedings, Gaithersburg, Maryland.* ACM. *The author considers some of the design alternatives for using menus. The principal question he addresses is which design alternatives lead to better performance? The author adopts a psychological approach to look at how different commands might be grouped together or "chunked". The author finishes by suggesting which menu arrangements might be better for which situations, and by outlining how users appear to search through menus.*

Gardiner, M. M. & Christie, B. (1987). Communication failure at the person-machine interface: The human factors aspects. In R. G. Reilly (Ed.), *Communication failure in dialogue and discourse.* Amsterdam: Elsevier. *This paper is concerned with input and output devices and techniques, and how they might be matched to appropriate tasks. This is a well written and wide-ranging review, where the authors consider many of the human senses and how they relate to different input and output devices.*

Knapp, B. G., Moses, F. L., & Gellman, L. H. (1982). Information highlighting on complex displays. In A. N. Badre & B. Shneiderman (Eds.), *Directions in human-computer interaction.* Norwood, New Jersey: Ablex. *This paper is concerned primarily with graphical displays. Different techniques for highlighting, simplifying and organizing are suggested and discussed. The authors go on to suggest a set of five guidelines for highlighting information in graphical displays.*

Michaelis, P. R. & Wiggins, R. H. (1982). A human factors engineers introduction to speech synthesizers. In A. N. Badre & B. Shneiderman (Eds.), *Directions in human-computer interaction.* Norwood, New Jersey: Ablex. *The paper is divided into two parts. The first describes how speech synthesizers work, while the second half is concerned with the human factors issues involved in using synthesized speech. Although often technical, the first part of the paper is interesting and easy to read. The second half of the paper in equally interesting and suggests when synthesized speech might be put to best use, as well as discussing issues such as voice quality and vocabulary limitations.*

Moody, T., Joost, M., & Rodman, R. (1987). The effects of various types of speech output on listener comprehension rates. In H. J. Bullinger & B. Shackel (Eds.), *Human-computer interaction–Interact '87: Proceedings of the second IFIP conference on human-computer interaction, Stuttgart.* Amsterdam: North-

Holland. The authors report the results of an experimental study into the effects of digitized, synthesized and human speech upon comprehension. They suggest-useful guidelines which relate to the content of speech messages.

Nickerson, R. S. (1986). *Using computers: Human factors in information systems.* Cambridge, Massachusetts: MIT Press. *The author describes and discusses communication media at the physical interface, including manual input devices, visual displays and graphics (pages 89–109). The author also discusses the use of speech, both as an input and output medium (pages 137–146). The author questions whether the issues associated with speech have been properly thought through, and suggests that the drive towards technological goals has obscured some of the wider issues relating to the use of speech.*

Reid, P. (1985). Work station design, activities and display techniques. In A. F. Monk (Ed.), *Fundamentals of human-computer interaction.* London: Academic Press. *This paper begins by considering input devices, and the different tasks for which they are suited. Display techniques are discussed and screen design guidelines are offered for the simplification and coding of displays.*

Rollins, A., Constantine, B., & Baker, S. (1983). Speech recognition at two field sites. In A. Janda (Ed.), *Human factors in computer systems: Proceedings of the CHI '83 conference, Boston.* Amsterdam: North-Holland. *The authors discuss the use of speech input (recognition) in two different working environments. Many studies of speech recognition are laboratory based, and so this study provides an interesting change. The results of the study suggest that although some operators are able to use voice automatic speech recognition to their advantage, some operators are not always as successful. The authors conclude, however, that success in using speech input is related more to overall work habits than to speech itself. This is an interesting and readable paper.*

Sauter, S. L., Gottlieb, M. S., & Jones, K. C. (1982). A systems analysis of stress-strain in VDT operation. In *Human factors in computer systems, conference proceedings, Gaithersburg, Maryland.* ACM. *The authors discuss some of the effects of visual display unit use upon the health, comfort and satisfaction of the user.*

Shneiderman, B. (1987). *Designing the user interface: Strategies for effective human-computer interaction.* Reading, Massachusetts: Addison-Wesley. *The author discusses interaction devices (pages 227–269). This includes keyboard layouts and function keys, cursor keys, the physical design of keys for a keyboard. Both direct and indirect pointing devices are considered, and various experimental comparisons of pointing devices are described. Shneiderman goes on to consider automatic speech recognition, digitization, and generation. Following this, visual displays and printers are considered. This forms an easy-to-read and wide-ranging discussion of interaction devices.*

Woods, D. D. (1984). Visual momentum: A concept to improve the cognitive coupling of person and computer. *International Journal of Man-Machine Systems, 21,* 229–244. *This paper is concerned with conceptually organizing displayed information. The author proposes the principle of "visual momentum" to allow users to integrate information across displays. He goes on to suggest four recommendations for improving visual momentum and comprehension. This stimulating and original paper is highly recommended.*

3 Human-Computer Dialogue

OVERVIEW

Firstly, the uses of the term *dialogue* are discussed as well as the difference between semantics and pragmatics. The concepts of dialogue style, structure and content are explained, and various dialogue styles are discussed. Following this, some of the dialogue design guidelines are considered and the question of whether HCI can be called a *dialogue* is raised. To elaborate this question further, the similarities and the differences between human dialogue and HCI are then examined. Leading on from this discussion, the desirable qualities of future human-computer dialogue are suggested. Finally, the reasons why we need to consider the user's knowledge of the task and system are explained.

INTRODUCTION

In the last chapter the hardware and software of HCI were discussed. The nature of this communication, however, was not considered. In this chapter the process of communication that occurs through the interactional media that were the subject of the last chapter is addressed. In other words, the character of human-computer dialogue is examined. But first, we may need to understand what is meant by the term *dialogue*.

What is Dialogue?

When two humans speak to one another we call this *dialogue*. Dialogue, however, is not just spoken words, but is the process of communication between two or more agents. When we communicate, we do not just swap words, we exchange information, and this exchange is dependent upon the meanings that are attached to the words involved.

Meaning can be considered in terms of *semantics* or *pragmatics* (Morris, 1946). We can consider the literal meanings of words and sentences, regardless of context, and this type of study is called *semantics*. *Pragmatics* on the other hand, is the study of meaning with regard to the individuals involved and the context of the situation (Gerrig, 1986). Both of these terms are used within the HCI literature, and so it maybe useful to understand practically the difference between them. For example, imagine that your friend, Phil, steps into your house. He is wet, which is not surprising as you know that it is raining. You ask him, "Have you been out in the rain?" Phil replies, "No, I jumped into the lake". The semantic interpretation of Phil's reply is that he jumped into the lake. Yet we know that this is probably not the truth, and might not be what Phil intended to be understood by his statement. A pragmatic interpretation of the situation, however, produces a different result. It may be that you know Phil well and that he intended the statement humorously. Alternatively, he may be annoyed at being wet, and have been irritated by a question that he perceived as being foolish. Thus, the interpretation depends not only upon the words used, but also upon the context of the utterances and the speakers involved.

From the example above, it is clear that analysing dialogue might not always be a straightforward case of assigning meanings to the terms and phrases employed by the parties concerned. Meanings depend not only upon the words themselves, but also upon the context in which they are communicated and the recipient's knowledge of language and the world generally. Consequently, dialogue might be thought of *as the exchange of symbols between two or more parties, as well as being the meanings that the participants in the communicative process assign to these symbols.* Human dialogue, however, is richer than this definition might imply. It involves active listening and responding. That is to say, that we search for information in another's speech and look to map this information onto our present knowledge structures (the notion of mapping will be dealt with in the next chapter). Human-computer dialogue, however, does not appear to possess this richness and activity.

DIALOGUE STYLE, STRUCTURE AND CONTENT

Within HCI a distinction is sometimes made between the *style, structure* and *content* of human-computer dialogue (Barnard & Hammond, 1983). The *style* of the dialogue refers to the "...character and control of the information exchange." (Barnard & Hammond, 1983). Command languages, menu selection, question-answering are all examples of different types of dialogue style (these styles will be explained later in this section).

The *structure* of the dialogue refers to the "...formal description of dialogue elements in terms of their constituent structure together with their ordering within and between dialogue exchanges." (Barnard & Hammond, 1983). For example, Fig. 3.1 shows a simple difference in dialogue structure for a command language statement. In the first case (1) the object is first and the operation to be performed upon it is second. In the second case (2) this ordering has been reversed. Most dialogue structure differences are likely to be more complicated than this simple example. The *content* of the dialogue refers to "...the semantics of the information exchanged – in terms of the user's general knowledge of the meanings of words and specific knowledge of the nature and consequences of computer representations and actions." (Barnard & Hammond, 1983).

More recently, some researchers have begun to suggest that we ought to consider the pragmatics of human-computer dialogue (e.g. Buxton, 1983; Norman & Draper, 1986). In other words, that we should look, not only at the literal meanings of the symbols within the dialogue, but also at what the user understands from the dialogue. What is communicated in human-computer dialogue may depend, not only upon the content of the dialogue, but also its style and structure. The context of any particular message is also important. Messages are not often delivered in isolation, but relate to the previous messages; Draper (1986) has termed this *inter-referencial input/output*. For example, if you were to type "delete myfile" into a computer, the system may respond with "Are you sure you want to delete this file?", and you might type, "yes". The last two statements each refer to the statements that preceded them. That is to say, that they cannot be understood without reference to previous statements; they have to be interpreted in the context of the whole dialogue exchange. Consequently, a pragmatics of HCI should consider, *not only the semantics of the words or symbols used, but also the style, structure and context of the dialogue.*

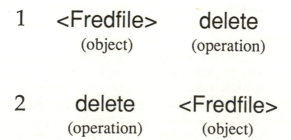

FIG. 3.1.   An example of a simple difference in command language dialogue structure.

Dialogue Style and Control

Much of the research into human-computer dialogue has considered the style of the interaction. In this subsection a few of the different dialogue styles will be briefly explained. To reiterate, the style of the dialogue refers to the "...character and control of the information exchange." (Barnard & Hammond, 1983). The notion of *control* in the dialogue should become clear as we proceed through the examples.

Command language is one of the oldest and most commonly used dialogue styles. (Some researchers, e.g. Moran, 1981, use the term command language to mean any form of user input other than programming or natural language. Here, and throughout the rest of the book, the term command language will be used to mean a specific dialogue style.) When using command language the user has to type in commands to the computer system and the computer system then carries out these commands. For example, the user may type:

> DELETE FREDFILE

and the system may respond with either a prompt to indicate that the command has been carried out, or with a message stating why this command could not be executed. Command language leaves the user in control of the interaction. That is to say that the computer simply implements the commands that the user issues. The difficulty with this approach is that the user has to remember many commands. Furthermore, the user has to know the correct syntax for these commands. For example, imagine that a user wishes to make a copy of a file called FREDFILE, and wants to call this copy BILLFILE. In this case, all of the following are legitimate commands on different systems:

> FREDFILE.BILLFILE COPY
> COPY FREDFILE, BILLFILE
> COPY FREDFILE; BILLFILE

The last line can be distinguished from the second line only by the use of a semicolon instead of a comma. Yet the order in which commands are written, and the placing and choice of separators, such as spaces, commas, colons and semicolons, is often crucial to whether the system will accept and execute a command.

An alternative to command language, that avoids the problem of re-membering commands, is to use menus (see Fig. 3.2). The user simply chooses the command from a list (menu) of possible commands. Menus are increasingly being used in preference to command language. Where there are many possible commands, and displaying them all might prove difficult, then menus are sometimes organized hierarchically in tree-like structures

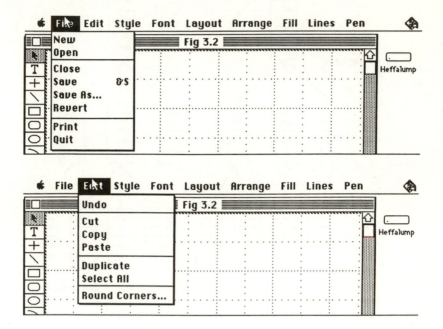

FIG. 3.2. Two examples of menus from the MacDraw package for the Apple Macintosh. By permission of Apple Ltd.

(see Fig. 3.3). In other words, a menu might not only contain commands, but also routes through to other menus. For example, we might choose "print commands" from menu 1 (see Fig. 3.3). This should take us to the "print commands" menu. We might then choose "printer set-up" which should take us to the "printer set-up" menu. From here we can choose the commands we need.

Like command language, menus leave the user in control of the interaction, although it should be noted that the user never has complete freedom within the dialogue. The user may choose the commands, but the total assemblage of possible command alternatives is dictated in advance by the design of the computer system.

A dialogue style that leaves the user with very little control is that of form fill-in (see Fig. 3.4). Here the user is presented with a form where the

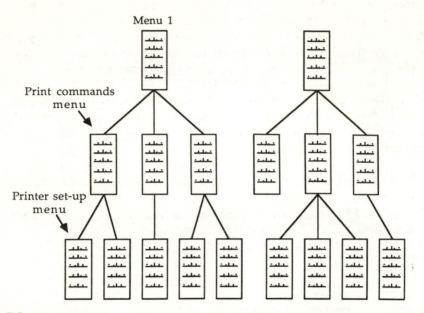

Menu 1

Print commands menu

Printer set-up menu

FIG. 3.3. A possible menu tree structure. In the higher menus the user can either select commands that perform actions or commands that allow access to other (lower) menus. To get to the commands in lower menus the user must first work through the menus above.

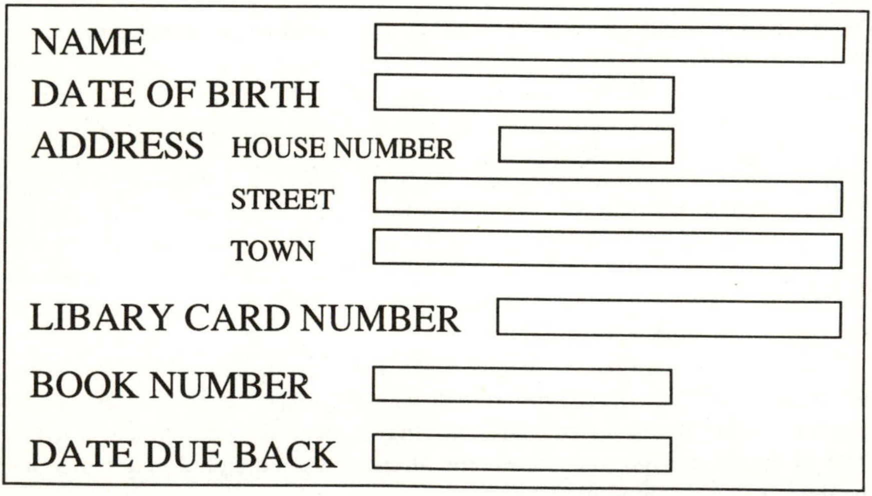

NAME

DATE OF BIRTH

ADDRESS   HOUSE NUMBER

STREET

TOWN

LIBARY CARD NUMBER

BOOK NUMBER

DATE DUE BACK

FIG. 3.4. A form fill-in interface. The user must fill each box, moving between the boxes using either the return, enter, tab or cursor keys.

various portions must be filled-in, leaving the user with few alternatives. Although the user has little control over the dialogue, this style has the advantage that the user rarely needs to remember commands or their syntax.

Direct manipulation is a dialogue style that is growing in popularity and use. This form of dialogue style has been particularly successful in computers such as the Apple Macintosh, although the concept and the term were suggested as long ago as 1974 by Shneiderman. The idea of direct manipulation is that the user's actions should directly affect what happens on the screen to the extent that there is a feeling of physically manipulating the objects on the screen. Shneiderman (1982) has listed the advantages of direct manipulation interfaces:

1. Novices can learn basic functionality quickly, usually through a demonstration by a more experienced user.
2. Experts can work extremely rapidly to carry out a wide range of tasks, even defining new functions and features.
3. Knowledge intermittent users can retain operational concepts.
4. Error messages are rarely needed.
5. Users can see immediately if their actions are furthering their goals, and if not, they can simply change the direction of their activity.
6. Users have reduced anxiety because the system is comprehensible and because actions are so easily reversible.

Although it may be thought of as a useful dialogue style, direct manipulation has its problems. Shneiderman (1982; 1987) suggests that graphical presentations, which are normally necessary for direct manipulation interfaces, are not suitable for all tasks, and in some situations may even mislead and confuse users. Nevertheless, in many situations direct manipulation leaves the user in control of the dialogue. Moreover, this *direct engagement* at the interface, as Hutchins, Hollan, and Norman (1986) call it, often provides the user with a feeling of confidence which results from this perception of control.

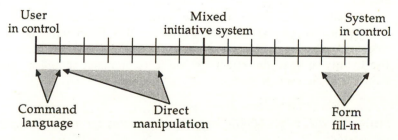

FIG. 3.5. A continuum of dialogue control with estimations of where some of the different dialogue styles might be placed.

So far, we have discussed control of human-computer dialogue as though it was a black and white issue. In reality, different dialogue styles are better thought of as being somewhere between these two extremes. However, as Fig. 3.5 shows, most dialogue styles tend to reside towards one end of this *control continuum* or the other.

Few, if any, dialogue styles can be described as *mixed initiative*. Mixed initiative systems are those where the user may control the dialogue up to a point. The computer system may then take control, possibly asking questions of the user, before handing control back. This idea of a mixed initiative dialogue or system, where dialogue control moves back and forth during the process of communication, is presently the subject of research. Mixed initiative systems are part of a future perspective, where systems are no longer tools, but collaborate intelligently with their users. This idea will be considered in greater detail in Chapter Eight.

Dialogue Design Guidelines

There has been a great deal of research into the structure, content and style of human-computer dialogue. This extensive research, however, has not produced any unified theory or explanatory framework. Nevertheless, general dialogue design guidelines have emerged, such as those proposed by McMillan and Moran (1985) for example:

1. A system should recognize any reasonable approximation of a command.
2. After a command is entered by the user the system should provide an acknowledgement of some sort which includes some reference as to how the system interpreted the command.
3. Syntax and commands should be kept simple and natural.
4. The number of commands in a system should be limited and in a limited format.
5. The amount of information passed by a command line should be limited.
6. The designer should consider the user when choosing command names. In other words, choosing command names that fit in with the other command names in the system is not the most important consideration.
7. The facility to undo the effects of the last command should be made available to the user.

Shneiderman (1987, pages 60–62) suggests eight rules for human-computer dialogue design:

1. Dialogues should be consistent.
2. Systems should allow users shortcuts through some parts of familiar dialogue.
3. Dialogues should offer informative feedback.
4. Sequences of dialogues should be organized into logical groups.
5. Systems should offer simple error handling.
6. Systems should allow actions to be reversed.
7. Systems should allow experienced users to feel as though they are in control rather than the system.
8. Systems should aim to reduce short-term memory load. In other words, users should not be expected to remember too much.

These sets of guidelines are only examples. Gaines & Shaw (1983) for example, suggest 17 rules for dialogue engineering. Although guidelines and rules may be useful to designers of computer systems, these guidelines are only partially about the dialogue at the interface, and are more often aimed at system design generally. Furthermore, such guidelines are often limited in their usefulness. Although they are helpful in guiding the designer towards a consideration of the relevant human-computer dialogue issues, they require interpretation. For example, McMillan & Moran's third guideline, that "Syntax and commands should be kept simple and natural." (McMillan & Moran, 1985), is open to a wide variety of interpretations. A designer's and a user's perspective on what is "simple and natural" may be considerably at odds.

Is "Dialogue" the Correct Term?

An alternative to guidelines might be a theoretically-based technique for designing dialogue at the interface. Indeed, this is often viewed as a desirable goal. However, if theory is to develop then there needs to be some common agreement about what is occurring at the interface. Furthermore, the terms that might be used to describe various aspects of the communicative process need to be agreed. As yet, there appears to be little overall agreement. There are even questions over whether the interaction between a user and a system might be correctly termed *dialogue*.

Although most people may understand the term *dialogue* to mean the exchange of information between two individuals, in HCI it sometimes takes on a slightly different meaning. Some researchers use the term *dialogue* interchangeably with the term *interface*, as may have become apparent in the last section. For example, Shneiderman's "Eight Golden Rules of Dialogue Design" could just as well be, "Eight Golden Rules of Interface Design". Gaines and Shaw (1983; 1984) also use these terms in this way. Although using the terms *dialogue* and *interface* interchangeably has become a common practice within HCI research, it is questionable whether it is useful to have two terms that have the same meaning. Consequently, in the following sections and chapters *the term "dialogue" will be used to mean the process of communication that occurs at the interface*. These two terms will not be used interchangeably.

Although *dialogue* in HCI has become an accepted and well used term, Smith (1980) and Sheehy (1987) question whether the term is really appropriate at all. They suggest that communication at the human-computer interface is not full or proper communication. In essence, they seem to imply that the computer is just a tool, not another intelligence with which we converse. The question may be; do all parties to the communicative process need to be intelligent for us to call the process dialogue? We might reply that the user does communicate with an intelligence; that of the designer embedded within the system. Sheehy may, however, be correct when he points out that communication at the interface requires us to *suspend belief* and to imagine that we are, indeed communicating with another human.

Sheehy (1987) and Sheehy and Chapman (1987) raise the further issue of nonverbal communication. When two humans communicate they use not only words, but physical gestures and signals. Within HCI only words are used (if we discount direct manipulation interfaces). Thus, communication at the interface is not complete. Furthermore, there is limited evidence that if some aspects of nonverbal behaviour were used as part of input to a system, then communication might be made more accurate (Bolt, 1980). Nevertheless, humans can still converse without nonverbal communication channels. Consider the telephone for example. However, as Sheehy (1987) points out, when humans are forced to communicate without visual contact their language becomes more task orientated, their conversation becomes less spontaneous and the chances of reaching a negotiated solution are decreased.

HCI AND HUMAN DIALOGUE

The process of considering the questions raised by researchers, such as Smith and Sheehy, serves to illuminate some of the issues in human-computer dialogue. By way of examining these issues further, let us consider some of the similarities and differences between human and human-computer dialogue.

First, human-computer interaction, like human dialogue, is a form of communication where a degree of understanding can be achieved. Admittedly, this understanding may be limited in some respects, but if designed properly a computer system will do as its user wishes, provided the user knows what is possible and how to give commands.

Second, communication requires agreement on the terms used in the dialogue. When humans successfully communicate they usually have a shared understanding of the words used and the concepts to which they refer. This is also true of human-computer communication. When a user gives commands to a system then the system must have an "understanding" of these commands if the interaction is going to succeed. Likewise, the terms and symbols a system displays must mean the same thing to the user as they do to the system. This goes back to the idea of *mutual knowledge* mentioned in the first chapter (Habermas, 1981).

Third, communication requires agreement, not only upon the terms and concepts used, but also upon the context of the communication. For example, if two people are speaking to one another then there needs to be an agreed understanding of what they are speaking about. To illustrate this point further let us consider an example where two individuals do not agree on the context of their conversation: Two people are sharing a car to travel to a conference. They stop at a garage for fuel and to check the car tyres. Bill is putting air into the tyres when Fred asks, "How's the pressure?" Bill replies, "Not too good, the boss keeps getting on to me." Fred explains, "Sorry, I meant the car tyre pressure, but how's work anyway?" In this simple example Fred and Bill did not share a common context for their brief exchange. In their separate contexts, the context of work and the context of car maintenance, some of the words can have different meanings (i.e. "pressure" can have both a literal and metaphorical meaning) and the result is a failure in the dialogue between the two individuals.

This sort of dialogue failure can also occur in human-computer communication. For example, consider a user of a word processing system who issues a command to print the document that is currently being edited. Following the printing process the user issues a command for the system to re-display the document on the screen, but instead nothing happens. The system, upon receiving the first command changed to the printing mode, but did not adequately inform the user who was unaware of the change in context and the subsequent legality of some of the commands.

The meanings that those involved in communication assign to symbols and terms depend upon the context in which they are communicated. The previous two examples show how communication breaks down as a result of misunderstandings of the context of the dialogue. These examples demonstrate that context is not only important in conversation between humans, but is also a significant factor in human-computer dialogue.

To summarize, HCI is similar to human dialogue as it is a form of communication where a degree of understanding is achieved, there must be agreement between individuals involved in the process of communication on the meaning of the symbols and terms used, and the context of dialogue is important, as it is the context that dictates the meanings of some of the symbols and terms used.

HUMAN AND HUMAN-COMPUTER DIALOGUE DIFFERENCES

Now we have examined how human dialogue is similar to human-computer communication we will examine the dissimilarities between HCI and human conversation.

The most obvious difference between human dialogue and human-computer communication is that the physical media of communication for HCI are different from that of human dialogue. Humans speak to one another whereas a user types in a statement to a system (or selects a command with a mouse or some other device) and usually receives information via a screen. Clearly, this affects the user's view of the system. That is to say, that the system is perceived by the user as being in a context where human-like dialogue may be inappropriate.

Second, humans communicate using natural language whereas human-computer communication usually takes place using an abstract or abbreviated language. (Here, natural language is not the same as spoken language. The term *natural language* refers to language which is grammatically correct such as that which is written rather than spoken. The term *spoken language* refers to the non-grammatical language used in normal speech.) Even in the case of abbreviated languages the notation and symbols chosen by designers of systems often does not seem logical or helpful from the user's point of view. While natural language systems are currently being investigated and developed as part of intelligent knowledge-based systems (IKBS) and HCI research projects it is unlikely that they will be in serious widespread use for many years. It appears as though the majority of the communication between computer systems and users will continue to take place via these abstract or abbreviated languages.

Third, we rarely speak using perfect grammar. People speak only half a sentence, miss words out, will interrupt one another once the message being communicated has been understood, and utter single words which may mean nothing to an outside observer, but have meaning in the context of the conversation for those involved. This form of communication is economical and fast, but it is beyond current knowledge to build a computer system that could converse about such vastly different topic areas in this way. Most systems require the perfect grammar of their own peculiar language, and even though some systems are being developed which are *error-tolerant*, these systems, although an improvement, are little different to previous systems when compared with how humans cope with dialogue.

Finally, humans appear to be able to repair dialogue failures whereas computer systems cannot. As has been mentioned in the previous section, both parties to the communicative process must have similar knowledge about the world and need to agree terms. However, when individuals do not have agreed terms then they usually negotiate common definitions. In other words, if one person does not understand another then they might stop the present flow of conversation and ask for a clarification of some of the terms or concepts used.

The difficulties in communication between computers and their users often arise because the definitions in a computer system are given and invariant and cannot be negotiated as they are in communication between humans. The means for negotiating these definitions may eventually be available in future computer systems, but for the present they do not exist, and consequently, human-computer dialogue sometimes tends to be inflexible and unfriendly.

In summary, human-computer dialogue differs from human dialogue in the physical media of communication, in the nature of the language, in the ability to repair dialogue failures and negotiate definitions, and in the inability on the part of computer systems to cope with non-grammatical language in the way that humans can.

THE DESIRABLE QUALITIES OF FUTURE HUMAN-COMPUTER DIALOGUE

The differences between human and human-computer dialogue may first be viewed as goals for future HCI development. However, the situation is more complex than it first seems. The issue is; are the characteristics of human dialogue desirable. In other words, what deficiencies does a consideration of human-computer and human dialogue differences highlight?

First, the present-day physical media of human-computer communication (i.e. keyboards, mice and VDUs) may be suitable for some tasks, but there is a widely accepted need to develop further means for human-computer communication. Many examples of this sort of research can be seen in current research programmes, and some were discussed in the previous chapter.

Second, the need for natural language systems has long ago been recognized. Natural language systems might not be suitable for all tasks, but certainly their envisaged advantages, with respect to naive users and those systems intended for use by the general public appears to justify much of the current interest and research. The question-mark that hangs over these systems is the extent to which they can cope with the wide variety of human expressions and phrases.

Third, the means by which computers could understand the kind of language used in normal communication between humans appears to be only a distant goal, rather than a practical reality. Such a facility might be very useful in some situations and for some tasks where economy of effort and speed are desirable. However, this form of communication lends itself easily to misinterpretation and misunderstanding, and could prove highly undesirable where aspects of safety (e.g. chemical process control) or precision are required. Imagine for example, the frustration a user on the stock exchange might experience if a system bought a large number of the wrong shares.

Finally, a mechanism for the negotiation of common definitions could prove highly desirable in systems where users were expected to define and design their own tasks. If perfected, such a facility could overcome at least some of the present problems of HCI. However, the means for negotiating these definitions may require much more research into the ways in which humans negotiate the meanings of terms and concepts.

To summarize, almost all of the aspects of human dialogue appear desirable, at least for some sorts of task. Being able to negotiate with a computer system and define your own tasks, speaking to computers instead of poring over a keyboard for hours on end, and having a system which does not require perfect English or worse still an abstract language are all appealing possibilities. All, however, require further research, all have their disadvantages and problems, and all appear to be suited to only a limited set of situations.

WHY HAVE WE NO THEORY OF HUMAN-COMPUTER DIALOGUE?

We have established that human-computer dialogue is more restricted and less flexible than normal human dialogue. Given that this is the case, we might expect the development of a theory of human-computer dialogue to be relatively easy. Unfortunately, this has not proved to be possible.

It has been found that the context of the interaction between the user and the system is a significant factor. The structure and content of dialogue, although important, does not affect the interaction between the user and the system in any simple and straightforward way (Barnard et al., 1981; Hammond et al., 1980; 1983b; 1987; Barnard & Hammond, 1982; 1983). Users tend to recruit information and knowledge from related domains depending upon the demands of the task. A user's knowledge of the task, knowledge of natural language, and knowledge of the machine can all potentially interfere with the interaction in subtle and complex ways. This interference can by represented by the Block Interaction Model of Morton, Barnard, Hammond, and Long (1979) shown in Fig. 3.6.

It has been the complexity of the effects upon the interaction between the system and the user, sometimes termed the *multi-determination of usability* (Barnard & Hammond, 1982), that led Barnard et al. (1981) to argue that linguistic principles alone were not enough to account for human-computer

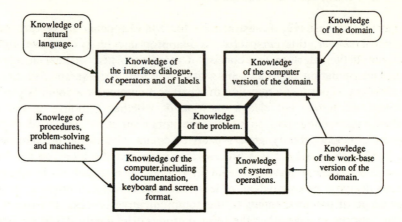

FIG. 3.6.   Morton *et al's* (1979) Block Interaction Model. The blocks with thick boundaries connected by thick lines indicate blocks of knowledge used by the ideal user. Other rounded blocks and arrows indicate possible sources of interference or facilitation (adapted from Hammond & Barnard, 1985).

dialogue. Furthermore, Hammond et al. suggest that any general design principle is likely to miss the "...detailed context-dependent aspects of user cognition" (Hammond et al., 1987), although they do agree that such principles might, nevertheless, be useful in design.

These views have led to a shift in emphasis within HCI. Researchers have begun to consider the effects of the user's knowledge of the task, the system and related domains. Moreover, researchers have begun to look for the means to model the way users employ their knowledge. This shift, from a consideration of straightforward dialogue towards a consideration of users' models, is best illustrated by Barnard and Hammond (1983), who state that:

> ...the cognitive context of a dialogue exchange includes mental representations and cognitive processes relating not only to the explicit structure and content of the dialogue, but also those representations and processes relating to the general cognitive demands imposed by the system, information extracted from the wider task environment, the specific question or problem motivating an exchange, and the cognitive strategies mobilized in the course of learning, use and remembering.

Some of these issues will be considered in the next chapter.

COMMENTARY

There is a tendency to regard dialogue design in HCI as the design of written messages. This projects a view of human-computer dialogue as consisting of a series of written statements that are passed between user and system. At one level of abstraction this view appears to be justified. Overall, however, this perspective is inappropriate on two counts. First, dialogue at the interface can consist of more than just written messages. Direct manipulation interfaces are a case in point. For example, syntax at the interface is not just a question of whether a comma or a colon is placed between two terms, but also a question of whether a mouse is double-clicked, etc. Second, and possibly more important, this view of dialogue appears to neglect the dynamic aspects of communication at the interface. In other words, dialogue is a process that occurs at the interface between two agents, where at least one is intelligent, and it is questionable whether we can design a process where at least one participant can produce such a wide range of potential inputs to the communicative process. In essence, I am not questioning whether the term *dialogue* adequately describes communication at the interface, but whether the term *dialogue design* is appropriate, and whether another term might be better suited. For example, it may be more useful to state that we design *scripts* for the communicative process that occurs at the interface.

Present script (or dialogue) design activity relies upon guidelines. However, there appears to be two problems with the "guidelines approach" to designing scripts (or dialogue). The first is that guidelines are frequently not used; a problem which is not peculiar to this area. The second is that present guidelines tend to be aimed at command language systems and that fewer guidelines exist for dialogue styles such as direct manipulation, etc.

While guidelines may suffice as an intermediate solution, they do not appear to be a long-term answer to the problems of designing scripts for the communicative process. Although there are presently checklist approaches for eliciting the issues that need to be considered during User Needs Analyses (see Chapter Five), we appear to have no means by which we can make explicit the issues that need to be considered in designing a communication script. In essence, we require a method or technique that can utilize data regarding tasks, users and situations to elucidate script (or dialogue) constraints and requirements. These requirements should specify, not only the steps that a profitable script might follow, but also the syntax most appropriate for the situation, task and user.

SUMMARY

Dialogue is the exchange of symbols between two or more parties, as well as being the meanings that the participants in the communicative process assign to these symbols. Dialogue is the process of communication that occurs at the interface.

Meaning can be considered in terms of semantics or pragmatics. Semantics is the study of the literal meanings of words and sentences, regardless of context. Pragmatics is the study of meaning in language, with regard to the individuals involved and the context of the situation.

The term dialogue style, within HCI, refers to the character and control of the information exchange, e.g. command language or menu selection. The term dialogue structure refers to the ordering of dialogue elements within and between dialogue exchanges, whereas, the content of dialogue might be considered as the semantics of the information exchanged. A pragmatics of human-computer interaction should consider, not only the semantics of the words or symbols used, but also the style, structure and context of the dialogue. Dialogue styles within HCI include command language, mixed initiative systems, menus and form fill-in.

HCI is similar to human dialogue in that it is a form of communication where a degree of understanding can be achieved, and it requires agreement between the two parties to the communicative process on the meanings of the terms used, as well as the context in which communication takes place. HCI differs from human dialogue in the physical media of the communication (i.e. speech compared with screens and keyboards), in the use of natural language, in the need on the part of computers for perfect or near-perfect grammar, and in the inability of computers to repair failures in dialogue.

The desirable qualities of future human-computer dialogue include a wider range of physical media for communication (including speech), natural language, the ability to understand language with imperfect grammar, and the means by which common definitions might be negotiated. Some of these facilities, however, might only be of use for certain types of tasks.

Many factors have been found to influence human-computer dialogue. Not only are the structure and content of the dialogue important, but users tend to recruit knowledge from domains which are both directly and indirectly related to the task and system. This finding has led to a shift in emphasis within HCI, away from a straightforward consideration of human-computer dialogue and towards research which focuses upon the user's model of the task and system.

A SELECTIVE ANNOTATED BIBLIOGRAPHY

Barnard, P. J. & Hammond, N. V. (1982). Usability and its multiple determination for the occasional user of interactive systems. In S. William (Ed.), *Pathways to the information society: Proceedings of the 6th international conference on computer communication, London.* Amsterdam: North-Holland. *This classic paper is one of the most cited in HCI. The authors argue that behaviour is highly task dependent and that usability is determined by the subtle interaction of many effects rather than a few straightforward main effects. This theme runs through many of the authors' papers, but this article is probably the most prominent.*

Barnard, P. J. & Hammond, N. V. (1983). *Cognitive contexts and interactive communication.* IBM Hursley Human Factors Laboratory Report. *Here the authors define what the style, structure and content of dialogue are, as well as considering cognitive contexts in HCI. After reviewing a number of their own experiments they conclude that the structure and content of dialogue are critical determinants of ease of use, but that these effects depend also upon many other factors, and that there is a need to account for cognitive context.*

Draper, S. W. (1986). Display managers as the basis for user-machine communication. In D. A. Norman & S. W. Draper (Eds.), *User centred system design: New perspectives on human-computer interaction.* Hillsdale, New Jersey: Lawrence Erlbaum Associates Inc. *The author introduces the idea of inter-referential I/O (input to output). This is where inputs and outputs directly refer to one another. In many ways, considering inputs and outputs separately has more in common with batch processing than direct manipulation, and the author introduces the concept of inter-referential I/O in an attempt to bring things up to date. The author suggests that display managers (or user interface management systems) allow these new forms of related inputs and outputs.*

Gaines, B. R. & Shaw, M. L. G. (1983). Dialogue engineering. In M. E. Sime & M. J. Coombs (Eds.), *Designing for human-computer communication.* London: Academic Press. *The authors review some of the work on dialogue engineering, stretching back as far as the 1960s. They go on to suggest 17 dialogue programming rules, which fall into four categories: Rules for system analysis and development, those concerned with the user's adaptation to the system, those concerned with minimizing the mental load on the user, and rules concerned with error detection and correction. This is an extensive, easy-to-read paper.*

Gaines, B. R. & Shaw, M. L. G. (1984). *The art of computer conversation: A new medium for communication.* Englewood Cliffs, New Jersey: PrenticeHall. *This book considers the conversation between the user and the computer. It is aimed as much at designers as academics, and provides a refreshing and wide-ranging discussion of many topics related to human-computer dialogue.*

Gerrig, R. J. (1986). Process models and pragmatics. In N. E. Sharkey (Ed.), *Advances in cognitive science.* New York: Ellis Horwood. *This paper is concerned with language understanding and what the author calls "meaning recovery tasks". This paper provides an interesting and readable introduction to some of the issues of language comprehension.*

Goodman, B. A. (1987). Repairing reference identification failures by relaxation. In R. G. Reilly (Ed.), *Communication failure in dialogue and discourse.* Amsterdam: Elsevier. *The author discusses dialogue failures and suggests a taxonomy of dialogue confusions.*

Hammond, N. V., Morton, J., Barnard, P. J., Long, J. B., & Clark, I. A. (1987). Characterizing user performance in command-driven dialogue. *Behaviour & Information Technology, 6. The paper reports three studies, the results of which are used to specify the development of the user's knowledge of the system. Using the Morton et al. (1979) framework for analysing user-system dialogue, a goal structure analysis and a process analysis, this paper shows the wide range of sources from which information and knowledge can be drawn. This paper is useful, not only for its findings, but also as a demonstration of the different types of analysis that can be performed.*

Hutchins, E. L., Hollan, J. D., & Norman, D. A. (1986). Direct manipulation interfaces. In D. A. Norman & S. W. Draper (Eds.), *User centred system design: New perspectives on human-computer interaction.* Hillsdale, New Jersey: Lawrence Erlbaum Associates Inc. *The authors consider the concept of direct manipulation, from the time when Shneiderman first suggested the term. The claims and supposed advantages of direct manipulation are critically examined and discussed.*

McMillan, T. C. & Moran, B. P. (1985). Command line structure and dynamic processing of abbreviations in dialogue management. *Interfaces in Computing, 3,* 249–257. *The paper reports an experiment which was concerned with the optimal lengths of command lines in a dialogue management system. Seven recommendations are made as to the design of dialogue.*

Nickerson, R. S. (1981). Some characteristics of conversations. In B. Shackel (Ed.), *Man-computer interaction: Human factors aspects of computers and people.* Rockville, Maryland: Sijthoff & Noordhoff. *The author discusses some of the features of human dialogue, with the aim of raising the question of whether these features ought to be present in human-computer dialogue. Bidirectionality, mixed initiative, control, nonverbal communication, and several other characteristics of human communication are discussed.*

Sheehy, N. P. (1987). Nonverbal behaviour in dialogue. In R. G. Reilly (Ed.), *Communication failure in dialogue and discourse.* Amsterdam: Elsevier. *The author first discusses language and gesture, leading on to a discussion of how nonverbal behaviour can be modelled. After briefly demonstrating the extent to which we rely upon nonverbal behaviour in normal human dialogue, the author considers human-computer dialogue and points out some of its present deficiencies. This paper is not only easy to read, but also provides an excellent discussion of some of the most important issues for future human-computer dialogue.*

Shneiderman, B. (1987). *Designing the user interface: Strategies for effective human-computer interaction.* Reading, Massachusetts: Addison-Wesley. *In chapters three, four and five the author deals with various dialogue, or interactional, styles. Menus, form fill-in, command languages, natural language, and direct manipulation are all considered. The discussion of these interactional styles is both extensive and readable.*

4 Cognitive Models in Human-Computer Interaction

In collaboration with Gill M. Brown
Department of Psychology, Manchester University

OVERVIEW

First, HCI is described from a cognitive standpoint. Much of the user's behaviour at the interface can be attributed to the cognitive or mental model that the user holds of the task and system. Consequently, the concept and characteristics of mental models are discussed, as well as some of the differences in terminology regarding *mental* and *conceptual* models. Following this, the use of metaphors to help users form their models of the task and system is considered.

While the term *user model* can sometimes be taken to mean the user's mental model of the task and system, this is not always the case. Therefore, the uses of the term *user model* are examined. We will then consider the different types of model that can be employed, as well as the purposes of modelling the user. Finally, three of the analytic techniques for modelling the user are described, and some of the problems with the modelling approach are discussed.

INTRODUCTION

In the last chapter some of the research into human-computer dialogue was considered. The overall finding of this research was that the context of communication strongly affected dialogue at the interface. Consequently, drawing straightforward and valid rules about dialogue design from this

65

research, without considering how context affects user behaviour, was not considered to be a realistic possibility.

This realization caused a shift of emphasis within HCI, as research began to concentrate on how users process information about a task and system. An example of this shift can be seen in Kidd's statement: "If interactive computer systems are to be easy and efficient to communicate with then their dialogue design must be compatible with the information processing characteristics of the human mind." (Kidd, 1982). This emphasis has led to one of the major themes in HCI; that of understanding human-computer interaction in cognitive terms. Storrs et al. epitomize this view: "The 'man' in MMI [HCI] is not primarily interacting with a machine but is interacting with information, program logic, knowledge, another intelligence. That this interaction takes place through computers and their peripheral devices should not be allowed to obscure that fact that it is essentially cognitive and that the most important issues are cognitive." (Storrs, Rivers, & Canter, 1984).

The character of this cognitive perspective has been summed-up by Green: "The special quality of a cognitive approach is, of course, that it starts from considering the mental life of the user, often using modelling techniques drawn from artificial intelligence and cognitive science to reveal what he or she knows about the interface and how this knowledge is put to use." (Green, 1986).

COGNITIVE PERSPECTIVE ON HCI

The cognitive perspective on HCI suggests a particular way of considering both the user and the interaction between the user and the computer system. Several researchers have considered what users do at an interface from this cognitive perspective, most notably Donald Norman.

Norman (1986) points out that many of the problems that we experience, in operating machinery of any sort, can be related to the difficulties of linking our psychological goals to the physical variables and controls of the task. To illustrate this point Norman gives the simple example of filling a bath with water. We have two psychological variables; the temperature of the water, and the rate at which the water flows into the bath. However, the physical variables that we can control are just two valves, one for the hot water and one for the cold water. Adjusting one of these valves changes, not just the temperature, but also the flow rate. In other words, our psychological variables do not directly *map* onto the physical variables of the task. If we had a bath where the flow rate control and the temperature control worked independently (e.g. such as those fitted to some showers), then these controls might *map* onto our psychological variables more accurately.

The term *mapping* is used widely in the psychological literature, but comes from the discipline of mathematics, where it is used to mean associating one element from one set to another element from another set. So we say that we *map* our psychological variables to appropriate physical variables, which means almost the same as saying that we *relate* our psychological variables to the physical variables of the task.

The problems of mapping our psychological variables onto the physical variables of the task might be expected to become greater as the complexity of the task increases. This problem has also been identified by other researchers, such as Young (1981) and Moran (1983). Mapping difficulties have been described by Norman (1986) as being the gulfs that prevent users from dealing easily and efficiently with computer-based tasks.

The *gulf of execution*, that Norman (1986) describes, is where the user knows what needs to be achieved, the user has a goal, but does not know which physical variables to adjust, or in what way to adjust them. The *gulf of evaluation* is where the system has altered, usually as a result of the user's actions, but the user cannot easily understand the change in the system's state. In other words, it is difficult for the user to work out what has happened to the system, and whether the change fits in with the initial goals and intentions. These gulfs are represented in Fig. 4.1.

Norman (1986; 1987) suggests that users engage in seven stages of activity. These stages span the gulfs of evaluation and execution shown in Fig. 4.1, and are as follows: Establishing the goal; Forming the intention; Specifying the action sequence; Executing the action; Perceiving the system

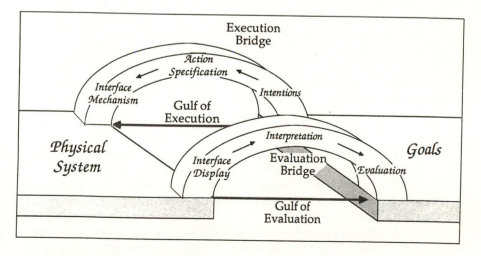

FIG. 4.1. The gulfs of execution and evaluation, together with the bridges that span these gulfs. Adapted from Norman (1986).

state; Interpreting the system state; and Evaluating the system state with
respect to the goals and intentions.

Norman has outlined the aspects of a task that might influence these
seven activities, and has provided some definitions of the terms used in his
approximate theory of action (what follows has been taken directly from
table 3.1 of Norman's 1986 paper):

Goals and intentions: A goal is the state the person wishes to achieve; an
intention is the decision to act so as to achieve the goal.

Specification of the action sequence: The psychological process of determining
the psychological representation of the actions that are to be executed by the
user on the mechanisms of the system.

Mapping from psychological goals and intentions to action sequence: In order
to specify the action sequence, the user must translate the psychological goals
and intentions into the desired system state, then determine what settings of the
control mechanisms will yield that state, and then determine what physical
manipulations of the mechanisms are required. The result is the internal,
mental specification of the actions that are to be executed.

Physical state of the system: The physical state of the system, determined by
the values of all its physical variables.

Control Mechanisms: The physical devices that control the physical variables.

Mapping between the physical mechanisms and system state: The relationship
between the settings of the mechanisms of the system and the system state.

Interpretation of system state: The relationship between the physical state of
the system and the psychological goals of the user can only be determined by
first translating the physical state into psychological states (perception), then
interpreting the perceived system state in terms of the psychological variables
of interest.

Evaluating the outcome: Evaluation of the system state requires comparing the
interpretation of the perceived system state with the desired goals. This often
leads to a new set of goals and intentions.

Norman (1983c) previously suggested four stages of activity, but has
since revised this to seven, and these stages form an approximate theory of
action. The theory is only approximate because the seven stages are not
necessarily discrete (separable), and because the stages might not necessarily
follow one another in a strict order.

What Norman has suggested is an account of how people interact with
computers. This is not necessarily intended as an empirical theory, but is a
useful way of thinking about the activities involved in performing a task.
However, although Norman's description provides a useful way of thinking

about the activities involved in HCI, it is difficult to see how such a description might be of practical use. The steps identified in the description are, in reality, difficult to distinguish. Consequently, it is not, and was never intended, as a theory that might be used within the design and development process.

There have, however, been other useful ways of considering HCI. Usually, these alternatives complement rather than contradict Norman's approximate theory. Moran (1981), for example, has suggested Command Language Grammar as a means of structuring and understanding the human-computer interface. In Chapter Two it was mentioned that *command language* might be thought of as a dialogue style. Moran, however, uses the term command language to mean any system where the user enters commands, whether this is via menu, form fill-in, or any other dialogue style. The only exceptions to this are natural language systems and programming languages.

Moran (1981) describes Command Language Grammar (CLG) as having three components and six levels (see Fig. 4.2), although only four of these levels are dealt with in any detail. In the paper, Moran describes the first four levels in the following way:

Task level : The user comes to the system with a set of tasks that he wants to accomplish. The purpose of the Task level is to analyse the user's needs, and to structure his task domain in a way that is amenable to an interactive system. The output of this level is a structure of specific tasks that the user will set for himself with the aid of the system.

Semantic level : A system is built around a set of objects and manipulations of those objects. To the system these are data structures and procedures; to the

Conceptual component:	Task level
	Semantic level
Communication component:	Syntactic level
	Interaction level
Physical component:	(Spatial layout level)
	(Device level)

FIG. 4.2. The three components and six levels of the Command Language Grammar from Moran (1981).

user they are conceptual entities and conceptual operations on these entities. The Semantic level lays out these entities and operations. They are intended to be useful for accomplishing the user's tasks, since they represent the systems functional capability. Thus, the Semantic level also specifies methods for accomplishing the tasks in terms of these conceptual entities and operations.

Syntactic level : The conceptual model of a system is embedded in a language structure, the command language, for users to communicate with the system. All command languages are built out of a few syntactic elements; commands, arguments, contexts and state variables. The Syntactic level lays out these elements. The "meaning" of each command of the system is defined in terms of operations at the Semantic level, and the methods at the Semantic level are recorded in terms of Syntactic level commands.

Interactional level : The dialogue conventions for the user-system interaction must ultimately be resolved as a sequence of physical actions–key presses and other primitive device manipulations by the user and display actions by the system. The Interaction level specifies the physical actions associated with each of the Syntactic level elements, as well as the rules governing the dialogue.

This division of the interaction into task, semantic, syntactic, and inter-actional levels has been widely adopted within HCI, often by researchers who do not necessarily use Moran's grammar. The purpose of the approach suggested by Moran (1981) is to distinguish the conceptual model (this will be explained later in the chapter) of a system from the command language, and so reveal the associations and connections between the two. The grammar itself will not be described here, but it can be thought of as providing a way of working through different parts of a system, making explicit both the relationships between the different components and the different levels within the system. (For a description of the grammar see Moran, 1981.)

The idea of separating out the different levels (i.e. the semantic and the syntactic) of interaction appears, at first, to be both theoretically and practically appealing. Nevertheless, in reality such an approach has the same drawbacks as Norman's (1986) division of activities. That is to say, that the semantic and syntactic aspects of interaction are sometimes difficult to distinguish. They are often so closely tied together that they cannot always be usefully considered in isolation. Despite this, both Moran's (1981) identification of the different levels of interaction and Norman's (1986) approximate theory of action provide a useful way of thinking about the activities and the issues involved in HCI. In this respect, approaches such as this, while not of immediate practical relevance, provide possible building blocks for more practically orientated theory and technique.

Neither Norman's (1986) approximate theory nor Moran's (1981) grammar have been described in great detail, and it is suggested that interested readers should refer to the original papers for more complete descriptions. However, both Norman's and Moran's ideas provide ways of breaking down what users do at the interface (for other models see Clarke, 1986; Nielsen, 1986). In essence, these different models or ideas provide a means by which we can structure how we think about the cognitive aspects of HCI.

However, while approaches such as Norman's approximate theory of action allow us to break down the different components of HCI, if we wish to understand and predict the user we may need to understand how the user thinks about the task and system. In other words, we may need to consider the user's *mental model* of a system.

MENTAL MODELS

It is commonly accepted within the psychological literature that people form mental models of tasks and systems, and that these models are used to guide behaviour at the interface. Norman (1983c) explains this in the following way: "In interacting with the environment, with others, and with the artifacts of technology, people form internal, mental models of themselves and of the things with which they are interacting. These models provide predictive and explanatory power for understanding the interaction." But what does the research show about mental models?

Research into Mental Models

Research that has focused upon how people think about problems can be traced back several decades. This work has considered many sorts of problems, from spatial problems (problems to do with 3-dimensional shapes, etc.), to problems to do with mathematics and logic. One of the most interesting findings that has arisen from this research is the discovery that we do not always reason logically.

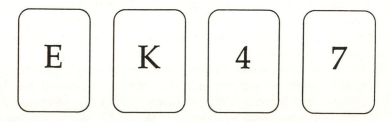

FIG. 4.3. Four cards shown to subjects in Wason's (1966) problem. There are four logical types in this problem; vowels, consonants, odd numbers and even numbers. Each card shows one of these types.

For example, Wason (1966) gave subjects a *four card* problem. The subjects were told, "...if a card has a vowel on one side then it will have an even number on the other side." Subjects were shown four cards (see Fig. 4.3) and were asked which cards they would turn over to make sure that the rule was valid. Most subjects select the "E" card to check that the rule is correct. Few subjects however, check the "7" card to see whether a vowel is shown on the other side. The "7" card is considered to be critical, as it will show whether the rule can be shown to be false. In other words, if we turn the "7" card over and it has a vowel on the other side then the rule stated above is false.

Johnson-Laird (1981; 1983) has taken this research further by demonstrating that not only does our reasoning not conform to formal logic, but furthermore, that our decision is dependent upon the domain of the problem. For example, if the same problem is presented in the context of bank cheques, and whether they have been signed on the back or not, then subjects produce a different answer. In short, *the problems may be logically identical, but the responses to the problems may vary according to the domain* (Johnson-Laird, 1981; 1983; Manktelow & Jones, 1987).

The work of Johnson-Laird has been particularly influential with respect to how we have come to think about mental models. For instance, Johnson-Laird has pointed out that mental models must not only allow us to deal with propositional statements and problems (e.g. the canary has wings, only birds have wings, therefore the canary is a bird), our models of the world must also allow us to understand spatial relations, such as the relative positions of people sitting around a table, for example.

Johnson-Laird, and other researchers in the field (e.g. Cheng, Holyoak, Nisbett, & Oliver, 1986), have used research into how we think about problems to inform their theories of how these problems are represented mentally. There are many theories of how we represent knowledge, and of how we form and use our mental models of the world. There is still, however, no generally agreed theory that can account for all of the psychological data. Most theories account for some of the data very well, but cannot account for other things that humans do. As such, these theories help us to move towards a better understanding of how we form and use our internal mental models, but we still do not know exactly how humans form and use their mental models.

The vast literature on mental models cannot be properly considered here, but interested readers are referred to books such as Aitkenhead and Slack (1985), Gentner and Stevens (1983), Gilhooly (1982), Kolodner and Riesbeck (1986), and papers such as Kieras and Bovair (1984), Manktelow and Jones (1987). Nevertheless, much of the research that has been conducted allows us to outline some of the general characteristics of mental models.

The Nature of Mental Models

The first thing we can say about mental models is that they are simpler than the entities they represent and as a consequence are incomplete (Johnson-Laird, 1983). When people encounter new machines, devices or computers they begin to construct mental models to represent their behaviour and operation. These internal models provide a means by which people can understand and predict the world around them, but we construct these models as we go along and as a consequence our models tend to be incomplete, unstable, do not have firm boundaries, are unscientific and parsimonious (Norman, 1983c).

Mental models are incomplete as it is rare that all of the subject matter concerning a task or system is known to the user. The instability of mental models can be seen by the way that people forget details, and confuse one system with another because of the lack of firm boundaries between models. What people do not know, they will work out and assume. One of the efficiencies of the human mind is the ability to use a small amount of knowledge to infer a great deal. Sometimes, however, we assume incorrectly, and the mistakes and misunderstandings that we make are characteristic of these incomplete and confusable models of the world.

Mental models are parsimonious, according to Norman, because they are no more complicated than they need to be, and possibly as a result of this people are apt to maintain superstitious beliefs in the way that they act towards a system. For example, once we feel we understand a system at least well enough to cope with it, we do not usually expend extra effort trying to understand it further. It is, after all, easier to maintain a super-stitious belief that apparently explains a system than find out how it really works.

Norman's (1983c) description of mental models fits the views held by many other researchers in the field. As was mentioned in the last chapter, Barnard and Hammond (1983) found that users recruited knowledge from related domains depending upon the perceived demands of the task. In other words, users appear to have blocks of knowledge relating to different domains (e.g. natural language understanding) and use parts of these knowledge blocks when they believe that it is appropriate (Morton et al., 1979). The idea that users have coherent and accurate models is unsupported by much of the available evidence. It appears as though *users proceed through a task picking and choosing from both appropriate and inappropriate areas of their knowledge, and only after much experience do users form a more precise and representative model of the system with which they are dealing.*

Differences in Terminology: Mental and Conceptual Models

Now that we have identified some of the key characteristics of mental models, what is the difference between a *mental model* and a *conceptual model?* The most disagreement is over the use of the term *conceptual model.* Young (1981) distinguishes between *conceptual knowledge*–used to interpret and understand the machine–and *procedural knowledge*–knowledge of what sequences of actions are appropriate for a particular task. Thus we have *conceptual models* which allow us to understand complex devices and *task-action mapping models* which relate what we understand to the physical variables of the device which are important for the task at hand. In short, task-action mapping models relate what we know (conceptual knowledge) to what we can do (procedural knowledge).

For example, a person may have a conceptual model of a car engine. This person will understand the basic principles of the internal combustion engine. Nevertheless, although this individual understands the principles of what is happening, it may not be possible for the person to relate what is known to the screws and adjusters which alter different aspects of the engine's performance. The individual does not have the model which maps the principles of what is understood to the physical variables of the engine. This is the task-action mapping model which relates the conceptual model to what can and should be done.

Norman (1983c), on the other hand, uses the term *conceptual model* to mean something which is not necessarily held by the user at all. A conceptual model, in Norman's terms, is an accurate, consistent and complete model of a system. It is the kind of model that the designer of the system might wish to present, and the type of model a teacher might attempt to convey. For Norman, a conceptual model is invented by an engineer, scientist, designer or teacher, while a mental model is a naturally evolving internal representation of a system. In other words, conceptual models are external and explicit whereas mental models, although they guide what we think and do, cannot be directly expressed. Furthermore, however well-developed a mental model might become, it will always remain confusable and inexact to some extent.

This disagreement is not a dispute about the nature of cognition, although disputes are plenty enough, but more a difference of opinion of how different terms should be used. As a rule of thumb, when writers are referring to Norman's work then a conceptual model should usually be thought of as a complete and coherent model which has been invented by someone such as a designer. When ideas relating to task-action mapping are being discussed, then a conceptual model should be thought of as something which sits on top of a task-action mapping model and provides the overall understanding of the task or system. Unfortunately, however, these are only very general guidelines. The terms *mental* and *conceptual model* are sometimes used interchangeably. Norman, in his 1986 paper, even uses the term *conceptual model* to mean something different to his earlier definition of 1983c. Sometimes only careful reading will show how the different terms are being used.

METAPHORS IN HCI

Now that we have identified some of the characteristics of users' mental models, as well as the different uses of some terms, the question that now arises is, *how can we ensure that users acquire an appropriate mental model of a system?* One approach to helping users form their mental model of a task and system is to provide a metaphor that explains the workings of the system. Over the past decade there has been a number of papers reporting research into the use of metaphors in HCI. Interest in the use of metaphors is increasing, but why are metaphors potentially useful?

Metaphors are used in everyday speech (Lakoff & Johnson, 1980), and because they are so commonly used, speaking without using a metaphor is particularly difficult. This may be partly because we do not always realize when we are using a metaphor. For example, if we are informed that the amount of money in our bank account has increased, we might say that our savings have *gone up*. The notion of *increase* is metaphorically associated with concepts such as *height* and *going up* (Lakoff & Johnson, 1981). Nevertheless, this still does not fully answer the question of *why are metaphors potentially useful?*

The answer involves the question of how we learn. It is commonly accepted that we learn by building upon existing knowledge, and this is where metaphors play an important role. If, for example, we need to explain the concept of an electron to someone, how might we do this? Firstly, we can say that it behaves *like* a wave, in that it shares certain properties that radio waves or light possess. Then we can say that an electron is *like* a particle, in that it has mass. Finally, we can say that an electron is *like* a cloud in the way that it surrounds the nucleus of an atom. Notice how we use the word *like* to suggest that it has properties with are similar to waves, particles, and clouds. In truth, of course, an electron is neither a cloud, particle, or wave; it is unique. But by identifying those features which the electron has in common with concepts that are already understood, we build a new concept based upon existing knowledge. In essence, metaphors enable learning, they provide short-cuts to understanding complex concepts; they can be used to shape users' behaviour in circumstances that are unfamiliar and that they might otherwise find confusing.

Analogy and Metaphor

Halasz and Moran (1982) have distinguished analogies from metaphors. They state that an analogical model: "...involves a structure mapping between two complex systems, one known and one unknown. The analogical model maps objects, relations, operations etc., in the known source system to corresponding objects, relations, operations etc., in the unknown target system." They go on to say that: "...only the most salient point need be drawn from a metaphor...In contrast, analogical reasoning requires considerable work to sort out the relevant mappings and allowable inferences."

In short, Halasz and Moran (1982) are suggesting that an analogy is where a whole unknown system is considered to behave, at some level of abstraction, in the same way as a known system. On the other hand, a metaphor only suggests that part of an unknown system is similar to a known system. This definition is used by Halasz and Moran to argue that analogy can lead, not only to faulty reasoning, but also to a limited view of a system, where the only parts of a target system that can be properly exploited are those that are explained by the analogy. Marshall, Nelson, and Gardiner (1987b) make a similar point when they state that: "...by tying an interface to concepts which prevail in non-electronic environments, one is not taking full advantage of the benefits that can accrue from using the electronic medium...For example, a *filing cabinet* can be as restrictive as the real-life filing cabinet."

Nevertheless, if analogies are potentially unhelpful, how can we explain the results of experiments where benefits were shown? One such experiment has been reported by Rumelhart and Norman (1981), who used three analogical models to improve performance. Halasz and Moran (1982) point out that the three models used by Rumelhart and Norman (1981) were only used to convey one concept each. In essence, they were used as metaphors rather than analogies. Halasz and Moran (1982) conclude that metaphors, which are used to explain only one or two aspects of a system, may be of use in HCI. Analogical models, on the other hand: "...can often act as barriers preventing new users from developing effective understanding of systems." (Halasz & Moran, 1982).

The Dimensions of a Metaphor

Rather than distinguish metaphors from analogies Hammond and Allinson (1987) suggest that a metaphor can be described along two dimensions, *scope* and *level of description*. The *scope* of the metaphor refers to the number of concepts that the metaphor addresses. Hammond and Allinson point out that some systems have many metaphors of narrow scope. That is to say, that each metaphor in the system explains just one or two concepts. Other systems, however, have fewer metaphors of wider scope, and they give the hydraulic metaphor as an example. This metaphor is used in the UNIX™ system, where files and messages are sent down pipes, etc. One of the most popular metaphors is the desktop metaphor, which has been exploited to its best commercial advantage in Apple's Macintosh personal computer, although this metaphor was used sometime ago in the Xerox Star system, and has also been used in systems developed by companies such as Hewlett Packard and DEC. In systems that use this metaphor the screen often consists of files, folders, waste-paper baskets, etc. (see Fig. 4.4). Users are encouraged to use their knowledge of how an office works to infer the correct operations on the system. For example, to delete a file or folder it is placed in the waste-paper basket.

The *level of description* of a metaphor is concerned with the type of information that a metaphor might be expected to communicate. For example, if we take the distinctions used in Moran's (1981) Command Language Grammar, a metaphor can be aimed at the task level, the semantic level, the syntactic level, or the physical level.

In summary, Hammond and Allinson (1987) offer a way of thinking about metaphors, while Halasz and Moran (1982) distinguish metaphors from analogies. The interest in metaphors, as models for the design of some systems, and in the way that they enable the user to understand a system, is presently growing. This expanding area of research within HCI is likely to

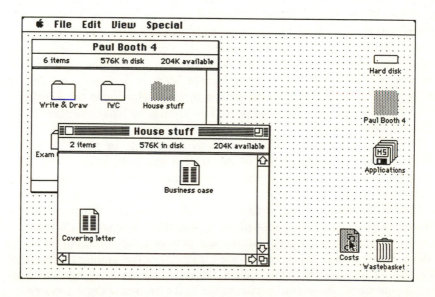

FIG. 4.4.   A screen from an Apple Macintosh, showing the desktop metaphor, with files, folders, wastebins, etc.

be directed towards the question of how we can use metaphors efficiently in *human-computer interaction*. While there may be a need for metaphors in HCI to help users understand systems, there is also the danger that poorly chosen metaphors can restrict a system and confuse users. One of the central issues regarding metaphors is how we can signpost the boundaries of metaphors within a system so that users know when a metaphor is no longer relevant and when another metaphor is appropriate.

USER MODELS

One objective of the research into HCI has been to find ways of identifying suitable metaphors for a system, so that it is properly explained, but not limited by the metaphor. An approach to this problem, as well as the question of understanding the user's model of the task and system, has been to employ analytic techniques to model the user. But what are user models?

Although the term *user model* may have originally been intended to mean the user's mental model of a task and system, the term has come to have a number of different meanings. Indeed, the term *user model* is often used in even more ways than the term *conceptual model*. Here, we will attempt to clarify the different uses of this term. Hammond et al. (1983b) distinguish three main uses of this term. First, the term *user model* can be used to mean a representation of the user embedded within a system. For example, a system for advising accountants on some aspect of the tax system might have a model of the user (the accountant) which dictates what the accountant can be assumed to know. This type of model is held within the system.

The second usage that Hammond et al. identify is that where a user model is something closer to what Norman calls a conceptual model. It is an ideal model which the ideal user might hold. It acts as a goal for the designer of a product during the design process. Hammond et al. refer to this as the *design interface image* (this is similar to what Norman (1986) calls the *system image*).

Third, and most common, the term *user model* can be taken to mean a model of the user's knowledge of the system and task. In this sense *user modelling* is taken to refer to the representation of the user's model of a system and task.

This distinction, although perfectly valid, is not the only view of the function and place of user modelling within HCI. Young (1985) makes a similar, but slightly different distinction between the different senses in which the term *user model* can be used. First, it is the designer's model of the user. This is a predictive model which helps guide design and aids predictions about the overall performance of the human-computer system.

Second, it is the user's conceptual model of the system. In other words, it is the internal model the user has of the system (note how the term *conceptual model* is used in Young's sense to mean a general model that facilitates understanding rather than in Norman's sense, where it means an invented model that is complete and consistent).

Third, the term *user model* can be used to mean an embedded user model. This is a representation of certain aspects of the user which is implicit within the software of the machine and is used to adapt the system to suit the user. It is possible to argue that all systems have an implicit model of the user embedded by the designers within the software. Here, however, Young is referring to *explicit* models within computer systems.

The view which appears to have been most commonly accepted within HCI as to the possible uses of the term *user model* has been expressed by Clowes (1987), who suggests that there are the following types of user models: the designer's model of the user; and the user's model of the task; the user's model of the system; and the system's embedded model of the user.

Although this view appears to be generally accepted, the degree to which the user's model of the task and the user's model of the system can be distinguished practically is in some doubt. Furthermore, it is important to recognize that views on user modelling which are alternative to these are not necessarily wrong; they represent different ways of considering the problems of HCI and as such are still potentially valuable contributions.

What is the Purpose of User Modelling?

Having reviewed some of the ideas relating to what comprises a user model, it may now be useful to explain the possible advantages and uses of user modelling. There is general agreement between researchers as to the purposes of user modelling. First user modelling can help in matching the facilities that a system provides to the needs of the user. As mentioned in Chapter One, many systems provide functions that are not required while facilities that are needed by users are often not present. Providing tools for matching what the system can do to the needs of the user is seen as one of the most important contributions HCI can make to systems design.

Second, user modelling can suggest metaphors to improve user learning. An example of a very popular metaphor, the desktop metaphor, was briefly described earlier.

Third, user modelling can guide design decisions and make design choices and assumptions explicit. In other words, user modelling can help to create a rational design (Young, 1985). Many of the decisions that designers make are based on intuition. Indeed, creativity and intuition are seen as being essential to good design. However, by making the reasons for these design decisions explicit the image that the completed system will project to the user can be more thoroughly considered.

Fourth, user modelling can provide a predictive evaluation of proposed designs (Young, 1985). During the design process there are very often alternative designs for different parts of the system. By providing predictions of user behaviour, user modelling techniques can help to choose between these competing options.

Fifth, user modelling can help to identify variations in the user population. For example, accountants and secretaries might have different models of a particular task and therefore require different interfaces to a system. The elucidation of these differences should help designers to direct their design.

Finally, user modelling can guide the design of experiments and help in the interpretation of the results (Young, 1985). In other words, user modelling can provide a theoretical framework for research in HCI.

Classes of User Model

Although user modelling might serve a number of purposes, not all of these objectives are likely to be fulfilled by just one modelling technique. Different modelling techniques provide different types of information, but what are these different types of models?

At a general level, user models can be either predictive, descriptive or normative (Clowes, 1987). In other words, they can provide information which allows us to predict the user, information that describes and explains what the user is doing, or information which provides overall norms (or perhaps just norms for particular user groups).

More specifically, three general classes of model can be identified; those that are concerned with performance, learning or reasoning. Young (1985) has charted the questions answered by different types of model, and these questions and answers can be seen in Fig. 4.5.

The different questions set out by Young are useful as a way of considering different types of model. It is unlikely, however, that any one modelling technique will provide all that HCI needs, as different modelling techniques provide the answers to different questions. It is hoped that these different modelling techniques, when taken together, will one day provide a wide-ranging view of the user and so produce the means by which the user's model of the task might be matched comprehensively with that embedded within the system by the designer.

MODELLING TECHNIQUES

So far we have considered the different uses of the term *user model*, we have looked at the purposes of user modelling, and the different types of model we might use. However, the question that we have not addressed is *what exactly are these modelling techniques?*

PERFORMANCE
System competence: Which tasks can be performed on the system?
User functionality: Which tasks can users perform?
Method choice: Which methods will users actually choose?
Time: How long will the task take?
Error sites: Where will errors occur?
Error types: What type of errors will occur?
Relative error frequency: What is the relative frequency of different classes of errors?
Probability of success: What is the absolute frequency of different error classes?
Loading: Where is the user over-loaded?

LEARNING
Generalizations and transfer: What new tasks can users perform because of past experience?
Learning time: How long will it take to learn a system?
Over-generalization and negative transfer: What errors will users make because of past experience?
Forgetting: What will be retained and what forgotten over time?
Long-term memory distortions: What distortions in system knowledge will occur?

REASONING
System prediction: Given a set of inputs, what will the system do?
Method invention: Given a goal, derive a method by which the goal can be accomplished on the machine.
In-principle method space: What is the space of in-principle methods?
Explanation: Given a set of inputs and outputs, explain why the outputs occurred?
Explanation space: What is the space of the explanations?

FIG. 4.5.   The questions that different types of model answer, taken from Young (1985).

The answer is that they are forms of task analysis. User modelling techniques to date have taken the form of formal grammars for describing the user's tasks at the interface. Implicit within these task analysis techniques are models of certain aspects of human cognition. That is to say, that an interface is described using the symbols and conventions of a grammar, and the number of rules within the grammatical description of the task or interface are assumed to reflect the cognitive complexity of performing the task.

To provide a better idea of what these modelling methods comprise three grammars will be briefly described. This should provide a flavour of some of the cognitive modelling work within HCI. However, the modelling techniques outlined here are by no means the only techniques that are worth considering. Many interesting and potentially useful techniques exist. Furthermore, the account of each model is intended to be illustrative rather than comprehensive. Readers who wish to know more about any particular modelling technique should refer to the original paper.

The three models or techniques that are described are GOMS (Goals, Operators, Methods, and Selection rules), BNF (Backus Naur Form), and TAG (Task-Action Grammar). The GOMS model was chosen because it is possibly the best known of the modelling techniques. BNF is described because it is the grammar that so many other grammars are based upon. TAG, on the other hand, has been chosen because its central goal is to relate what the user knows to the actions that the user needs to perform. Consequently, TAG attempts to tackle a problem that is seen by many researchers as being of great theoretical importance.

The GOMS Model

The Goals, Operators, Methods, and Selection rules (GOMS) model was developed by Card, Moran and Newell in the mid-1970's (Card et al., 1980; 1983). It was intended as an approximate cognitive model of human information-processing. It is approximate because its predictions were never intended to be completely precise. The purpose of the model was to provide reasonably accurate predictions of human behaviour at the interface without requiring a great deal of effort on the part of those involved.

The GOMS model has four components: *Goals, operators, methods*, and *selection rules*. Card et al. (1980) describe these components in the following way:

> Goals: "A goal is a symbolic structure that defines a state of affairs to be achieved, and determines a set of possible methods by which it may be accomplished."
>
> Operators: "Operators are elementary motor or information-processing acts, whose execution is necessary to change any aspect of the user's memory or to affect the task environment."
>
> Methods: "A method describes a procedure for accomplishing a goal. The description of the procedure is cast as a continual sequence of goals and operators, with conditional tests on the contents of the user's immediate memory and on the state of the task environment."
>
> Selection rules: "When a goal is attempted, there may be more than one method available to the user to accomplish the goal." The choice of method is

governed by selection rules which depend upon the features of the task environment.

It may be useful to consider a simple example. Suppose that we have typed a piece of text using a word processor (see Fig. 4.6). The window shows some of the text that we have typed. Not all of the text that we have entered can be shown, and so there is a scroll bar to the left-hand side of the window. In the middle of the scroll bar is a scroll marker, that indicates our position within the text. If we take the pointer to the scroll bar using a mouse, or some similar input device (see Chapter Two for details), and move the scroll marker to the top of the scroll bar, then the window will move to the beginning of our text. If we move the scroll marker to the bottom of the bar, then we will see the end of our text. However, we may not wish to move such large distances. We may wish only to see the portion of text below the text that is presently being displayed. If this is the case, then we can click, using the mouse button, directly on the scroll bar, below the scroll marker. This will cause the next window of text to be displayed.

In short, we have two strategies; we can move the scroll marker up or down large distances, or we can click on the scroll bar itself to move the text a screenful at a time. Now let us consider a GOMS model interpretation of editing a line in this text (see Fig. 4.7). The first feature of the notation that stands out is the dots towards the left. These dots indicate the positions

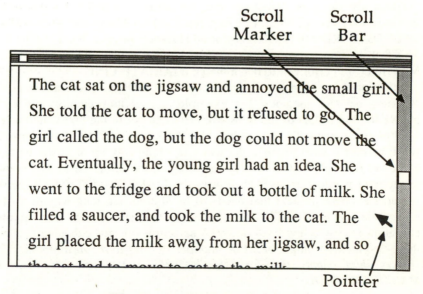

FIG. 4.6.   A window from a text editor.

GOAL: EDIT-MANUSCRIPT					(goal)
•	GOAL: EDIT-UNIT-TASK				(goal)
•	•	GOAL: GET-UNIT-TASK			(goal)
•	•	•	GET-UNIT-TASK		(operator)
•	•	GOAL: DO-UNIT-TASK			(goal)
•	•	•	GOAL: LOCATE-LINE		(goal)
•	•	•	•	[select: USE-MARKER-METHOD	(operator)
				USE-BAR-METHOD]	(operator)
•	•	•	GOAL: MODIFY-TEXT.		(goal)
•	•	•	•	[select: USE-D/LINE-METHOD	(operator)
				USE-D/WORD-METHOD]	(operator)
•	•	•	•	VERIFY EDIT	(operator)

FIG. 4.7.   A task description using GOMS, adapted from Card et al. (1980). The operators, USE-MARKER-METHOD and USE-BAR-METHOD, mean that the scroll marker is moved, or the scroll bar is clicked respectively. The operators, USE-D/LINE-METHOD and USE-D/WORD-METHOD, mean that the command to delete a line is used, or the command to delete a word is used respectively.

of the goals. For example, the goal EDIT-UNIT-TASK is a subgoal of EDIT-MANUSCRIPT. In other words, EDIT-UNIT-TASK is part of EDIT-MANUSCRIPT.

Goals are states or objectives that we want to achieve. Operators are those actions we perform to reach our goals. Therefore, the operator DELETE-WORD-METHOD is performed to reach the goal GOAL: MODIFY-TEXT. Likewise, the operators USE-MARKER-METHOD or USE-BAR-METHOD are performed to reach the goal LOCATE-LINE.

Selection rules form the final component of GOMS. These are rules for choosing between methods. For example, a user may employ either the MARKER-METHOD or the BAR-METHOD to get to the text which might need to be changed. To recapitulate, the MARKER-METHOD is where the scroll marker is used to move the window a long way up or down the text, while the BAR-METHOD involves clicking on the scroll bar to move down to the next window of text. Therefore, the MARKER-METHOD might be preferable where the text that needs to be altered is a long way down the file, while the BAR-METHOD may be best when the text that requires alteration is only a few lines down. A selection rule for choosing between these two methods might be: *If the number of lines to the next modification is less than twenty then use the BAR-METHOD, otherwise use the MARKER-METHOD.*

The GOMS model works by breaking the task down into a goal stack (see Fig. 4.7), and specifying the operators, methods, and rules for selecting between alternative methods. This way the model can be used to predict times and users' routes through tasks. In their experimental evaluation of GOMS Card et al. (1980) concluded that a user's behaviour at a particular word-processing task could be described using 1–20 goals, 1–13 operators, 4–6 methods, and 1–4 selection rules. As we might expect, the numbers of goals, operators, methods, and selection rules depends upon the *grain of analysis* (the extent to which we break the task down) and the text editor that is being studied. Card et al. also found that the user's choice of methods could be accurately predicted in about 80% to 90% of all cases.

However, GOMS is unfortunately limited with respect to the extent to which it can be applied. The model assumes expert behaviour. In other words, it cannot account for a novice's or intermediate-level user's behaviour. Furthermore, the model assumes performance which is substantially error-free. Card et al. suggest that routine errors will degrade the accuracy of the model. It appears unlikely, however, that the GOMS model will remain useful as a predictor where more substantial errors occur.

The GOMS model is important because it was the first significant cognitive model of HCI. Even now, over a decade from when it was first conceived and developed, it is still considered to be of some interest and value.

Backus Naur Form

In 1981 Phyllis Reisner suggested that Backus Naur Form (BNF) might be used as a means by which HCI could be formally described, although the possibility of formally describing human-computer interaction had been raised earlier (Embley, 1978; Ledgard & Singer, 1978; Reisner, 1977). BNF is a production rule grammar, similar to the type of grammar used by Chomsky (1957) in linguistics, because it describes a language in terms of the rules that describe correct *strings* or sentences. Reisner seems to best describe the typical features of a production rule grammar:

"Traditionally, a production rule grammar consists of:
1. a set of terminal symbols (the words in the language);
2. a set of non-terminal symbols (invented constructs used to show the structure of the language, e.g. *noun phrase*;
3. a starting symbol (e.g. S for sentence);
4. the meta symbols +, |, and ::= (some common meanings for these are *and, or*, and *is composed of*, respectively);
5. rules constructed from the above (e.g. S ::= noun phrase + verb phrase).
(Reisner, 1981).

---

7   shape ::= discrete shape | continuous shape | text shape

This rule can be translated as saying: a shape may be a discrete shape, a continuous shape, or a text shape.

8   discrete shape ::= separate d-shape | connected d-shape

This rule can be translated as saying: a discrete shape can consist of a separate discrete shape or a connected discrete shape.

FIG. 4.8.   Two rules taken from Reisner's (1981) description of a graphics package.

Using BNF, it is possible to describe all of the rules which govern the interaction with a system. For an example of how the notation is used see Fig. 4.8. In the figure, the two rules and their translations are shown. Although the two rules are concerned with defining shape entities in a graphics system, nevertheless, the advantage of this type of notation, according to Reisner (1981; 1982) is that it can be used to make predictions regarding the time to complete certain tasks, and the errors that might occur. Predictions are made according to the number of different terminal symbols, the lengths of the terminal strings for particular tasks, and the number of rules necessary to describe the structure of some set of terminal strings.

Therefore, BNF provides a means by which alternative design choices might be compared. In other words, if there are two possible ways of designing part of a system then BNF can be used to describe both alternatives. By using BNF to make predictions about times and errors for each of the possible alternatives it is possible to see which design might be better.

However, as Reisner (1981; 1982) notes, to show all of the structure of a language it is necessary to have some near-redundant rules. Furthermore, a large number of these rules are usually required to describe any system completely. Indeed, the importance of such a notation may not be the notation itself, but that context-free re-write rules are being used to describe interaction with a system. The answer that Reisner (1981; 1982) suggests to these problems, is to build on notations like BNF and develop better grammars for describing HCI.

Task-Action Grammar

One such notation, built on BNF, has been developed by Payne and Green (1986), (and see also Payne, 1984). Moran's (1981) Command Language Grammar has been described by Payne as being: "...the first serious attempt at cognitive modelling in HCI." (Payne, 1984). Some may consider this judgement to be a little unfair to models such as Card et al.'s (1980) GOMS. Nevertheless, Command Language Grammar (CLG) was the first model to attempt to break interaction down into its task, semantic, syntactic, and interactional levels.

This breakdown was used by Young (1981) when considering how people use different forms of calculators. According to Young, many of the difficulties users experience with a system are due to the lack of an adequate *task-action mapping* model. This idea has already been discussed earlier in this chapter, where Norman (1986) described these difficulties as gulfs which prevent the user interacting easily with the system. A *task-action mapping* model is one that maps the different levels in Moran's (1981) Command Language Grammar onto one another. In other words, a *task-action mapping* model relates what we know onto what we can do. An example was given earlier, where a person may understand the principles of how a car engine works, but may not be able to adjust the engine in any way. This may be due to a lack of a mapping model to relate what is understood to what can be done.

Task-Action Grammar (TAG) is a model proposed by Payne and Green (1986) to account for how we map our conceptual model of a system onto our actions towards that system. In other words, it is a model of how we relate what we understand onto what we can do. Rather than examine the specific grammar of TAG, we will outline the general concepts, in a simplified way, to provide an idea of how this model works. Payne and Green describe the purposes of the model in the following way: "The central aim of TAG is to formalize [the mapping from the task level to the action level] in such a way that simple metrics over the grammar, such as the number of rules, will predict aspects of the psychological complexity of the mapping." They go on to say: "A secondary aim of TAG is to help the analyst appreciate the structure of a task language." (Payne & Green, 1986).

When Payne and Green use the term *task language* they mean, in effect, the same as Moran (1981) when he used the term *command language*. They do not use Moran's term because *command language* has now come to mean a particular dialogue style, as was explained earlier.

TAG uses a notation similar to BNF, except that the task language is described in terms of *simple tasks* and *rule schemata*. (Schemata can be thought of as active and dynamic structures in memory.) By *simple tasks*, Payne and Green mean tasks that are cognitively automated, such as those we might use for a word processing system; *move the cursor one letter to the right*, or *move the cursor one word to the left*. These are tasks that are well known to the user and performed in a routine fashion. The rule schemata are memory structures where the *simple tasks* are represented according to their features. These structures enable task descriptions to be

---

1   get spoon from drawer
2   open drawer
3   remove the kettle lid
4   replace the kettle lid
5   take the substance from the jar and place it in the cup using the spoon
6   undo the lid of the coffee jar
7   unplug the kettle
8   plug kettle in and switch on
9   get cup
10   undo lid of sugar jar
11   put lid on coffee jar
12   when boiling, pour water into cup
13   put lid on sugar jar
14   fill the kettle with water from the tap
15   close drawer

FIG. 4.9.   A list of simple tasks, some of which can be used to make a cup of coffee.

mapped onto action specifications. In other words, *simple tasks* (represented in the rule schemata) are selected and ordered according to their features to provide an action specification. An action specification can be thought of simply as a list of actions to perform. It may be helpful if we illustrate this point with a simple example.

Imagine that we have been set the task of making a cup of coffee, with no milk and no sugar. Firstly, what related *simple tasks* do we perform routinely? The list of tasks in Fig. 4.9 is somewhat arbitrary, but should illustrate the ideas nevertheless. This list of *simple tasks* is clearly meaning-less as it stands. It would not be possible to make a cup of coffee with the *simple tasks* using the order shown in the figure. Furthermore, some of the *simple tasks* in Fig. 4.9 are not necessary for making a cup of coffee without sugar or milk. It is up to the rule schemata, not only to select the *simple tasks* that are required, but also to put these tasks in the correct order, as in Fig. 4.10.

The essential characteristic of Payne and Green's (1986) model is how *simple tasks* are selected and ordered. They suggest that *simple tasks* are selected and ordered according to their features. This is achieved by the rule schemata, in which the simple tasks are represented. The rule schemata are active and dynamic memory structures. Payne and Green (1986) call these *feature-tagged schemata* because the *simple tasks* are represented in

1   unplug the kettle
2   remove the kettle lid
3   fill the kettle with water from the tap
4   replace the kettle lid
5   plug kettle in and switch on
6   get cup
7   open drawer
8   get spoon from drawer
9   close drawer
10 undo the lid of the coffee jar
11 take the substance from the jar and place it in the cup using the spoon
12 put lid on coffee jar
13 when boiling, pour water into cup

FIG. 4.10.   A list of simple tasks, in the order in which they are required to make a cup of coffee.

the schemata according to their features. Payne and Green suggest that the actions of these *feature-tagged rule schemata* must perform can be modelled according to certain rules which relate to the grammar of TAG.

These ideas, of rule schemata and simple tasks, may be useful as a way of thinking about tasks, but what advantage does TAG have over other grammars such as BNF? In other words, why should we bother to use TAG? The answer provided by Payne and Green (1986) is that TAG can be used to expose inconsistencies that BNF does not detect. For example, a system may require the user to select an object (e.g. a file) and then an operation (e.g. delete) for each act that needs to be performed. Alternatively, a system may require the user to select the operation (e.g. delete) and then the object (e.g. a file) for each act. A system that required the user to select the object first in some cases, and the operation first in other cases is clearly less consistent than a system that requires the user to select always the object or always the operation first. However, BNF appears to have no way of expressing this inconsistency, whereas TAG does. That is to say, TAG provides a better approximation to user knowledge than BNF as it can detect inconsistencies that BNF cannot (Payne & Green, 1986). Another example, taken from Green (1987), may be useful in illustrating the use of the grammar.

Consider the MacDraw™ package on the Apple Macintosh. To draw an ellipse the user must select the "ellipse" tool from the side of the window. The user must then use the mouse to position the cursor on the screen, press the mouse button, and move the mouse to another position to create the ellipse. The position to which the mouse is moved will determine the size and shape of the ellipse. However, the user may wish to draw a circle. The MacDraw system treats a circle as a special-case ellipse. To draw a circle the user must follow the same series of actions as before, but the "shift" key must be held down while the operation is executed. The series of actions for drawing a rectangle are the same as those for drawing an ellipse, except that the "rectangle" tool is selected instead of the "ellipse" tool. Again, to draw a square, which is treated as a special-case rectangle, the shift key must be held down as the operation is performed. Intuitively, it appears as though there is a consistency between these two operations. That is to say, that to draw a square or a circle requires the use of the "shift" key. These actions can be represented as a single rule in the TAG grammar:

$$task_{[effect \; = \; insert, \; type \; of \; entity \; = \; ANY, \; special \; case \; = \; ANY]}$$
$$\rightarrow special \; action_{[special \; case]} + draw \; object_{[type \; of \; entity]}$$
$$draw \; object_{[type \; of \; entity]} \rightarrow select \; tool_{[type \; of \; entity]} + move \; mouse...$$

This example has been taken from Green who states: "The important thing is that such a compact representation is only possible when two conditions are fulfilled: the interface language has a consistent structure; and that structure fits the user's mental representation." (Green, 1987).

However, it may be useful if we explain this rule in more detail. The "effect = insert" means that entities (rectangles or ellipses) are being added to the picture, not moved or deleted. The "type of entity = ANY" means that the rule stands for any entity, whether it is a rectangle, ellipse, or whatever else. The "special-action [special case]" means that if it is a special case (i.e. a square or circle) the special action is performed, which means holding down the "shift" key.

From this explanation of the rule it can be seen that the consistency of the system is that the rule holds for any entity. If it did not then another rule would be required to describe the system. To re-iterate a point made earlier, the number of rules that are required to describe a system is a guide to the cognitive complexity of that system. In short, the less consistent a system is the more rules that are required to describe it. The advantage of TAG is that it detects inconsistencies that BNF misses. Its disadvantage, however, is that small inconsistencies are given as much prominence in the grammar as large inconsistencies (Green, personal communication).

In summary, Payne and Green (1986) are proposing a model that accounts for how our intentions are converted into action specifications. These action specifications are made up of building blocks called *simple tasks*. These *simple tasks* are selected and ordered, for any intention or goal, according to their features.

The TAG model is more sophisticated than the short explanation that has been provided here might suggest, and interested readers are referred to Payne and Green's (1986) paper. However, from the description that has been provided, it can be seen that one of the attractive features of this model is that it accounts for how we convert what we know, and what we want to do, into concrete actions that affect the task at hand.

Other Models and Approaches

For reasons of space only three techniques have been briefly described. Here, some of the other techniques will be mentioned to provide an indication of what is available.

Moran's (1981) Command Language Grammar has already been mentioned several times in this chapter, and provides a foundation upon which many other techniques have been built, such as TAG and the whole notion of task-action mapping. As mentioned earlier, one of the problems with Command Language Grammar (CLG) is that it does not support the mapping between its different levels. In response, Moran (1983) proposed ETIT (mapping the External Task space to the Internal Task space). ETIT is a form of task analysis for mapping between the user's own representation and the system's representation of the task. It is not a cognitive model of the user. The difficulty with ETIT is that it assumes that a user comes to the system with a clearly structured view of the task domain (Payne, 1984).

Kieras and Polson (1985) and Polson (1987) have suggested the use of GTNs (Generalized Transition Networks) to analyze cognitive complexity in interaction. The model is built upon the GOMS model approach, in that it breaks goals and tasks down into sub-goals and unit tasks. In recent years, this approach has been particularly influential.

Another area of interest relates to the question of how users plan their actions. As Green points out, in an ideal system users should not have to plan their activity: "At the appropriate moment, each part of the system offers itself naturally to the use it was meant for." (Green, 1986).

Unfortunately, few systems do this. One possible route towards such systems has been suggested by Riley & O'Malley (1984). They propose planning nets as a means by which a designer can work through a design and decide which parts of a system need to be shown to a user. If the correct parts are shown, then users should be able to construct an appropriate mental model and plan their actions accordingly (for a discussion of planning in HCI see Young & Simon, 1987).

The Problems With the Modelling Approach

One of the difficulties associated with almost all modelling techniques is the question of what *grain of analysis* to employ. For example, it may be possible to break down the task of making a cup of coffee into 13 subtasks, 30 subtasks, or even 50 subtasks. The extent to which the task is broken down (the *grain of analysis*) should affect the number of rules that are needed to account for interaction with the task or system. In other words, the greater the number of components to a task, the greater the number of rules that are required to account for how these components fit together.

The problem that this creates becomes more obvious when we remember that the most common predictor of cognitive complexity is the number of rules that are required to describe a task. Unfortunately, the number of rules that are generated by any modelling technique may be dependent, not only upon the true complexity of the task, but also upon the *grain of analysis* employed.

A further problem with modelling techniques is related to the purpose to which they might be put in design. Ideally, a task that the user might have to perform on a system can be described using a notation, and this should show us how complex and consistent our task is. However, this assumes that we have a clear view of how the task might be performed. Often, a task on a system that is being developed is not explicitly designed, but develops as it is programmed. Consequently, our understanding of any particular task might not be good enough for us to apply one of the cognitive notations (modelling techniques) at that point in design where they might be most useful.

Another potential shortcoming of modelling techniques is that they do not directly involve the user. The modelling techniques or procedures that presently exist do not directly inform the designer of what the user wants or needs from a system. These techniques may show inconsistencies in the way that the system is constructed, they may show the relative complexity of competing designs, but they do not show where the user has a conceptualization of the task which is markedly different to that of the designer.

Finally, these techniques are often time consuming and produce lengthy, and some would say unusable, notations. If grammars are to be widely used then they must be easy to produce and easy to understand. At present there is some question over whether existing grammars fulfill these criteria.

In summary, many of the modelling techniques that have been suggested offer the designer a way of analyzing a system without directly involving the user. The advantage of this is that involving users is often time-consuming. The disadvantage is that modelling techniques only inform us of the potential difficulties that users might encounter, they do not inform us of the real problems that users experience. Nevertheless, many researchers believe that cognitive models of the user offer the designer a potentially valuable tool in the development of usable systems, providing that the designer has a good understanding of the user's tasks, time to learn a notation or grammar, and a clear view of those parts of a proposed system that require analysis.

COMMENTARY

The cognitive approach to HCI has, without doubt, received the most attention in recent years. This attention is reflected in both the number of HCI papers that are published from a cognitive perspective, and the proportion of research funding that is devoted towards cognitively orientated projects. This concentration upon the cognitive aspects of HCI may be justified given that the majority of the problems in *human-computer interaction* appear to be cognitive (cf. Storrs, Rivers, & Canter, 1984). However, one weakness with the cognitive approach is that its goals within HCI do not always appear to be clearly defined. It is with this lack of clarity in mind that we will argue for two related points: Firstly, that the central aim of the cognitive approach within HCI should be to develop a theoretical framework for understanding what occurs at the interface, and that this framework should be used to contribute towards the development of techniques where the cognitive issues are addressed in the context of physical (ergonomic), social and organizational issues. Secondly, following from the first argument, that cognitive grammars should be viewed as research tools or theoretical test-beds, not as practical techniques for design.

The first aspect of our argument, that the cognitive approach should aim to develop a theoretical framework for the process that occurs during interaction, is not particularly contentious. But how far are we from developing a usable theoretical framework for considering HCI? At first glance it appears as though little has been achieved. However, if we look further we can see that the earlier work of the 1980s (cf. Barnard & Hammond, 1982; 1983) appears to define the problem, while contributions such as Norman's (1986) approximate theory of action would seem to provide a beginning for this theoretical framework. Furthermore, the models developed as part of some cognitive grammars, such as TAG (Payne & Green, 1986), also have a contribution to make in understanding particular aspects of interaction (i.e. task-action mapping).

The second aspect of our argument concerning the role of the cognitive approach within HCI was that its theoretical framework should contribute towards general methodologies or techniques where the cognitive issues are addressed in the context of physical, social and organizational issues. But why not develop techniques that address the cognitive issues alone?

The first reason is that cognitive problems cannot be divorced from the social and organizational context in which they arise. In other words, social norms and group work practices may well determine an individual's knowledge and cognitive approach to a particular task. In turn, an individual's model of a task will determine the physical actions that are performed and the physical media that are required to accommodate these actions. In short, cognition does not operate in isolation and, if we are to understand the problems of HCI, it cannot be fruitfully considered outside its everyday context.

The second reason is that techniques that account for cognitive issues in a comprehensive and detailed manner may not be practically usable. That is to say, that if we were to develop techniques that explicitly and fully address the cognitive issues, it appears probable that these techniques might be so laborious and long-winded that they would never be used in the design and development process.

A third reason against an isolationist cognitive approach is that designers may be reluctant to use a number of different techniques when addressing a set of related issues. They may prefer a single methodology or an integrated set of tools and techniques, to a piecemeal approach to human factors.

However, given that techniques that address cognitive issues alone might not be suitable for the design process, what role might cognitive grammars play? We view cognitive grammars as research tools. They are a means by which we can test our cognitive models of the various aspects of interaction, such as task-action mapping. However, these grammars often address only one or two aspects of the cognitive process of interaction. Furthermore, they are often perceived as being complex and difficult to use. These problems, together with the drawbacks of an isolationist cognitive approach outlined above, appear to suggest that they might not be suited as practical tools for design.

This perspective is undoubtedly contentious, and some researchers who have developed grammars clearly intend them to be used during design and development. Other researchers, however, are more clear about their goals. Payne and Green (1986), for example, make it quite clear that their goal in developing TAG was to advance a particular model of one aspect of cognition in HCI, while providing a usable design tool was identified as being a secondary aim. However, not all appear to have been quite so forthright in prioritizing their goals, and some may still feel that developing cognitive notations for the design process is both desirable and potentially fruitful. Much of the industrial community may, nevertheless, remain to be convinced of this.

However, if the cognitive approach is not advance grammars or notations for use during design, what has it to contribute towards the design of usable systems? Most of all the cognitive approach can offer an explanatory framework for understanding HCI. Furthermore, it might provide a terminology to accompany this theoretical framework. In turn, this framework can be used as a basis for developing more general techniques for bringing human factors into the design process. For example, many design teams now prototype their systems and test them with users. An explanatory framework for analyzing and understanding the model mismatches (or misunderstandings) that occur between the user and the system might be of great use in helping to identify the central causes of these misunderstandings. Overall, the central aim of the cognitive approach might be to provide a description of the cognitive process of interaction, together with a terminology, that can be incorporated into techniques that address the social, organizational, physical (ergonomic) and cognitive issues together.

This has not been an argument for a radical shift within the cognitive HCI movement, but a case for a re-appraisal of its goals. The direction this movement has taken may be correct and justified, but it appears as though we need to be clearer about our goals, and the means by which we intend to achieve these goals. If we cannot easily justify what we do, then there is a danger that sceptical designers will dismiss a cognitive approach altogether. In other words, if we present unusable grammars as "handy tools" that can reveal the inconsistency and cognitive complexity of a system's interface, we may, in reality, discourage designers from exploring the cognitive issues properly. Furthermore, we may be diverting effort away from more desirable goals; those of developing a usable theoretical framework of HCI, and contributing towards comprehensive human factors analysis and design methods.

SUMMARY

The realization that the user's knowledge of the task and system has a profound effect on behaviour caused a shift in emphasis within HCI. This new emphasis has led to one of the major themes in HCI; that of considering the user in cognitive terms.

Norman (1986) points out that many of the problems that users experience can be related to difficulties of linking psychological goals to the physical variables and controls of the task. These difficulties are like gulfs, where the users find it difficult to both execute their intentions and evaluate the consequences of the actions. The *gulf of execution* is where the user knows what needs to be achieved, but does not know which physical variables to adjust. The *gulf of evaluation* is where the system has altered, but the user cannot easily understand the change in the system's state. Norman (1986) suggests that users engage in seven stages of activity that span the gulfs of evaluation and execution; establishing the goal, forming the intention, specifying the action sequence, executing the action, perceiving the system state, interpreting the system state, and evaluating the system state with respect to the goals and intentions. Alternatively, Moran (1981) suggests describing interfaces on a task level, a semantic level, a syntactic level, and an interactional level.

Within the HCI literature it is accepted that people form mental models of tasks and systems, and that these models are used to guide behaviour at the interface. A user's mental model of a system is incomplete, unstable, lacks firm boundaries, is unscientific and simpler than the system it represents. Users' models develop as they proceed through a task, picking and choosing from both appropriate and inappropriate areas of their knowledge. Only after much experience do users form a more precise and representative model of the system with which they are dealing.

The term conceptual model is used by Young to mean the model the user possesses which provides an overall understanding of the task or system. Norman, however, uses the term to mean those models invented by designers, teachers and scientists. These models are complete, coherent and consistent. Within the HCI literature the term *conceptual model* can be used in either of these ways.

Metaphors are potentially useful because they are already commonly used within everyday speech and other forms of communication. Metaphors enable learning–they provide short-cuts to understanding complex concepts. Halasz and Moran (1982) have distinguished between a metaphor and an analogy. They suggest that an analogy is where a whole unknown system is considered to behave in the same way as a known system, while a metaphor only suggests that part of an unknown system is similar to a known system. Hammond and Allinson (1987) have suggested that a metaphor can be described according to its *scope* and *level of description*. *Scope* refers to the number of parts of a system that a metaphor explains. *Level of description* refers to the level on which the metaphor operates (i.e. task level, semantic level, etc.).

Most commonly, user models can be of one of four entities: They can be of the designer's model of the user, the system's embedded model of the user, the user's model of the task, and the user's model of the system.

Six purposes of user modelling were identified: To help match the system's facilities to the user's needs, to suggest metaphors to improve use learning, to guide design decision and make these decisions and assumptions explicit, to provide predictive evaluations of proposed designs, to identify variations in the user population, and to provide a framework for designing and interpreting experiments.

User models can be either predictive, descriptive or normative. Furthermore, user models can be performance, learning or reasoning models. These different types of models answer different questions within HCI and alone, no one modelling technique is expected to adequately satisfy all of the demands we might make of user modelling.

The GOMS model considers the user's goals, operators, methods and selection rules for choosing between alternative methods, and the model was suggested by Card, Moran and Newell (1980). GOMS can be used to predict routes through tasks and task times. However, the model cannot account for a novice's or intermediate-level user's behaviour. Furthermore, the model assumes performance which is substantially error-free.

Reisner (1981) suggested that BNF (Backus Naur Form) might be used as a means for describing *human-computer interaction*. BNF is a production rule grammar. The guide to the cognitive complexity of any system is assumed to be the number of rules needed to describe a system's action language. However, to adequately show the structure of a language it is necessary to have some near-redundant rules. Consequently, there is currently research aimed at building on the notation of BNF to provide better grammars for describing HCI.

Payne and Green (1986) have suggested TAG (Task Action Grammar) as a model that accounts for how our intentions are converted into action specifications. They suggest that action specifications are made up of building blocks called *simple tasks*. These *simple tasks* are represented in *feature tagged schemata*. These schemata select and order the *simple tasks* according to their features. One of the attractive aspects of this model is that it accounts for how we convert what we know, and what we want to do, into concrete actions that affect the task at hand.

Other modelling and task analysis techniques that have been suggested include, Moran's (1981) Command Language Grammar, Moran's (1983) ETIT (mapping the External Task space to the Internal Task space), Kieras and Polson's (1985) model based on GTNs (Generalized Transition Networks), Riley and O'Malley's (1984) Planning Nets, Johnson et al.'s (1984) TAKD (Task Analysis for Knowledge Descriptions), and Barnard's (1985; 1987) Interacting Cognitive Subsystems model.

Three major problems with cognitive modelling were identified. The number of rules that are generated by any modelling technique may be dependent, not only upon the true complexity of the task, but also upon the grain of analysis employed. Modelling techniques do not show where the user has a conceptualization of the task which is markedly different to that of the designer. Finally, it is questionable whether some of the modelling techniques suggested are really usable in the design process.

We argue that we should not aim to develop cognitive grammars for use in the design process because a technique that adequately accounts for the cognitive factors is likely to be too difficult and time-consuming to use, and because the cognitive issues should be addressed in the context of organizational, social and ergonomic issues, not in isolation. The alternative to developing cognitive notations aimed at design is to provide a terminology and a theoretical framework that might contribute towards methodologies or techniques that address human factors generally in the design process.

A SELECTIVE ANNOTATED BIBLIOGRAPHY

Aitkenhead, A. M. & Slack, J. M. (Eds.) (1985). *Issues in cognitive modelling.* Hillsdale, New Jersey: Lawrence Erlbaum Associates Inc. *The book is a collection of previously published papers that have been edited. This book offers readable and interesting accounts of various areas of cognitive modelling. This is an excellent introduction to many of the issues of cognition.*

Barnard, P. J. (1987). Cognitive resources and learning of human-computer dialogues. In J. M. Carroll (Ed.), *Interfacing thought: Cognitive aspects of human-computer interaction.* Cambridge, Massachusetts: MIT Press. *After a discussion of the need for applicable theory in HCI, the author presents a model of "interacting cognitive subsystems", that he first suggested in 1985. This is a model of human cognition, and the idea is that there are different subsystems, such as the visual subsystem, the object subsystem, the propositional subsystem. This model is currently being used to attempt to construct an expert system that can predict problems that users might have with different interfaces and systems (see Green, 1986).*

Black, J. B., Kay, D. S., & Soloway, E. M. (1987). Goal and plan knowledge representations: From stories to text editors and programs. In J. M. Carroll (Ed.), *Interfacing thought: Cognitive aspects of human-computer interaction.* Cambridge, Massachusetts: MIT Press. *The authors consider how we use our knowledge of goals and plans to understand written stories. They then consider how we then use our knowledge in planning our interactions with a computer. In particular, they consider computer programming as a planning activity. It is possible to question why programmers should be considered in HCI. The answer is that they are users of computer systems, although they are certainly a different class of user. The authors use their consideration of programmers to draw general conclusions about human goal and plan representation.*

Card, S. K., Moran, T. P., & Newell, A. (1980). Computer text-editing: An information-processing analysis of a routine cognitive skill. *Cognitive Psychology, 12,* 32–74. *The authors propose and detail support for the GOMS model, which has been discussed in this chapter. This paper is well-written and worth reading.*

Carroll, J. M. & Mack, R. L. (1985). Metaphor, computing systems, and active learning. *International Journal of Man-Machine Studies, 22,* 39–57. *The authors discuss how metaphors and analogies are used. Of particular concern are the arguments provided by Halasz and Moran (1982). Carroll and Mack suggest that learning is not possible without at least some reference to known systems, and that even presenting users with graphical representations of conceptual models of systems involves users drawing upon their knowledge of these types of graphical representations.*

Carroll, J. M. & Thomas, J. C. (1982). Metaphor and the cognitive representation of computer systems. *IEEE Transactions on Systems, Man, and Cybernetics, SMC-12* (2), 107–116. *The authors discuss how people learn, as well as how we use metaphors. This is an interesting and wide-ranging discussion of metaphors in human-computer interaction.*

Foley, J. D. & van Dam, A. (1982). *Fundamentals of interactive computer graphics.* Reading, Massachusetts: Addison-Wesley. *The authors present a picture of design that begins with task analysis, and then moves through conceptual, semantic, syntactic and lexical levels. This book is seen as a major work and, despite its age, is well worth reading.*

Gentner, D. & Stevens, A. L. (Eds.) (1983). *Mental models.* Hillsdale, New Jersey: Lawrence Erlbaum Associates Inc. *This book provides a number of well-written and important articles. The central concern is the nature, representation, and use of mental models.*

Green, T. R. G. (1986). Cognitive aspects of HCI. *Computer Bulletin, September. This short article concentrates on summarizing the cognitive approach to HCI. Again, this is an easy-to-read article that provides a stimulating perspective on human-computer interaction.*

Halasz, F. & Moran, T. P. (1982). Analogy considered harmful. In *Human factors in computer systems, conference proceedings, Gaithersburg, Maryland*: ACM. *The authors distinguish between analogies and metaphors. They argue that metaphors may be of use within HCI, but that analogies can limit systems development and mislead users. This is an interesting and well-written paper.*

Hammond, N. V. & Allinson, L. J. (1987). The travel metaphor as design principle and training aid for navigating around complex systems. In D. Diaper & R. Winder (Eds.), *People and computers III, proceedings of the third conference on human-computer interaction.* Cambridge: Cambridge University Press. *The authors suggest that a metaphor can be described according to its scope and level of description. They go on to suggest a model of metaphor use, that is intended for use by designers.*

Hammond, N. V., Morton, J., MacLean, A., & Barnard, P. J. (1983b). Fragments and signposts: Users' model of the system. In *Proceedings of the 10th international Symposium on human factors in Telecommunications, Helsinki. This article is concerned with how users form models of the systems they use. Three uses of the term "user model" are identified and then a definition is offered. It is suggested that users form models by pulling together fragments of knowledge from related domains.*

Johnson, P., Diaper, D., & Long, J. (1984). Task, skills and knowledge: Task analysis for knowledge based descriptions. In B. Shackel (Ed.), *Human computer interaction–Interact '84: Proceedings of the first IFIP conference on human-computer interaction, London.* Amsterdam: North-Holland. *The authors describe a form of task analysis that involves representing knowledge in action-object pairs. The aim of the technique is to establish the knowledge that is required for any particular task.*

Kieras, D. E. & Bovair, S. (1984). The role of a mental model in learning to operate a device. *Cognitive Science, 8, 255–273. The authors show that those who have a model of the underlying operation of a device (a control panel) learn to operate the system much faster than those who do not. Furthermore, the benefit of a model is only achieved if that model supports direct and simple inferences as to the exact steps required to operate the device. This supports Young's (1981) and Norman's (1986) ideas, where a person can only operate a device if their conceptual model can be mapped onto the physical variables of the device.*

Kieras, D. E. & Polson, P. G. (1985). An approach to the formal analysis of user complexity. *International Journal of Man-Machine Studies, 22 (4), 365–394. The authors suggest an approach to analyzing cognitive complexity. Their technique involves using Generalized Transition Networks to analyse the mapping between different task states. This technique uses a goal structure analysis approach similar to that employed in the GOMS model.*

Langacker, R. W. (1986). An introduction to cognitive grammar. *Cognitive Science, 10, 1–40. The author explains what cognitive grammars are intended for and how they work. Although the author is principally concerned with human language, the discussion nevertheless has relevance to HCI modelling techniques. This paper is useful as an introduction to grammars, but the reader should be aware that a particular theory is being proposed. Not all of what the author proposes is necessarily accepted.*

Manktelow, K. I. & Jones, J. (1987). Principles from the psychology of thinking and mental models. In M. M. Gardiner & B. Christie (Eds.), *Applying cognitive psychology to user interface design.* Chichester: Wiley. *The authors review much of the research into mental models and then suggest principles for HCI based upon this research.*

Moran, T. P. (1981). The Command Language Grammar: A representation for the user interface of interactive computer systems. *International Journal of Man-Machine Studies, 15, 3–50. This paper has become something of a classic. The structure that Moran proposes for HCI is still the dominant theme within HCI research. The author suggests breaking the interaction into its task, semantic, syntactic, and interactional levels. The paper is easy to read and highly recommended for anyone who intends to work in the HCI field.*

Norman, D. A. (1983c). Some observations on mental models. In: D. Gentner & A. L. Stevens (Eds.), *Mental models.* Hillsdale, New Jersey: Lawrence Erlbaum Associates Inc. *The author outlines a view of what constitutes a conceptual model and discusses some of the characteristics of a mental model. This easy-to-read article provides an excellent introduction to the question of, what are user's mental models and how they are formed?*

Norman, D. A. (1986). Cognitive engineering. In D. A. Norman & S. Draper (Eds.), *User-centred system design: New perspectives on human-computer* interaction. Hillsdale, New Jersey: Lawrence Erlbaum Associates Inc. *Firstly, the author defines cognitive engineering. He argues for approximate models of HCI and suggests that the user's needs should dominate the design of the interface, and the needs of the interface should dictate the rest of the system. This is an interesting and well-written paper where Norman's approximate theory of action and gulfs of execution and evaluation are presented. These have already been discussed in this chapter.*

Payne, S. J. & Green, T. R. G. (1986). Task-action grammars: A model of the mental representation of task languages. *Human-computer interaction, 2,* 93–133. *The authors outline their theory, and this has already been discussed in this chapter. This interesting paper requires careful reading if it is to be fully appreciated.*

Reisner, P. (1981). Formal grammar and human factors design of an interactive graphics system. *IEEE Transactions on Software Engineering, SE7 (2),* 229–240. *The paper illustrates how a formal grammatical description can be used as a predictive tool. These ideas and this paper have already been discussed in the chapter. However, this paper is particularly well-written. Its explanations are clear and it is well worth reading.*

Riley, M. & O'Malley, C. (1984). Planning nets: A framework for analyzing user-computer interactions. In: B. Shackel (Ed.), *Human-computer interaction--Interact '84: Proceedings of the first IFIP conference on human-computer interaction, London.* Amsterdam: North-Holland. *The authors suggest a framework for analyzing the user's planning activity. Their approach considers the mapping between the user's goals and the available commands of the system. This is an interesting, practical and readable paper.*

Winograd, T. & Flores, C. F. (1986). *Understanding computers and cognition: A new foundation for design.* Norwood, New Jersey: Ablex Publishing Corporation. *The authors outline a view of cognitive science and then go on to argue that it is limited in its scope. They suggest that current theoretical discourse about computers is based upon a misinterpretation of the nature of human cognition and language. They view language as the key, not the rationalistic tradition. This seminal piece of work is well-written and interesting.*

Young, R. M. & Harris, J. E. (1986). A viewdata-structure editor designed around a task-action mapping. In M. D. Harrison & A. F. Monk (Eds.), *People and computers: Designing for usability, proceedings of the second conference on human-computer interaction.* Cambridge: Cambridge University Press. *The authors do not propose a theory of task-action mapping, but report the use of a system designed around the general principles of task-action mapping. They report that the system they developed was able to anticipate the user much of the time, and that the users were generally pleased and impressed with the system.*

5 Usability in Human-Computer Interaction

In collaboration with Chris J. Marshall
Hewlett Packard Ltd., Pinewood

OVERVIEW

The term *usability* is sometimes used to indicate a particular approach to the issues of HCI. With this in mind, the concepts that make up *usability* are considered, and a number of definitions of usability are outlined and discussed. The usability approach is concerned with both obtaining user requirements in the early stages of design, and with evaluating systems that have been built. Consequently, a process for performing a *User Needs Analysis* is outlined. The issue of how to evaluate the usability of systems is then addressed. Finally, some of the problems with the usability approach are considered.

INTRODUCTION

In the last chapter we considered the cognitive approach to modelling the user, and to HCI in general. In contrast to this heavily theoretical approach to HCI, this chapter will concentrate upon the usability or process ergonomics approach.

The usability perspective might be characterized as an approach that first addresses the practical issues and second theoretical issues, although some might dispute this, and argue that the two go hand-in-hand. This focus on usability does not just include information technology (IT) products, but also other types of systems, devices, machinery or work environments. This may, in part, account for why *usability* is such a commonly used term. Not only is the term *usability* employed widely within the HCI community, it is even beginning to be used in the newspapers and on television. This may be because usability is now being seen as an important issue, as well as a potential selling point for many products. For example, how many times do we hear people complain that their video recorder or washing machine is so complicated that they cannot properly operate it?

It seems as though the issue of usability has grown more important as greater numbers of technically complicated products have become available to a wider population of, what Eason (1976) has termed, *naïve users*. While manufacturers have concentrated upon increasing the functionality of their products (increasing the numbers of things they can do), users have grown steadily more confused and frustrated that they cannot operate the machinery that they have bought.

Within the IT industry this problem has been even more serious. Many software products have had to be abandoned, not because they did not work, but because the users could not or would not use them. This may be because IT products are generally more complicated than household products such as video recorders and washing machines.

Usability problems appear to afflict all manner of complicated products, from complex IT systems to everyday household items. The issue of concern is how to mitigate the effects of these usability difficulties, or better still, how to ensure that usability problems never arise. This challenge is best expressed in the statement: *Today we are just as capable of producing an unusable product or system as we have always been.* In other words, the challenge is this: although we might recognize usability as a central issue in the design of complex products, how can we ensure that future products do not suffer from these problems?

The usability approach to this issue is to provide better HCI education for designers, and to permanently change the design and development process. This notion of a two-pronged attack, in the areas of education and the design process by incorporating human factors techniques, may be useful as an overall view. However, what does this approach entail in reality? In other words, in practical terms, what is the *usability* approach to the problems of HCI?

CONCEPTS FOR USABILITY

A useful starting point is provided by Gould (in press) who sets out a list of the components of usability (see Fig. 5.1). Gould's list implies the notion of usability to be a broad concept that involves many of the stages and aspects of design and implementation. In essence, Gould is suggesting the areas that a study of usability should cover. He is not only considering the end-user or operator (the person at the computer terminal), but also all of the other types of *user*. This includes programmers, systems engineers, installation engineers, the people who support the users, etc. These are the aspects of system development and implementation that directly affect the total usability of a system.

SYSTEM PERFORMANCE
  Reliability
  Responsiveness

SYSTEM FUNCTIONS

USER INTERFACE
  Organization
  Input/output hardware
  For end users
  For other groups

READING MATERIALS
  End-user groups
  Support groups

LANGUAGE TRANSLATION
  Reading materials
  User interface

OUTREACH PROGRAMME
  End-user training
  On-line help system
  Hot-lines

ABILITY FOR CUSTOMERS TO MODIFY AND EXTEND

INSTALLATION
  Packaging and unpacking
  Installing

FIELD MAINTENANCE AND SERVICEABILITY

ADVERTISING
  Motivating customers to buy
  Motivating user to use

SUPPORT-GROUP USERS
  Marketing people
  Trainers
  Operators
  Maintenance workers

FIG. 5.1.   Gould's (in press) list of usability components.

Nevertheless, although Gould's list is undoubtedly helpful, it does not suggest concepts that might contribute to a definition or better understanding of usability. Such concepts may be needed if we are to understand what makes a usable system easy to understand and operate. The reason for this is that usability is not determined by just one or two constituents, but is influenced by a number of factors (cf. Barnard & Hammond, 1982). These factors do not simply and directly affect usability, but interact with one another in sometimes complex ways. Eason (1984) has suggested a series of concepts that explain what these variables might be (see Fig. 5.2).

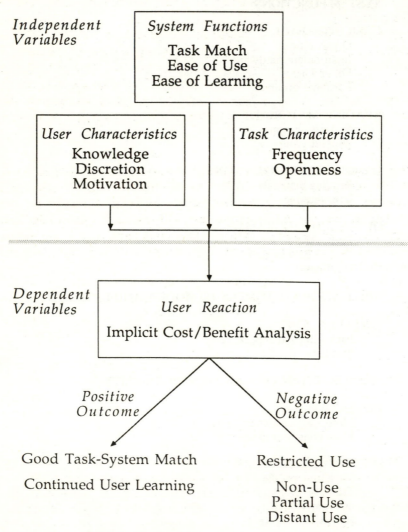

FIG. 5.2. Eason's (1984) causal framework of usability.

Task Characteristics

First we will consider the two task variables that Eason identifies; *frequency* and *openness*. The term *frequency* simply refers to the number of times any particular task is performed by a user. Eason (1976) points out that if users perform a task infrequently then they will expect a dialogue that guides them through the task. On the other hand, such a dialogue may not be appropriate for a task that is performed routinely. For a frequent task users may well expect an economic dialogue. This is because they can easily remember the steps that are required for the task and do not usually require help or prompting.

The second term *openness* refers to the extent to which a task is modifiable. An open task is one where the information needs of the user are variable. Consequently, the task must be structured to allow the user to acquire a wide range of information. Alternatively, the user's information needs may be fixed. If this is the case then the task need not be open and flexible, as the same information is required each time the task is performed.

System Functions

The three major system variables are *ease of learning, ease of use,* and *task match*. The term *ease of learning* refers to the effort required to understand and operate an unfamiliar system. Clearly, this will depend upon the knowledge the user possesses and the ease with which this knowledge can be mapped onto the unfamiliar system. The second term, *ease of use*, refers to the effort that is required to operate a system once it has been understood and mastered by the user.

At first, *ease of use* and *ease of learning* appear to be indistinguishable concepts. However, it is quite possible to have a system that is easy to learn but difficult to use, or a system that is difficult to learn but easy to use. For example, consider a system that is easy to learn. This system may be thoughtfully explained and its dialogue may guide the user easily through the various tasks. However, once the user has come to know the system well, the dialogue that was initially so helpful could become obstructive and time consuming. In other words, by not allowing the user short-cuts through tasks, and by insisting that everything is repeatedly explained to the user, the system becomes frustrating to use, although it was initially easy to learn.

On the other hand, a system that has many abbreviated commands and little explanation may be difficult to learn, but easy to use. For example, the UNIX™ operating system requires a user to type "cd" to change from one file directory to another. All of the major commands in UNIX are of this sort; abbreviations that are difficult to remember but easy to use once memorized. This sort of system is often frustrating and difficult for users to learn, but relatively easy and straightforward for users once they have mastered the system (although some may argue that UNIX is never easy to use). The dialogue of such a system provides little explanation of how the system works for first-time users. Nevertheless, such a dialogue does not obstruct the experienced user. In short, the concepts *easy to learn* and *easy to use* can be distinct and relatively independent.

The third system concept is that of *task match*. This term refers to the extent to which the information and functions that a system provides matches the needs of the user. In short, a system may be easy to learn and easy to use, but does it do the job? This is a question of whether the system provides the necessary functions that are required, as well as the information that the user needs.

User Characteristics

The final set of variables are those that belong to the user. These are *knowledge, motivation* and *discretion*. The user's knowledge of the task and system have already been discussed in Chapters Three and Four. However, to reiterate a little of what was stated earlier; the knowledge that the user chooses to apply to a task, whether that knowledge is appropriate or not, can be considered as a variable that contributes towards the ultimate usability of a system.

The second variable is *motivation*. This term is used with respect to the user's motivation to use the system. If the user has a high degree of motivation then more effort will be expended in overcoming problems and misunderstandings. Alternatively, if the user is not strongly motivated to complete a task on the system then the user's commitment to the system may wane, and there may be a reluctance to learn or use complicated parts of the system.

The third variable, *discretion*, refers to the user's ability to choose not to use some part, or even the whole of a system. A user has discretion every time a choice is presented. However, in some circumstances this choice may be limited. For example, many shop assistants in supermarkets use systems that recognize bar codes on the foods they sell. They appear to have little discretion as to whether and how they use the system. On the other hand, a statistician in a business may have more discretion. Besides the large number of statistical techniques that a statistical software package will offer the user, the statistician will also have the ultimate choice of not using the system at all, as long as the information that is required is produced.

The essence of what Eason (1984) suggests is that the usability of a system will depend, not only upon the nature of the user, but also upon the characteristics of the task and system. That is to say, that the variables of task, system and user all combine to determine the usability of a system (see Fig. 5.3).

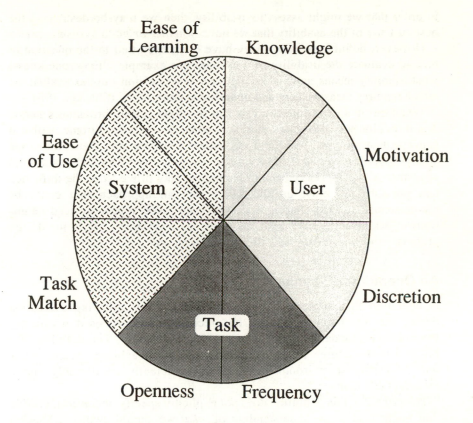

FIG 5.3.   A re-iteration of Eason's (1984) interacting task, system and user variables.

Eason's stance has been to consider usability from the perspective of how systems are used in a work environment. While such a view is undoubtedly useful from a global standpoint, it is not the only perspective on usability, although it may be one of the more comprehensive.

DEFINITIONS OF USABILITY

The global definition of usability suggested by Eason (1984), and implied in the last section, is that: The "...major indicator of usability is *whether* a system or facility is used..." He goes on to say: "It is the [user's] act of choice which is the essence of usability which suggests that the crucial measure [of usability] is the pattern of [the user's] responses to options and the way ...[these responses] build into a learning or non-learning strategy." The argument in favour of this view, and against trying to measure usability in the laboratory, goes as follows: If we force an individual to use a system in order that we might assess its usability, then we may be destroying the best measure of the usability that we have, *whether or not a system is used.*

However, definitions of usability have often been tied to the question of how to evaluate the usability of a system. For example: "Everyone knows what usability means until its recognition as a criterion implies evaluation, which requires measurement and operational definition." (Shackel, 1981.)

When Eason's definition is viewed in this light certain problems emerge. The difficulty with this ideal approach, when taken to its extreme, is that it suggests that we must build and implement a system, and then wait to see what happens if we wish to evaluate its usability. Although data from systems that have already been implemented may prove to be the most rich and possibly the most useful, this is not an approach that could be recommended to cost-conscious design teams. We appear to need definitions of usability that will allow us to evaluate systems early in the design process, as well as during and after implementation.

An Operational Definition

A definition that appears to point the way towards allowing evaluation during the development process has recently been proposed within the International Standards Organization (ISO), and states: "The usability of a product is the degree to which specific users can achieve specific goals within a particular environment; effectively, efficiently, comfortably, and in an acceptable manner."

Nevertheless, this definition does not explicitly specify operational criteria that might lead to an understanding of *what* we should evaluate. Shackel (1986), however, has suggested just such an operational definition of usability. This definition can be seen in Fig. 5.4. The essence of this definition is that all its constituent elements are measurable. What Shackel is suggesting is that any system should have to pass the usability criteria of *effectiveness, learnability, flexibility*, and user *attitude*.

A system must be *effective*, in that a certain proportion of target users must be able to use the system in a number of environments, within a certain time and without too many errors. A system must be *learnable*, in that users must be able to learn the system after a certain amount of training. Furthermore, users who do not frequently use the system must be able to re-learn the system within a certain time. A system must be *flexible*, in that user performance must not deteriorate by more than a certain percentage across tasks and environments. Finally, a system must provoke user *attitude* ratings where a certain percentage are positive towards the system.

Usability can be specified and measured via the operational criteria defined below. The terms should be given numerical values when the usability goals are set during the design stage of 'requirements specification'.

For a system to be usable the following must be achieved -
The range of required tasks must be accomplished -

EFFECTIVENESS

- at better than some required level of performance (e.g., in terms of speed and errors),
- by some required percentage of the specified target range of users,
- within some required proportion of the range of usage environments.

LEARNABILITY

- within some specified time from installation and start of user training,
- based upon some specified amount of training and user support,
- and within some specified re-learning time each time for intermittent users.

FLEXIBILITY

- with flexibility allowing adaptation to some specified percentage variation in tasks and/or environments beyond those first specified.

ATTITUDE

- and within acceptable levels of human cost in terms of tiredness, discomfort, frustration and personal effort.

FIG. 5.4.   An operational definition of usability. Source: Shackel (1986).

To date, Shackel's (1986) definition is one of the most useful operational statements of usability that we have, although it is certainly not the last word on the subject. Nevertheless, it has been this sort of operational definition of usability, suggested by Shackel (1986) and others (e.g. Bennett, 1984; Bury, 1984; Gould, in press; Gould & Lewis, 1985) that is beginning to receive considerable attention within the industry.

However, despite the interest that Shackel's definition has aroused, it appears to have limitations. First, *flexibility* is particularly difficult to specify, communicate and test in a real product development environment. Second, Shackel appears to omit an element that would seem to be fundamental to any definition of usability; that of *usefulness*. A *useful* system is one that helps users to achieve their goals. For example, a system may be easy to learn, it may be effective for the tasks that it addresses, and it may provoke good user attitude ratings. However, if the functions of the system do not match the users' goals in their everyday work environments then the system will not be used. As a result, it can be seen that a system might fulfill Shackel's criteria, yet remain unused because it does not help users to achieve their goals. In other words, the system might fail because it was not *useful*. Consequently, we suggest that Shackel's definition be amended to include the criteria of *usefulness* (see Fig. 5.5). Furthermore, it is suggested that for practical purposes the criteria of *flexibility* should not be included.

Future Development of the Concept of Usability

Unfortunately, despite the gradual refinement of the term *usability*, it appears unlikely that a generally agreed definition of usability will emerge within the next few years. The main reason for this is that the term *usability* is used by many researchers to mean many different things. Indeed, some researchers have argued that the concept is so vague and ambiguous that it ought to be abandoned. However, as the term is now in general use, and has entered the vocabulary of the media, it seems unlikely that it can be easily forgotten.

USER NEEDS ANALYSIS

The definition of usability, however, should not be viewed as the only contribution that the usability approach has made towards HCI. Much of the work from this background has concentrated upon how information about users, their tasks, their needs, etc., might be gathered and incorporated into the design process. It may be useful, therefore, to outline an analysis that

---

USEFULNESS

EFFECTIVENESS (or ease of use)

LEARNABILITY

ATTITUDE (or likeability)

FIG. 5.5.   An amended set of criteria for usability.

can be performed to identify the key factors that need to be considered when designing a system.

A *User Needs Analysis* is assumed to have a number of stages. Our suggested approach is to divide the analyses as follows:

User Characterization: There must be an understanding of who the users are, together with an appreciation of their relevant characteristics.

Task Analysis: There needs to be an understanding of the user's goals and activities, as well as the tools they use and the environment within which they work.

Situational Analysis: There needs to be an appreciation of the situations that commonly arise as part of the user's normal activities.

Acceptance Criteria: There needs to be an understanding of the user's requirements and preferences.

These areas clearly overlap to some extent, as do the checklists that accompany them, and some may choose to partition a *User Needs Analysis* differently. However, we find the above division to be both convenient and useful.

User Characterization

The first stage in a *User Needs Analysis* is to attempt to capture all of the information about the target user groups that is relevant to the proposed system (sometimes called a *product opportunity*). This process of user characterization is repeated for both primary and secondary user groups. The issues that might be considered in this user characterization can be seen in Fig. 5.6. Some researchers would object to the inclusion of personality traits within this checklist, and the questions of user traits and user classification are presently contentious issues. However, despite our reservations, we have chosen to include these factors and to leave it for others to judge whether a consideration of personality traits might usefully contribute towards user characterization.

Task Analysis

In the previous chapter the issue of task analysis was considered with respect to the cognitive grammars that can be used to describe interaction. Here, however, the term *task analysis* is used in a slightly different sense. In the last chapter *task analysis* meant breaking the task down by describing it using a grammar. Here, *task analysis* means identifying the user's goals and tasks by a slightly less formal means. Nevertheless, it can be seen that this distinction between these cognitive (using grammars) and usability approaches to task analysis is, in many respects, only slight.

USER DATA
  Identify the target user group
  Proportion of males and females
  Average age/age range
  Cultural characteristics (including language, etc.)

JOB CHARACTERISTICS
  Job role description
  Main activities
  Main responsibilities
  Reporting structure
  Reward structure
  Schedules
  Status/quality
  Turnover rate

USER BACKGROUND
  Relevant education/knowledge/experience
  Relevant skills
  Relevant training

USAGE CONSTRAINTS
  Voluntary versus mandatory use
  Motivators versus de-motivators

PERSONAL PREFERENCES AND TRAITS
  Learning style
  Interactional style
  Aesthetic preference
  Personality traits
  Physical traits

FIG 5.6.   A checklist for user characterization.

Task analysis, in the usability sense of the term, involves listing the user's goals. In this list the overall goal is usually the end-result the user might wish to achieve using the proposed system, while the user's sub-goals can provide a perspective on the tasks that need to be performed to achieve the overall goal. Furthermore, these sub-goals provide some idea of the order in which tasks need to be performed.

However, listing the user's goals, although useful, cannot be considered as a comprehensive and thorough approach to task analysis when taken alone. Consequently, practitioners may find it useful to have a checklist of issues to guide their analysis. Such a checklist is shown in Fig. 5.7. Once again, however, this list can only be taken as our guide to what might be considered, it should not be viewed as being a final definitive statement on the subject.

GOALS
> Identify goals and list important supporting tasks

For each important task:

TASK INTRINSICS
> Identifier information (identify the task uniquely)
> Inputs and outputs
> Transformational process
> Operational procedures
> Operational patterns
> Decision points
> Problem solving
> Planning
> Terminology
> Equipment

TASK DEPENDENCY AND CRITICALITY
> Dependency on other tasks, systems, etc.
> Concurrent effects
> Criticality of task (linked to dependency)

CURRENT USER PROBLEMS (in performing the task)

PERFORMANCE CRITERIA
> Speed
> Accuracy
> Quality

TASK CRITERIA
> Sequence of actions
> Frequency of actions
> Importance of actions
> Functional relationships between actions
> Availability of functions
> Flexibility of operation

USER DISCRETION (can the user control or determine)
> Pace
> Priority
> Procedure

TASK DEMANDS
> Physical demands
> Perceptual demands
> Cognitive demands
> Environmental demands
> Health and safety requirements

FIG. 5.7. A checklist for task analysis.

Situational Analysis

The third stage in a *User Needs Analysis* entails an analysis of the situations that can arise in the work context, and a consideration of how these might affect both the user's performance and the user's needs. While issues such as task analysis and user characterization have been the focus of much attention within the literature in recent years, considering the various situations that might arise during the use of a product has received less consideration. However, by analyzing the situations that might render the system less usable, it is possible to gain some idea of how the product might be used in the everyday work environment. A checklist of situations that might effect the use of the system can be seen in Fig. 5.8. The central question that is addressed using this checklist is *if this situation arises how will it affect the use of the system?* Once adverse effects upon the use of the system have been identified then strategies to avoid certain situations, or mitigate their effects, can be planned and built into the system.

What are the likely situations that could arise during system use?

EQUIPMENT
does not meet performance target
does not meet specification
fails

AVAILABILITY
missing data
missing materials
missing personnel
missing support

OVERLOADS
too many people/machines using resource
too much data, information, materials, etc.

INTERRUPTIONS
process breakdown
things missed/forgotten
restart required

SURROUNDINGS
change in physical or social environment

POLICY
changing laws, rules, standards, guidelines

FIG. 5.8.   A checklist for situational analysis.

Acceptance Criteria

While an analysis of the user's tasks and goals may show us what the user needs to achieve, it is often users' own perceptions of their needs, together with their perceptions of how the system matches these needs, that will determine whether the system is used. Consequently, there is a need within a *User Needs Analysis* to elicit the user's stated requirements and preferences. These requirements and preferences form, to some extent, the acceptance criteria for the system. That is to say, that they are the user's acceptance criteria. If a system matches these requirements then it stands a better chance of being accepted into the everyday work environment as a valued tool or assistant.

USABILITY TESTING

While the *User Needs Analysis* described above may help to identify some of the issues and concerns that should be considered when specifying and designing a system, there are still likely to be usability problems with the system. This is because it is rarely possible to anticipate every problem or pitfall. Consequently, many of the IT manufacturers have taken the lead in moving towards the idea of *usability testing* their products. In essence, this usually entails building prototypes of the system and testing it on users in a laboratory. Frequently users are filmed and the video-tapes are then played back to the designers to demonstrate where users experienced problems. The main reasons for adopting this approach are as follows: It can be used to measure user performance and satisfaction; it can be used to identify and assess usability defects; it can be used to provide ideas as to how a system might be improved; it can be used to educate design teams.

These usability tests can take place throughout development, and are generally considered to be relatively easy to perform, although the purpose of the test may vary according to the stage at which the system is being tested. A table of the different stages of system development and the purposes of *usability testing* can be seen in Fig. 5.9.

Task Scenarios

Usability testing products often requires task scenarios. These are descriptive stories about the intended use of the product. They provide a design vision, illustrate tasks that the system is intended to support, and provide the raw materials for usability assessments. For example, a task scenario may look something like this: "You are a system administrator for a software system which schedules and allocates resources such as company cars, meeting rooms, etc. Unfortunately, one of the meeting rooms has been unexpectedly scheduled for re-furbishment, which will take two months, beginning in

Phase	Purposes	Objects
Investigation	• set usability objectives • discover opportunities	• existing solutions
Design and build	• resolve conflicts • answer questions • debug • measure against objectives	• early concepts • simulations • prototypes • partial products • training • documentation
Post-release	• get data for sales/marketing • input to next release • competitive analysis	• finished product • competitive products

FIG. 5.9.   Phases of product usability testing.

July. Your task is to notify those people who have booked the room, and to provide alternative resources."

From the example above it can be seen that task scenarios embody a goal, information about the task and information about the situational context in which the system is to be used; they are not detailed specifications of task steps. Such scenarios can be used to explore the boundaries of use for both frequent and critical conditions, and as such, they form a useful basis for *usability testing* within human factors laboratories.

Usability Defects

While a task scenario sets the context for usability testing, the notion of a *usability defect* can provide a means by which the performance of a system can be considered. This concept, of a *usability defect*, can be defined as *anything in the product which prevents a target user completing a target task with reasonable effort and within a reasonable time*. Usability defects can be considered as analogous to reliability and performance problems with products. The advantage of this sort of concept is that it allows us to focus upon those aspects of a product that require attention and alteration. The strength of this type of approach is that the notion of defects, i.e. those parts or aspects of a system that cause difficulties for the user, appears self-evident.

However, the difficulty with this approach, and with user-testing in general, is that wider issues may be overlooked. That is to say, that it is possible that all of the problems that users experience may be fixed, yet a system may remain substantially unusable because the use of the system cannot be explained using a consistent conceptual model. In other words, while looking at the detail of the design we may miss the larger issues that will ultimately determine whether a system is likely to be used outside the laboratory. This does not mean, however, that an approach that explicitly considers usability defects is flawed, only that it is practically limited in what it can achieve.

EVALUATING THE USABILITY OF A SYSTEM

The utility of usability definitions such as Shackel's (1986) is that they provide a means for structuring usability goals. For example, taking Shackel's amended scheme, we require effectiveness, learnability, usefulness and attitude goals for any product. A *User Needs Analysis* provides the means by which these goals can be identified. But how can we evaluate a product against these goals?

Formative and Summative Evaluation

Hewett (1986) distinguishes two forms of evaluation; *formative* and *summative*. The difference between these two types is in their purpose. Formative evaluation helps the designer to refine and *form* the design. Because of this objective certain types of evaluative measure might not be appropriate for this type of evaluation. For example, an overall score, however it is derived, is unlikely to tell a designer what should be done to improve the design. Formative evaluation is more likely to require qualitative information that can be used to help the designer pinpoint those parts of the systems that require alteration.

Alternatively, summative evaluation is more likely to require quantitative information rather than qualitative data. As Hewett explains: "Summative evaluation involves assessing the impact, usability and effectiveness of the system – the overall performance of user and system." (Hewett, 1986).

Hewett goes on to suggest that different types of evaluation may be suited to different stages in the design process. For example, qualitative data may be required when a design is being refined. Designers will need to know more about why errors or misunderstandings occurred rather than just their absolute numbers. In the later stages of design quantitative information may be required. This will allow the designers to assess the usefulness of changes to the design. If problems are shown to exist within a design at this stage then more qualitative data may be required to inform further changes.

This distinction between formative and summative forms of evaluation also serves to highlight one of the problems with Shackel's (1986) definition. It is not clear where the evaluation proposed by Shackel is supposed to take place. If it is in the earlier stages of design then simply acquiring user attitude scores and error counts may not properly inform the designers of the type of changes that are required. In essence, Shackel's operational statement of usability appears to be aimed only at the summative evaluation of a system.

What Measures Can We Use to Evaluate the Usability of a System?

Time. One of the most commonly used measures of usability is the time it takes a user to perform a task. Measures of time have the advantage that they are easy to measure and suitable for statistical analysis. The problem with using simple measures of time is that it is not always clear what these measures should be considered against. Often the time it takes a novice user to perform a task is compared to the time it took an expert user to perform the task. A more sophisticated means of calculating user performance has been suggested by Whiteside, Jones, Levy, and Wixon (1985), who have proposed a work rate metric for assessing the usability of systems. This metric is as follows:

$$S = \frac{1}{T} PC$$

where: S = the user's performance score,
T = time spent on task,
P = percentage of task completed,
C = arbitrary constant based on the fastest possible task solution for a practised system expert.

This metric gives an overall indication of work rate performance by taking account of what can be achieved (the expert's performance, C), the time the user takes (T), and the percentage of the task the user manages to complete (P). Consequently, this can be thought of as a more sophisticated metric than a simple measure of time.

However, there is no need to restrict measurement to the time it takes a user to perform a task. Bennett (cited in Shackel, 1981) has suggested that we might also measure the time it takes to adequately train users to use a system, the time that is required before the user can perform actions automatically, the time it takes users to *warm-up* after a period of non-use of a system, and the time the user requires to recover from errors. The problem with using time as a measure of learning, is that people often learn at different speeds and even in different ways.

Errors.   The errors that occur at user interfaces are potentially one of the most useful sources of information. Measures such as time only provide gross indications of where the user experienced difficulties. Errors, on the other hand, have the potential to show where problems exist within a system. Moreover, a study of user-system errors may also suggest the cause of a difficulty.

However, as Norman (1983b; Lewis & Norman, 1986) points out, the term *error* may not be the most appropriate for describing misunderstandings at the human-computer interface. The word *error* seems to apportion blame, whereas the terms *misunderstanding* or *dialogue failure* seem to more accurately characterize what happens when a user and a system fail to properly communicate with one another. For the moment, however, we will continue to use the term *error* because it is so commonly used within the literature.

Errors are unusual as a form of data as they provide both quantitative and qualitative information about usability (see Fig. 5.10). For any task simple counts of errors, or counts of particular error types can be made. Error counts for novices can be compared with error counts for experts or intermediate users. The problem with using errors in this way is that it is sometimes difficult to decide what is and what is not an error. Used qualitatively, errors can be a rich source of information. This is possibly because errors can often be related to points in the design that do not match either the user's needs or the user's understanding of the task.

In order that we might better understand user-system errors Norman (1983b) has suggested a means for classifying them into different types. Norman (1983b) suggests that an error in a user's intention is a *mistake*, while an error in carrying out an intention is a *slip*. These types of classification arise from the psychological study of human error (see also Norman, 1981a; Reason & Mycielska, 1982). Norman (1983b) also suggests the categories of *mode* errors and *description* errors. Mode errors are the type that occur when users believe that they are in one mode, when they are really in a different mode (for a discussion of mode errors see Monk, 1986). Description errors occur where there is insufficient specification of an action and the confusion leads to the wrong action. For an example of the use of Norman's classification scheme see Riley and O'Malley (1984) who used it in their approach to planning nets, that was mentioned in the last chapter.

Verbal protocols. Verbal protocols are written statements of what a user has said either during or after a task. There are two types of protocol; *concurrent* and *retrospective.* A concurrent protocol is one that is taken while the user performs that task. A retrospective protocol is one that is taken once a task has been completed.

A concurrent verbal protocol has the advantage that it is likely to produce more data about a task and system. Distortions may arise in this type of protocol, however, as the act of providing the protocol may influence the user's view of the task and, consequently, the user's behaviour. A retrospective protocol has the advantage that it is less likely to affect the user's behaviour at the task. Unfortunately, distortions in the protocol may occur as the user will only remember parts of the information that might have been provided by a concurrent protocol. For a discussion of verbal protocols and their relative advantages and disadvantages see Ericsson and Simon (1980).

One alternative to using single user protocols, described by Gould (in press), is that of using two users simultaneously (sometimes called *co-explorational studies*). The users speak to one another about the system they are using and their dialogue provides the data for analysis.

Visual protocols. These can be taken using a video camera. As with verbal protocols the information that this sort of measure can produce is qualitative and requires interpretation. Distortions in behaviour can arise as users may behave differently when they know that they are being filmed. The advantage of this technique within industry is that design teams can be shown where users experienced difficulties with a system.

Visual scanning patterns. Saccadic eye movement studies can show where a user's eyes fixated on the screen and for what duration of time. In other words, this sort of data can show us what information the user was looking at, at what time, and for how long. However, such data requires careful interpretation. For example, if we know that a user was looking at a certain piece of information shortly before an error was made what does this tell us? It may be that this information was crucial to the error. On the other hand, the user may have been thinking about the problem and just happened to be looking at that particular part of the screen. Nevertheless, this sort of data can show scanning strategies and demonstrate when some of the information on the screen is viewed for greater periods of time. For an example of this sort of study see Graf, Elsinger, and Krueger (1987).

Patterns of system use. Earlier in this chapter Eason's (1984) definition of usability was explained. The essence of this definition was that the

Measure	Can be used qualitatively	Can be used quantitatively
Time	No	Yes
Errors	Yes	Yes
Verbal protocols	Yes	Sometimes
Visual protocols	Yes	Sometimes
Visual scanning patterns	No	Yes
System use patterns	No	Yes
Attitude	Yes	Sometimes
Cognitive complexity scores	No	Yes

FIG. 5.10.   A table of evaluation measures, together with the types of information that they can be used to produce.

ultimate measure of usability was whether a system was used. By placing prototype systems in work environments and studying their patterns of use it is possible to assess which parts of a system are more frequently used. Such an approach may indicate that certain sections of a system are easier to use, or that certain tasks are more amenable to automation. Moreover, it may be possible to see which user groups prefer a system and which user groups avoid it.

Attitude measures.   These sorts of measures are usually elicited using questionnaires or interviews (for an example see Brooke, 1986). These measures often cover a wide range of areas. For example, questions may be asked about the user's opinion of the learnability of the system, the ease with which the system could be used, and whether the system adequately performed the task. Other types of questions that are often asked are whether the user felt in control of the task and situation, or whether the user felt frustrated and not in control of the interaction.

Although attitude measures require careful construction and validation, and may be open to bias, they nevertheless provide a valuable source of information. This type of user feedback can serve as an indication as to whether a system is likely to be used and appreciated in the work environment.

Cognitive complexity measures. These measures are produced by using some of the modelling techniques described in the last chapter. They can be used to assign cognitive complexity scores to various parts of a design. This is done by counting the number of rules that were required in cognitive grammar to describe a particular part of a system. Some of the advantages and disadvantages of this sort of approach have already been discussed earlier, in the last chapter. It is difficult to argue that the cognitive complexity scores that are produced using the modelling techniques can be used in any other way than quantitatively. However, the proponents of the cognitive modelling approach argue that the process of producing the grammar describing part of a system provides qualitative information. In other words, the modeller gains an insight and a better understanding of the system.

Methods of Evaluation

Hewett (1986) points out that not only does a system, and the design of that system require goals, but also any evaluation requires goals. By specifying the objective of an evaluation it is possible to identify what measures and what methods should be used. We have outlined some of the measures in the last section, but what methods might we employ, besides testing with naïve users?

Concept test. A concept test is where the ideas and concepts for the proposed system are laid out on cards or storyboards and presented to the user. This sort of test is also often referred to as *paper-and-pencil testing*. The objective of the test is to identify those concepts that the user finds acceptable and those that are likely to cause confusion.

Friendly users. It is commonly accepted that most evaluation programmes should involve users at some point, but what sort of users? Evaluation should certainly involve users from the different user groups that have interests in the system. However, other alternatives to using naïve users include using friendly users who have some technical knowledge to make suggestions as to possible alterations that might be made to a system. The advantage of this is that people can be used who have a reasonably good knowledge of how systems work, whereas naïve users are often unable to suggest how the design might be changed from an informed point of view. Unfortunately, as Hewett (1986) points out, these users tend to miss aspects of a system that often cause difficulties for naïve users.

Hostile users. A possible alternative to using either naïve or friendly users is to use hostile users. This is the sort of user that has no investment in the system. In other words, the sort of user who does not care if the system fails. When hostile users attempt to destructively use and criticize a system they often expose many inconsistencies and flaws that would have created difficulties for naïve users (Hewett, 1986).

Simulating users. Another possibility suggested by Hewett (1986), is that of simulating users. If the progress of several naïve users is charted, then later their routes through the system can be replicated by the designers. The advantage of this approach is that the designer is taken through the system in a way that may not have been previously envisaged. This way problems within the system can be identified and rectified.

Structured walkthroughs. An approach which is very similar to simulating users is for the designer to work through a series of tasks the user might be expected to perform, looking for sources of potential difficulty. The difference between this and simulating users is that a structured walk-through is based upon envisaged routes through tasks, whereas simulating users is based upon the actual routes through tasks that users took.

Expert review. A review such as this is where a system is examined by either a human factors expert or a designer who has not been directly involved in the project. The advantage of such a review is that comments and criticisms are made from a position of knowledge. The disadvantage of this sort of approach is that the expert is often immersed in the same technical culture as the designer, even if not to the same extent. Consequently, although such examinations can provide useful information about system inconsistencies, there is also the likelihood that difficulties that will hinder a naïve user will not be detected.

Simulation trials. A simulation trial is where a system is tested using rough prototypes or mock-ups of the intended system. When a system is built a great deal of effort, time and expense is put into creating and implementing a design. Understandably, designers are sometimes reluctant to change their designs, which often include elegant solutions to difficult technical problems. If a system can be tested before the majority of this effort and time is expended then the first iteration of the design is likely to be closer to the eventual usable design. The advantage of this approach is that time and money is less likely to be wasted in designing a system that is substantially unusable, as mock-ups (e.g. using pencil and paper type tasks) and rough prototypes do not need the technical elegance of the final design.

Iterative informal laboratory experiments. This approach is based around iteratively refining mock-ups or prototypes of a system (Twigger, 1986). The iterations of the system are refined using predominantly qualitative information gained through usability testing, expert review and the like.

Formal laboratory experiments. The advantage of formal experiments is that they control the environment. As a result, experimenter effects (e.g. the biases of the design team) are less likely to affect the results. This sort of approach tends to be based around collecting quantitative data to confirm or refute hypotheses. The disadvantage of formal laboratory experiments is that they are often far removed from the work environment in which systems are used. Consequently, there are always doubts as to whether the user's behaviour in an experiment can be taken as a reliable indicator of behaviour outside the laboratory. Moreover, they tend to explore the user's initial responses to the system, and learnability issues, rather than the longer-term issues of ease-of-use and efficiency.

Audits. An audit is where the system is considered against checklists of criteria that have been developed within the ergonomics or human factors literature. These checklists may cover a variety of areas such as: hardware, software, documentation, screen layout, etc.

Field trials. A field trial is where a system is placed within an organization prior to its formal release so that its use can be studied. Measures such as patterns of system use and user attitude questionnaires can be used to assess the potential success and usability of the product. This information can then be used to refine design. The disadvantage of this sort of approach is that it tends to be time consuming, particularly if data is required on long-term use of a system. Furthermore, arranging data collection can be problematic, while the information that this method provides is often too late to effect significant change.

Follow-up studies. Once a system has been designed and implemented within an organization there would appear to be little that might be done to improve its design. However, many systems are refined over time and updated versions of systems are often produced and released by manufacturers. By following a product into an organization and using attitude scales and interviews with users it is possible to provide qualitative data that can be used to refine the next release of a system. Several of the large IT companies have adopted this approach (Twigger, 1986).

Field studies. These are studies of systems in organizations. They tend to be more rigorous than simple follow-up studies or field trials, although as formal experiments they are difficult to control. The advantage of this approach is that it can be seen as an ultimate measure of the usability of a system; *whether or not the system is used in the work environment* (Eason, 1984). Moreover, this type of study also provides information that can help us to understand why some systems are used and others are not.

The list that has been presented may be of some use in considering the different methods that are presently used to evaluate systems. However, this list, although a potentially useful way of considering evaluation methods, is not a definitive statement. In reality, these methods are seldom used in a *pure* form, but evaluation tends to be something of a *mix and match* as far as methods are concerned.

THE DIFFICULTIES WITH THE USABILITY APPROACH

The usability approach has been characterized as one that begins by analyzing the user's needs and setting usability goals for the intended system (or product). The idea of setting usability goals for products has been well accepted within both academia and industry. Unfortunately, the question of who sets usability goals and how they are set, has received less attention. One argument is that a system might only be as usable as its usability goals. In other words, if we choose inappropriate goals then, no matter how well we meet these goals, the system will still fall short of being usable. Furthermore, the degree to which a system fails to meet usability demands may be proportionate to the gulf between the goals we set and the needs of the user.

By setting usability goals we are supposedly making usability a specific design objective. However, it is possible that when we set usability goals, without some process to inform how these goals are formulated, we are placing the usability problem one step back, rather than making a genuine contribution to the usability of the proposed system. One approach to this, that is commonly accepted (cf. Damodaran, 1983; Eason, 1985b), but not always made explicit, is to incorporate the user into the process of how usability goals are set, and not just when and how a system is measured against these goals.

A further problem with the usability approach is with the definitions of usability. As mentioned earlier in this chapter, Shackel's (1986) operational definition of usability does not appear to take account of how we might use qualitative data to inform and refine the design of systems. Although quantitative data is required to accurately assess the usability of a system, it is the qualitative information that informs designers how to change an unusable system. In other words, operational definitions such as Shackel's suggest how we might practically measure usability, but do not give any indication how we might improve the usability of a design. While it may seem a nonsense to suggest that we might quantitatively specify how designers might use qualitative information, we nevertheless need to acknowledge the important role of qualitative information within iterative design.

These criticisms, that usability definitions are only concerned with quantitative information, also serve to highlight another related problem. The usability approach suggests how we can measure the usability of a system, but does not say how a system might be changed in order to improve its usability. One reply to this sort of criticism is that a formal consideration of usability can only suggest where problems exist, it cannot suggest how to design and refine a system as this is a creative process. However, an approach that provided a means for understanding what happens when humans interact with computers could suggest how systems might be improved, although design solutions might always require a degree of creativity from the designer. In essence, the criticism is this; *the usability approach may show us how to measure usability, it may suggest what evaluation methods we should use and it may allow us to improve products in practical terms, but it does not provide a complete framework for understanding HCI.*

COMMENTARY

The general criticism of the usability approach, that it offers no real explanatory framework for understanding HCI, appears to be generally accepted within some quarters of the HCI community. For many, the definitions of usability, even the operational statements, appear to be too vague. Furthermore, it is possible to argue that human factors within the design and development process, whilst guided by the usability approach, is not systematic, but relies upon intuition and subjective judgement. For example, even the definition of a usability defect we suggested earlier leaves room for many interpretations. To re-iterate, a usability defect can be defined as *anything in the product which prevents a target user achieving a target task with reasonable effort and within a reasonable time.* However, the important question that such a definition raises is, what is *reasonable*?

However, we believe that this view ignores the practical contribution of the usability approach to theory within *human-computer interaction*. It appears to be generally accepted that theory within HCI needs to be applicable (cf. Card et al., 1980; 1983). Those human factors practitioners within industry, that approach their role from a usability perspective, provide practical feedback as to the nature of the design and development process, they set the limits for what might be practically applicable, and they provide the ultimate test of the worth of a theory.

Moreover, it has been the usability approach that has concentrated upon the problem of practically improving systems in the commercial environment. Both designers and users alike might complain that they cannot wait for a comprehensive theory of HCI, they need to improve their systems now. It has been the usability approach that has satisfied this need. Furthermore, the human factors practitioners have not only helped to develop more usable systems, but also educated the designers and engineers. They have argued the need for human factors issues to be considered throughout the design process, not just at the beginning or, more often, the end, where the contribution is frequently ineffectual.

Nevertheless, there remains a rather naïve assumption, amongst some system developers and ergonomists, that usability is something that can be sprinkled on a product once it is more or less complete. This misplaced perspective may arise from an understanding of usability as something that is determined solely by the human interface of a product, and not the product as a whole. Yet excellence in usability, in common with all aspects of product quality, requires a total commitment to improvement that extends right throughout the product development lifecycle. An example of how some companies are institutionalizing this commitment is illustrated in Fig. 5.11.

It is our belief that a required degree of usability can be engineered into products. Obviously the availability of specialist skills (human factors skills) is useful and can save time, effort and mistakes. However, it is not essential, nor does it, in itself, guarantee usability. Usability may be a little more difficult to define, measure and engineer than say, reliability or performance. Nevertheless, fundamentally, it is little different. It is another product attribute that can be improved, provided that there is a commitment to certain activities. We have represented these activities using the acronym OPTICS:

Objectives: management backing and clear objectives to produce a usable product;

Planning: making plans and time to address the usability issue and apply human factors techniques and tools;

Techniques: apply the relevant human factors tools and techniques (on a cost/benefit basis) at the right time in the development process;

Interest: continually strive to put yourself in the user's position, understand the user's needs and involve representative users in design, review and testing;

Care: reflect concern for usability in all aspects of the product, and take care to fix important usability problems that are discovered; and

Specialists: make use of specialist human factors help.

PRODUCT LIFECYCLE PHASES	INVESTIGATION
HUMAN FACTORS PHASES	**Needs Analysis**
OBJECTIVE	Identify need for product by studying characteristics of the user, task and work environment
HUMAN FACTORS ACTIVITIES	• Identify target users and characteristics that will affect product success • Identify and analyze user tasks • Identify physical and organizational environment • Identify usability problems with similar or existing products • Develop initial product feature list
EXAMPLE HUMAN FACTORS METHODS	• Observation • Interview • Survey • Focus group • Task analysis • User diaries

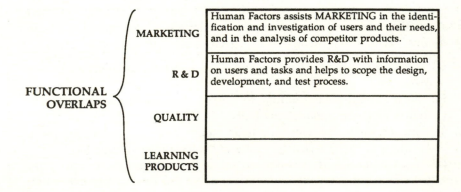

FUNCTIONAL OVERLAPS	MARKETING	Human Factors assists MARKETING in the identification and investigation of users and their needs, and in the analysis of competitor products.
	R & D	Human Factors provides R&D with information on users and tasks and helps to scope the design, development, and test process.
	QUALITY	
	LEARNING PRODUCTS	

FIG. 5.11a.   Usability in the design and development process. By permission of Hewlett Packard Ltd.

INVESTIGATION	DESIGN
Requirements Specification	**Conceptual Design**
Specify requirements products must satisfy to meet user needs successfully in the identified market and define system usability goals	Develop user interface specifications to meet previously identified product usability requirements and performance objectives
• Identify ergonomic and market-based require -ments • Define and develop product usability and user acceptance goals • Define criteria for measuring usability and acceptance • Develop product localization plan • Develop testing schedule	• Develop user interface requirements • Define users model(s) which describes system from user's perspective • Determine allocation of function between user(s) and system • Interpret Human Factors data, principles, and guidelines • Test Concept models with representative users
• Literature review	• Empirical investigations • Observation • Video/audio taping • Structured walkthroughs

Human Factors provides MARKETING with information about product requirements that will satisfy user needs.	
Human Factors and R&D work together to set usability goals and specify requirements for each target group.	Human Factors assists R&D in exploring the usability implications of the intended implementation of the design concepts.
QUALITY works with Human Factors to help determine usability and quality metrics for the product.	In this and subsequent phases, QUALITY monitors and documents with Human Factors help, ergonomic requirements and compliance.
LEARNING PRODUCTS works with Human Factors to identify support materials which will facilitate learning and effective use of the product.	Human Factors helps LEARNING PRODUCTS to integrate support materials into the development process.

FIG. 5.11b.   Usability in the design and development process. By permission of Hewlett Packard Ltd.

DESIGN		Construction/ Implementation	Testing and Release	Support
Prototype Development & Test		**Product Evaluation**		
Test product with representative users performing benchmark tasks to ensure a usable and functional interface		Verify that product meets customers needs and gather information for future product development		
• Provide technical support in the development of product prototypes or simulations • Review production prototypes for ergonomic compliance • Test usability of hardware, software, documentation, and training components • Provide feedback to designers on results of usability tests		• Review final product specifications to ensure that user interface issues have been addressed satisfactorily • Field test product usability • Provide marketing with data on user interface advantages • Conduct evaluations at customer site to determine how effectively product meets users' needs and necessary improvements • Perform analysis for next generation of products		

• Empirical testing of:
 	
  - Written scenarios of productuse
  - Early versions of user manuals
  - Simulations, demonstrations, and mock-ups
  - Early prototypes
  - Production prototypes
		• Field testing		

MARKETING helps Human Factors to identify test subjects and benchmark tasks, and helps to collect usability data.	MARKETING and Human Factors collect field data about product usability in order to support the marketing, sale, and support of the product.
R&D develops hardware and software prototypes for usability and user acceptance testing by Human Factors.	R&D updates hardware and software as necessary and provides updates for user testing.
	QUALITY reviews design methods and approach with Human Factors and discusses improvements
LEARNING PRODUCTS submits user documentation, on-line help, classroom and computer-based training for usability testing.	LEARNING PRODUCTS updates support materials as necessary and conducts usability testing with Human Factors.

FIG. 5.11c. Usability in the design and development process. By permission of Hewlett Packard Ltd.

We suggest that when such a strategy is present, a minimally acceptable level of usability can be guaranteed, on the grounds that the first 80% of improvement comes with the first 20% of effort. Notice how the OPTICS formula relates to the process of ergonomics or human factors. Notice also, that it is assumed that everyone who contributes to a product has some responsibility for usability. Specialist human factors help is brought in when and if available, but the burden of responsibility does not fall upon the specialists; it is the responsibility of the whole design and development team. The real challenge of the usability approach is to embed or institutionalize these good practices into existing development processes.

SUMMARY

It is commonly accepted that issues of usability should cover all types of user. In other words, programmers, systems engineers, maintenance engineers, end-users, etc., are all considered to be users of the system.

Eason (1984) has suggested eight variables that contribute towards the usability of a system. These include two task characteristics (frequency and openness), three that are functions of the system (ease of learning, ease of use and task fit), and three user characteristics (knowledge, motivation and discretion). Eason suggests that the variables of the task, system and user all combine to determine the usability of a system.

Eason (1984) argues that usability is best measured in the work environment where a system is normally used. The argument he proposes against trying to measure usability in the laboratory is this: if we force an individual to use a system in a laboratory then we may be destroying the best measure of the usability that we have; whether or not a system is used.

Shackel (1986) has defined usability in operational terms of effectiveness, learnability, flexibility and user attitude. A system must be effective, in that a certain proportion of target users must be able to use the system within a certain time. A system must be learnable, in that users must be able to learn the system after a certain amount of training. A system must be flexible, in that user performance must not deteriorate by more than a certain percentage across tasks and environments. Finally, a system must provoke user attitude ratings where a certain percentage are positive towards the system.

There appear to be limitations to Shackel's definition. First, *flexibility* is particularly difficult to specify, communicate and test in a real product development environment. Second, Shackel appears to omit an element that would seem to be fundamental to any definition of usability; that of *usefulness*. Consequently, it is suggested that Shackel's definition be amended to include the criteria of *usefulness*. Furthermore, it is suggested that, for practical purposes, the criteria of *flexibility* should be excluded.

It is proposed that a *User Needs Analysis* has the following stages: user characterization, task analysis, situational analysis and identifying acceptance criteria. The purpose of a *User Needs Analysis* is to identify some of the issues and concerns that should be considered when specifying and designing a system.

Usability testing usually involves testing prototypes on users in a laboratory. Such testing can be used to measure user performance and satisfaction, to identify and assess usability defects, to provide ideas as to how a system might be improved and to educate design teams. Furthermore, this sort of testing is considered to be relatively easy to perform.

Usability testing of products often requires task scenarios. These are descriptive stories about the intended use of the product. They embody a goal, information about the task and information about the situational context in which the system is to be used. Such scenarios can be used to explore the boundaries of use for both frequent and critical conditions, and as such, they form a useful basis for *usability testing* within human factors laboratories.

The concept of a usability defect can be defined as anything in the product which prevents a target user achieving a target task with reasonable effort and within a reasonable time. The advantage of this sort of concept is that it allows us to focus upon those aspects of a product that require attention and alteration. However, the difficulty with this approach, and with user-testing in general, is that wider issues may be overlooked.

Hewett (1986) distinguishes two forms of evaluation; *formative* and *summative*. Formative evaluation helps the designer to refine and *form* the design and is more likely to require qualitative information to help the designer identify problems. Summative evaluation is more likely to require quantitative information rather than qualitative data as its purpose is to assess the usability and impact of a system.

The measures we can use to evaluate a system include; time, errors, verbal protocols, visual protocols, patterns of system use, user attitude measures, and cognitive complexity measures. Methods of evaluation include; concept tests, using naïve, friendly, or hostile users, simulating users, structured walkthroughs, expert reviews, simulation trials, iterative informal laboratory experiments, formal laboratory experiments, audits, field trials, follow-up studies, and field studies.

The usability approach appears to have a number of drawbacks. One problem is the question of who sets usability goals for systems and how are they set. A further problem is with operational definitions of usability. These tend to define usability using only quantitative measures and ignore the contribution of qualitative informationally, the usability approach may show us how to measure usability, it may suggest what evaluation methods we should use and may allow us to improve products, but it does not provide a framework for understanding HCI.

A SELECTIVE ANNOTATED BIBLIOGRAPHY

Bennett, J. L. (1984). Managing to meet usability requirements: Establishing and meeting software development goals. In J. L. Bennett, D. Case, J. Sandelin, & M. Smith (Eds.), *Usability issues and health concerns*. Englewood Cliffs, New Jersey: Prentice-Hall. *This provides an interesting and easy-to-read introduction to some of the practical issues associated with designing usable systems.*

Bury, K. F. (1984). The iterative development of usable computer interfaces. In B. Shackel (Ed.), *Human-computer interaction–Interact '84: Proceedings of the first IFIP conference on human-computer interaction, London*. Amsterdam: North-Holland. *The author suggests how user interface prototypes can be used to test usability early in the design process. This paper describes a practical approach to iterative design and is well worth reading.*

Carroll, J. M. & Rosson, M. B. (1985). Usability specifications as a tool in iterative development. In H. R. Hartson (Ed.), *Advances in human-computer interaction*. Norwood, New Jersey: Ablex. *The authors are concerned with the use of usability specifications as part of iterative design. However, the paper also points out some of the problems with the cognitive modelling or analytic approach. This readable article provides an interesting and valuable perspective on usability in the design process and is highly recommended to readers from both academia and industry alike.*

Eason, K. D. (1984). Towards the experimental study of usability. *Behaviour and Information Technology, 8 (2)*, 133–143. *The author outlines the factors that contribute towards the usability of a system. Later it is argued that usability cannot always be measured in the laboratory as the ultimate test of the usability of a system is whether or not it is used.*

Good, M., Spine, T. M., Whiteside, J., & George, P. (1986). User-derived impact analysis as a tool for usability engineering. In M. Mantei & P. Orbeton (Eds.), *Human factors in computer systems–III: Proceedings of the CHI '86 Conference, Boston*. Amsterdam: Elsevier. *The authors build on the work of researchers such as Carroll & Rosson, Shackel, Bennett, and Glib to formulate an approach they term "usability engineering". This approach is concerned with defining usability through metrics, setting planned levels of usability and iterating design until the levels of usability are met. This is a well-written and interesting paper.*

Gould, J. D. & Lewis, C. H. (1985). Designing for usability–key principles and what designers think. *Communications of the ACM, 28*, 300–311. *The authors set out four principles for designing usable systems. These principles are that the designers must know who the intended users of the systems are, a panel of users must work with the design team, the design must produce prototypes, and problems found during usability testing must be rectified. Once again, this paper advocates iterative design, and by way of assessing how likely it is that this sort of design might be adopted, the authors describe some of the designers' attitudes towards their four principles.*

Hewett, T. T. (1986). The role of iterative evaluation in designing systems for usability. In M. D. Harrison & A. F. Monk (Eds.), *People & computers: Designing for usability. Proceedings of the second conference of the BCS HCI specialist group*. Cambridge: Cambridge University Press. *The author describes experiences in developing a particular system. In doing so, several different types of evaluative methods are discussed as well as the types of information that these methods produce. This is an interesting, wide-ranging and easy-to-read discussion of the role of evaluation in design.*

Howard, S. & Murray, D. M. (1987). A taxonomy of evaluation techniques for HCI. In H. J. Bullinger & B. Shackel (Eds.), *Human-computer interaction–Interact '87: Proceedings of the second IFIP conference on human-computer interaction, Stuttgart.* Amsterdam: North-Holland. *A number of evaluative measures and methods are discussed and placed within an overall evaluation framework. This paper provides a short and useful discussion of evaluative techniques within HCI.*

Lewis, C. & Norman, D. A. (1986). Designing for error. In D. A. Norman & S. W. Draper (Eds.), *User centred system design: New perspectives on human-computer interaction.* Hillsdale, New Jersey: Lawrence Erlbaum Associates Inc. *The authors point out that the term "error" is inappropriate for describing dialogue failures at the human-computer interface. Nevertheless a classification of errors is suggested. This classification is partly based upon human error research and partly around errors of misunderstanding that occur between systems and users. This is an interesting and clearly-written paper.*

Lund, M. A. (1985). Evaluating the user interface: The candid camera approach. In L. Borman & W. Curtis (Eds), *Human factors in computer systems–II: Proceedings of the CHI '85 conference, San Francisco.* Amsterdam: North-Holland. *A practical approach to evaluation is described that centred around video taping users. This paper may be of particular interest to designers and practitioners within industry who would like a down-to-earth description of an approach to evaluating a system.*

Roberts, T. L. & Moran, T. P. (1983). The evaluation of text editors: methodology and empirical results. *Communications of the ACM, 26 (4)*, 265–283. *The authors describe evaluating a text editor using a four dimensional methodology. This measures time, errors, learning and functionality. This is an interesting paper that discusses some of the different methods that can be employed to evaluate a system.*

Shackel, B. (1986). Ergonomics in design for usability. In M. D. Harrison & A. F. Monk (Eds.), *People & computers: Designing for usability. Proceedings of the second conference of the BCS HCI specialist group.* Cambridge: Cambridge University Press. *An operational definition of usability is suggested and explained. Following this, the different aspects of ergonomic design, from user centred design to user supportive design, are outlined and discussed. This paper is easy to read and essential for those who wish to know more about usability.*

Wright, P. & Bason, G. (1982). Detour routes to usability: A comparison of alternative approaches to multipurpose software design. *International Journal of Man-Machine Studies, 18*, 391–400. *One of the objectives of evaluation is to discover whether a system provides what the user wants. However, this paper asks the question; should the designer incorporate new functions and features into a design or just provide users with what they request? The authors discuss this ever-present issue in an interesting and stimulating way.*

6

The Design and Development Process

OVERVIEW

A generalized description of the design and development process is considered along with designers' views of this process. The deficits of design and development, and the question of how to make good these shortfalls is the central theme that runs throughout this chapter. The terminology regarding cognitive modelling and formal methods is reviewed, and formal mathematical methods are considered with respect to the design and development process. Following this, some of the problems of using formal methods within design are considered. The non-formal cognitive approach to design and development is then discussed, from guidelines to techniques. Finally, the usability approach to socio-technical design is described, and some of the guidelines and methodologies for incorporating human factors into the design and development process are outlined.

INTRODUCTION

The design and implementation of systems is considered to be the major focus of work within HCI. The issue of introducing systems within an organization will be dealt with in the next chapter. In this chapter the usability, cognitive and mathematical approaches to the problems of design and development will be discussed. That is to say, that here we will address the question; how can we apply the work that has been discussed in previous chapters to the design and development process? First, however, the question of how design and development is currently approached will be briefly addressed.

PRESENT DESIGN AND DEVELOPMENT PRACTICE

A simplified view of the stages of development is presented in Fig. 6.1. In the first stage, information is collected about the tasks a system will have to perform, and who its users will be, although discussion also frequently focuses upon competitor products and justifying a return on the investment. In the next stage the system is designed and specified. In other words, the questions of how the system is going to work and what it is going to do are set out in detail. Part of this stage is to partition different parts of the design

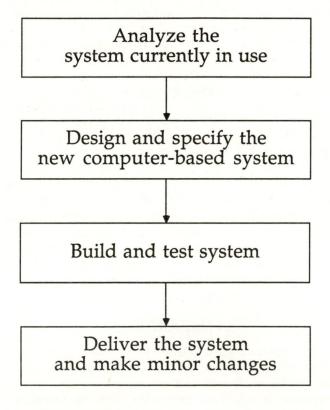

FIG. 6.1.   A simplified view of the development process.

to different engineers and to state how these different subsystems are going to link together to build into the system as a whole. The third stage is to build the system, and to test both the parts, and the system as a whole to see if it works. The final stage is to deliver the system to the user. Once the system has been implemented within an organization it may require adjustments, and minor changes are often made (sometimes these changes are more substantial).

The major problems with this traditional design and development process are: a) the information that is received about an organization does not provide adequate information about users; and b) designers are unable to properly understand the non-expert user (see Chapters One and Five). The inadequacies of present design and development practice lead to the kind of problems mentioned in Chapter One; users are required to remember too much information, systems are intolerant of minor errors, systems seem confusing to new users, interactional techniques are used inappropriately, systems do not provide the functions users require, systems force users to perform tasks in undesirable ways, and new systems cause unacceptable changes to the structure and practices of organizations.

The question that comes to mind when considering these problems is; why are present systems analysis and design methodologies failing to account properly for the user? One answer is that systems analysis techniques such as Structured Systems Analysis and Design Methodology (SSADM) are primarily concerned with information and object flow within a system. Although users are considered to some extent, the central focus is upon the system and the information and objects it must deal with. These sorts of methodologies do not describe users or usage very well. Consequently, these types of methodologies have been labelled *system-centred*.

In essence, it is suggested within HCI research that present systems analysis and design methodologies are inadequate to meet the needs of users. Furthermore, it is argued that many system usability problems are a consequence of these inadequacies. However, this sort of criticism is not intended to imply that present design and development practice is totally *wrong*. For example, the Jackson method of program design (Jackson, 1983), where the inputs and outputs to a program are represented as labelled trees, fulfills an important function within design and development. The argument is; that present design practice is inadequate with respect to the extent to which the interests and needs of the user are considered and represented. But if this is the case, how can we engineer a shift from *system-centred* design to *user-centred* design? Furthermore, what is meant by the term *user-centred* design?

The answer to this last question is that the term *user-centred* design is a statement of intention; the desire to make the user the central focus of the design and development process. This aim is commonly shared within HCI research, and a more appropriate question is; how can we best achieve this? If we are to begin to move towards an answer to this question, then we may need to understand the major features of the design and development process a little better.

THE CHARACTERISTICS OF DESIGN AND DEVELOPMENT

Carroll and Rosson (1985), using the earlier work of Carroll, Thomas, and Malhotra (1980), have suggested four aspects of design that essentially characterize it:

1. Design is a *process*, it is not a state and cannot be adequately represented statically.
2. The design process is *non-hierarchical*, neither strictly bottom-up nor top-down.
3. The process is *radically transformational*, involving the development of partial and interim solutions which may ultimately play no role in the final design.
4. Design intrinsically involves the *discovery of new goals*.

The essence of what Carroll and Rosson are trying to convey is that the design of a system evolves throughout the design and development process, a system is not simply specified and built. We might like to think of design beginning at a high level, where overall goals are chosen for the system. The rest of the development process might be thought of as a straightforward process of meeting these goals in the detail of the design. However, in reality this does not occur.

At the beginning of the design process some of the low-level goals are known as well as some of the high-level goals. Throughout the design and development process, through compromises and trade offs, these goals build into a more complete and coherent picture, as goals are added, changed or discarded. Solutions to design problems often require creativity, and consequently, the process of design and development, both in the emergence of goals and the development of solutions, cannot be described as completely rational or logical.

Other research into design has tended to produce results that generally agree with the characteristics outlined by Carroll and Rosson (1985). Rubinstein and Hersh (1984), for example, state that: "Design is seldom an orderly or linear process. System building occurs in a real world with constraints, interruptions, distractions, emotions, personalities, and politics. Any guidelines used for systems development must operate within these complex conditions." They go on to say: "Because design is an art as well as a science, it is never a completely rational process."

This view of design has been further supported by the opinions designers express about their role in creating systems. Figure 6.2 shows a perspective on the design process that emerged from interviews with designers (Hammond et al., 1983a). Notice how the needs of the user are not represented explicitly in Fig. 6.2; the major focus is upon how to build the system, rather than how to match the system to the user's needs.

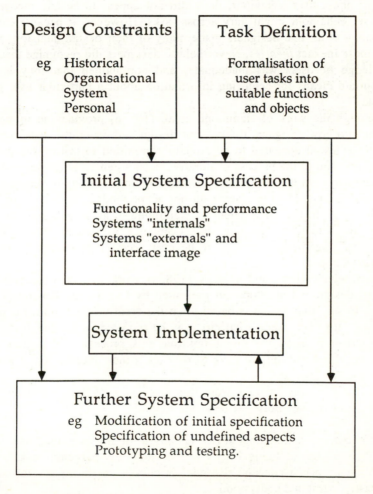

FIG. 6.2. A simplified framework for the sequence of design steps based upon evidence obtained from interviews with designers. Original source: Hammond et al. (1983a).

Hammond et al. (1983a) found that the task analysis the designers were likely to perform was based around considering the logical structure of the task, and was not concerned with the user's view of the task. Furthermore, designers were particularly concerned with "clean" internal architectures and "clean" interfaces that were consistent across different parts of the system. The difficulty with this approach is that this desire to be "clean" may cause the designer to ignore the user's needs with respect to performing the tasks that are required.

Moreover, designers' *theories* of users tended to consist of broad generalizations about user behaviour, there did not appear to be any recognition that user behaviour might vary across tasks. However, it became clear to Hammond et al. that designers made many of their design decisions based upon these inexact *theories*. Nevertheless, designers did recognize that their knowledge of users was inadequate, and complained that they had no appropriate means for acquiring information about a particular user group or task.

Although the work of Hammond et al. (1983a) provides an interesting insight into how designers think about design and users, the designers that they interviewed appeared to be already committed to testing the product with users, and to the process of iterative design generally (iterative design is where a system is built, tested, and built again according to the results of tests with users). Most engineers do not acknowledge the role of the user within design to the same extent as Hammond et al.'s designers. In other words, the situation regarding the acceptance of human factors within design and development appears to be even worse than Hammond et al.'s interviews imply.

Nevertheless, Hammond et al.'s (1983a) work generally supports the view of design and development presented by Carroll and Rosson (1985). That is to say, that design is based upon the creativity and intuition of the designer. However, while creativity may be required within the design and development process, we might improve this process if designers were better informed and did not have to rely upon their intuitions and guesses about tasks and users.

The question that emerges from this discussion of design and development is; how do we inform the designer so that:

1. The correct interactional device is chosen for any particular task.
2. The most useful dialogue style is chosen for any particular task.
3. An appropriate conceptual model is chosen so that a system can be easily learnt and understood.
4. Users are allowed to perform a task in the way that they choose.
5. The information that users require is provided in the form that is acceptable.

THE CHARACTERISTICS OF DESIGN AND DEVELOPMENT

6. The systems fits easily into the working practices of an organization.

There are three approaches to this problem, all of which stem from different disciplines; a cognitive approach, a mathematical approach, and a usability approach. The mathematical approach and parts of the cognitive approach employ analytical methods, while the usability approach is based around the notion of iterative design and informing the designer's intuition rather than providing formalisms. (Parts of the usability approach were dealt with in the last chapter, while some aspects of formal or analytical methods were considered in Chapter Four).

A Note on Terminology

Before, we consider the first of these approaches, that of formal mathematical methods, it may be useful to clarify some of the uses of the term *formal method*. The terms *formal method* or *analytic technique* are often used within the HCI literature, although these terms are often used to mean different things, depending upon who is using them.

A formal method is quite simply a notation for describing some aspect of a system or user behaviour. The idea of these approaches is that they break down the system's or the user's behaviour into manageable chunks and show where inconsistencies arise, or where the task is too complex. It is possible, however, to distinguish two different types of formal method. First, there are the methods or notations that attempt to cognitively model the user. The purpose of these approaches is to show how complex any particular task might be in cognitive terms. Some of these techniques were mentioned in chapter four (i.e. Card et al.'s (1980; 1983) GOMS model, and Payne and Green's (1986) Task-Action Grammar). Second, there are notations such as Z notation and Reisner's (1981) BNF (this last grammar, BNF, was also discussed in Chapter Four). These are notations that have often been adopted or derived from other fields, and applied to HCI, although some are now being developed specifically for HCI. The purpose of these notations is to expose logical inconsistencies within a system, and within a system's interfaces. They are not primarily concerned with the cognitive aspects of HCI.

This division may be viewed as a split between the cognitive scientists and the mathematicians. However, although this is a convenient way of thinking about different types of formal method, it is also a gross over-simplification. This difference between mathematical and cognitive formal methods might be better thought of as a continuum upon which we can place different formalisms (see Fig. 6.3).

Many cognitive scientists are concerned about consistency within a system's interfaces, and some mathematicians are just as concerned with

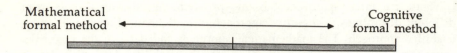

FIG. 6.3.   A simple representation of the continuum between the different types of formal method (or analytic technique).

the cognitive aspects of HCI as they are with the formal logic of the interface. The exact position where any notation may be placed upon the continuum (shown in Fig. 6.3) is largely determined by the individual who is using it. In other words, the difference between the two types of notation is in the purpose to which they are put; whether their central aim is to consider cognitive complexity or interface consistency, although these two concepts are clearly closely related.

FORMAL METHODS IN DESIGN AND DEVELOPMENT

Now that we have established that the distinction between cognitive and mathematical formal methods is somewhat vague, we will consider the role of formal mathematical methods in design and development. First, we need to outline the purpose of using formal mathematical methods. Sufrin (1986) provides this explanation: "...it is only by understanding the essence of the purpose of an information system—abstracting from the details of any proposed implementation—that one can begin to judge the validity of design choices concerning the user-system interface." In other words, mathematical methods can allow us to expose the workings of a system, and show a system in a new light that allows direct comparisons to be made between alternative design choices.

The aim of the mathematical approach is to reduce a system to its basic elements. By exposing the logical relationships between the different elements of a system we provide information that should make it easier for us to reach rational judgements about a system. For example, imagine that we have been given the task of designing a hospital information system. If we are presented with competing designs for that system how can we judge which alternative is best? There is a danger that our decision may be biased by our knowledge of how a hospital presently operates. In other words, because of our preconceptions, we may not make a rational decision and choose the best design. However, by describing each alternative mathematically we can break away from a decision that is clouded by our view of existing hospital structure. In essence, by describing a design mathematically we provide ourselves with new information and a new perspective upon which we can base our decision.

However, this argument does not imply that design decisions should be based solely on the evidence from mathematical descriptions. The advantage of using formal mathematical notations in design is that they increase the amount, type and quality of information that is available when making a decision. Design decisions are likely to be based on a variety of information sources, but by using an analytic description (a formal specification technique) we can expose unrecognized weaknesses, and confirm or refute suspicions about potential problems.

Different Formal Notations

Having decided that formal notations are potentially useful in HCI, we might now ask; what are these notations, and how do they differ from the techniques described in Chapter Four? The answer is that these techniques do not differ significantly from those described in Chapter Four. Moreover, the most common notation used is Backus Naur Form (BNF), and the major symbols and concepts used in such a grammar were outlined in Chapter Four. Commonly, this notation, or variations on it, are used with state transition diagrams (Edmonds & Guest, 1984; Jacob, 1985; Wasserman, 1985). State transition diagrams, as the term suggests, are diagrams that are used to show the changes from one situation or state to another.

However, BNF is by no means the only notation that can be used to formally describe a system. For example, Sufrin (1986) demonstrates how Z notation (Morgan & Sufrin, 1984; Sufrin, Morgan, Sørensen, & Hayes, 1985) can be used to describe an office mail system, together with its interface, from different points of view (from the designer's, from the user's point of view, etc.). Other types of notation have included using production systems (Durrett & Stimmel, 1982), and techniques that describe primitive steps or events in HCI (Alexander, 1986; Benbasat & Wand, 1984). (For a brief description of a formal notation see the section on modelling techniques in Chapter Four.)

Design Principles

Now we have briefly mentioned some of the different types of notation that are currently used, we need to understand how a formalism can be used to judge a design. In other words, once we have described a system using a notation, what do we do next? The answer is that we use these notations to check our design against various design principles. Bleser and Foley (1982) suggest the following principles for evaluating a design: completeness in design; consistency in syntax; consistency of lexical characteristics; minimization of visual and tactile alternatives.

IHCI—F

It is noticeable that these principles are not stated in cognitive terms, it is the logic of the interface that is the central concern. This can also be said to be true of the application of formalisms such as Z notation (Sufrin, 1986) to HCI. Monk and Dix (1987) take a similar non-cognitive approach, and in their paper adopt the principles of: predictability; simplicity; consistency; reversibility.

Monk and Dix (1987) suggest a *black box* approach where the principles they apply are considered with respect to the inputs and outputs from a system. In other words, the internal workings of the system do not interest them, nor are they directly concerned with the cognitive aspects of the interaction between the system and the user. In many ways, this sort of approach is akin to the behaviourist approach in psychology, where only the inputs and outputs to and from an organism (or system) are considered.

The advantage of Monk and Dix's (1987) semi-formal method is that it appears to be usable, while many formal mathematical methods are denounced for being too complex. On the other hand, formalisms that do not account for the cognitive features of HCI, such as Monk & Dix's notation, have been criticized for avoiding one of the most essential characteristics of *human-computer interaction*; the cognitive aspect. This argument is based around the idea that HCI is cognitively mediated. That is to say, that interaction is dependent upon what a user understands of a system. It appears unlikely that users will behave in accordance with simple action-effect rules. Consequently, much of the work from a formal methods standpoint has been based around developing notations that account for the cognitive aspects of HCI.

Formal Cognitive Notations

An example of the cognitive orientation of some approaches to formal methods is provided by Jacob (1982), who describes the desired properties of a formal specification technique:

1. The specification of a user interface should be easy to understand. In particular, it must be easier to understand (and take less effort to produce) that the software that implements the user interface.
2. The specification should be precise. It should leave no doubt as to the behaviour of the system for each possible input.
3. The specification technique should be powerful enough to express non-trivial system behaviour with a minimum of complexity.
4. It should separate what the system does (function) from how it does it (implementation). The technique should make it possible to describe the behaviour of the user interface, without constraining the way in which it will be implemented.
5. It should be possible to construct a prototype of the system directly from the specification of the user interface.

6. The structure of the specification should be closely related to the user's mental model of the system itself. That is, its principal constructs should represent concepts that will be meaningful to users (such as answering a message or examining a file), rather than internal constructs required by the specification language.

All of the formal notations that have been proposed for use in HCI to date would fail to meet at least one of these criteria. Jacob's (1982) criteria, however, are probably best viewed as a goal or ideal for formal notations within HCI. Nevertheless, what immediately stands out is that formalisms such as Z notation (Sufrin, 1986) do not fulfill Jacob's criterion regarding the representation of the user's mental model. The last criterion suggests that a notation should represent concepts that are meaningful to the user, and not just reflect the internal architecture of a system. Yet Z notation was originally developed with the central aim of representing the internal structure of systems.

While notations such as BNF, although not originally intended as a cognitive notation, have been applied as cognitive performance models within HCI, other formalisms have been developed that are specifically aimed at representing the cognitive aspects of interaction. The advantage of these cognitively orientated techniques is that they specifically address some of the most important cognitive issues in HCI. For example, the question of how users understand a system and then go on to formulate a sequence of actions to execute an intention is currently of particular interest. This issue has already been discussed in Chapter Four and will not be discussed again. Nevertheless, it should be mentioned that notations such as Task-Action Grammar (TAG) address just this problem (TAG was also described and discussed in Chapter Four).

THE ROLE OF FORMAL METHODS IN THE DESIGN AND DEVELOPMENT PROCESS

Formal methods, whether aimed at describing the logical or cognitive aspects of HCI, appear to offer a means by which alternative designs can be analyzed. Within the literature, many of the discussions of these techniques have focused upon questions of whether a notation sufficiently describes a system, or accurately characterizes human cognitive processes and representation. However, a question that is less frequently addressed is; can these methods be used in design and development?

In short, the answer to this question is not entirely clear, although many researchers are confident that usable notations that accurately describe HCI will be developed sometime in the future. Indeed, as new notations and variations on old notations are suggested and refined, we appear to be moving gradually towards the ideal, defined by Jacob's (1982) criteria. Nevertheless, there are criticisms of formal methods, and these criticisms provide an indication of the distance between present formal notations and Jacob's (1982) ideal.

Criticisms of Formal Methods

The area where formal methods have appeared to be most strongly criticized has been with respect to their usefulness in design and development. For example, it was noted in Chapter Four that none of the proposed modelling techniques or grammars directly involve the user. Therefore, there is a risk that these methods cannot detect when a user's conceptualization of the task is significantly different from that held by the designer or engineer who applies the notation.

Moreover, Carroll and Rosson (1985) have argued that current formal methods or modelling techniques do not fit easily into present design and development practice. They argue that: "...the formal evaluation of a given set of design specifications does not provide the kind of detailed qualitative information about learnability, usability, or acceptance that designers need in order to iteratively refine specifications, rather it assigns a figure...of merit to the design [i.e. the number of rules needed to describe part of the system]. This could be used to order a set of alternative designs, but contrasting alternative designs is an extremely inefficient means of converging on the best solution." Carroll & Rosson go on to say: "In a word, analytic approaches [modelling techniques/formal methods] do not support the process of design...The initial definition of design specifications can often rely on analytic methods. But this initial definition is only the beginning of the design process. Unfortunately, this is where the analytic approaches stall."

In essence, Carroll and Rosson (1985) are arguing that current modelling techniques (or analytic approaches) are almost irrelevant to the process of design and development. Of course, this does not necessarily mean that all future formal notations are unlikely to be of use, only that present methods may have serious shortcomings.

At first glance this debate may appear to be a simple and straightforward divide between those ergonomists (or human factors engineers) who believe in a usability rather than a cognitive or mathematical approach, and those cognitive scientists and mathematicians who cannot agree to an approach that does not consider the cognitive issues or rely upon formal logic. Such a characterization, however, would be unfair to all concerned, as there is no clear boundary between cognitive scientists, mathematicians and ergonomists. Many cognitive scientists and mathematicians accept the criticisms of current formal notations, and are trying to provide methods that involve the user and support design and development. However, not all cognitive psychologists and scientists have adopted this formal approach.

THE NON-FORMAL COGNITIVE APPROACH

Some researchers have attempted to embody the cognitive aspects of HCI within design guidelines or methodologies. Green (1986) even reports a project where the aim is to develop an expert system to advise designers on aspects of user cognition, based on Barnard's (1985; 1987) interacting cognitive subsystems model. An alternative, and less exotic approach, is to develop *programmable user models*.

Programmable User Models

Thimbleby (1986) explains the notion of programmable user models by asking the following question: "Would designers make better systems if, in addition to writing computer software, they had also to write user software and demonstrate it could (in some precise sense) operate their design? If a designer had to program a *programmable user*, perhaps as part of the proposed system's acceptance tests, then this would help to redress the unequal balance of attention normally loaded for the computer. It would make designers consider the user and the user's needs more carefully."

Runciman and Hammond (1986) make the same point, and go into the question in more detail. They suggest that a programmable user model, or user program, should be written in the same programming language as the system that it is intended to operate. They also propose a cognitive architecture on which to base these programs (see Fig. 6.4). So far, this idea has been mainly confined to being the subject of research projects and has not yet reached the design and development process.

Cognitive Design Guidelines

A more traditional method for incorporating new ideas into the design and development process is to express these ideas as guidelines. Marshall, Nelson, and Gardiner (1987b) have suggested a series of design interface guidelines based upon the cognitive psychology literature. An edited summary of these guidelines follows:

Design procedures and tasks
Task sequences should be kept short, or broken down into sub-sequences.
A user should not be asked to perform two complex tasks together.
Action sequences for different tasks should be unique.
Make important information explicit.
If the user has to remember and then use information, do not fill the time between these tasks with irrelevant distracting information or activity.
Define all terms relevant to the completion of a task early in the dialogue.
Ensure that users can utilize well-learned, generic (system-wide) commands for routine or repetitive actions.

Present information in the order in which it will be used.

When users need to progress rapidly through a series of transactions use familiar labels or sequences of actions.

To engender quick and accurate performance of tasks such as decision-making, reasoning or planning; encourage the user to complete one task at a time,

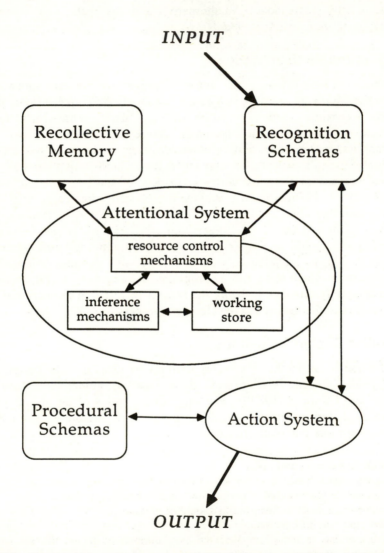

FIG. 6.4. The cognitive architecture suggested by Runciman and Hammond (1986) for developing user programs. This architecture is loosely based upon a mode proposed by Reason and Mycielska (1982) and influenced by the work of Anderson (1983).

avoid using nested loops within these tasks, and provide linear task structures.

Analogy and metaphor

Use familiar procedures when introducing new concepts so that existing bodies of knowledge can be used.

Use text materials to invoke relevant domains of user knowledge.

Use text material to supply useful analogies and to help users to understand what they have done and how effective it has been.

Do not mix metaphors.

Ensure that the metaphor will match the type of work the system will be used for.

Provide information to delineate the boundary of application of the analogy or metaphor.

Use metaphors that are clearly defined and well-bounded.

Identify those parts of an interface where a particular metaphor does not apply.

Make explicit the nature of any mismatch between the actual system functions and the analogy or metaphor.

Avoid automatic interaction; where the consequences of inappropriate actions are serious, where the user needs to keep track of a long series of operations, or remember what happened in a given situation, or where sequences of actions have similar starting points, but different consequences.

Require a confirmatory input prior to 'fatal' operations.

Provide a powerful undo and redo key.

Verbal labels alone are not sufficient to make users think to best effect in terms of the metaphor.

Aim to provide a framework for using the system, rather than trying to teach the user every system feature.

Training and practice

For systems incorporating novel concepts, provide online tutorials which provide (textual) information step by step.

Do not use text instruction as a short-cut to skill acquisition, practice is essential.

Training modes should protect users from the consequences of errors.

Consider restricting the initial options novice users can access to a few basic choices.

Make feedback positive not negative.

Consider combining the HELP function with some kind of computer-assisted learning that allows the user to try out different available courses of action.

Start gradually and encourage users to try out more complex facilities only as they gain experience, although this progression to more complex facilities must be under user control.

Where default values exist, make it obvious to the user and make the default more prominent than specifying non-default parameters.

Task-user match

Reduce the amount of information that the user has to remember; minimize the number of commands, objects et cetera that a user has to remember to perform a task, and if the user has to remember information for some time then the total number of items should not normally exceed five.

Try to arrange information that has to be remembered into meaningful chunks.

When it is anticipated that a significant number of older users (over 55 years) will have to use the system then reduce the amount of information that has to be kept in mind.

Feedback

Alert users to specific courses of action, system rules and particular dependencies amongst dialogue elements as they become relevant to the task.

Feedback should tell users; what effect their action had on the system, any possible consequences of that action, the new system state, and their new location in the system.

Selecting terms, wording and objects

Avoid using prefixes that qualify the meaning of sentences within a dialogue.

When presenting instructions or feedback use affirmative sentences rather than negatives. Never use double negatives or nested negatives.

Construct sentences that are open to only one interpretation.

Highlight important information.

If essential information needs to be remembered highlight it in an unusual way.

Do not use icons or pictures to represent abstract items or concepts.

Use simple, familiar concrete pictures to represent information and to act as memory prompts.

When it is important for users to remember and make associations with a visual pattern, keep that pattern simple.

Command languages should have the syntax of normal speech.

Consistency

All procedures and component elements in a dialogue should have consistent properties, names and relationships with other elements; and be used consistently throughout the dialogue. If this is not possible, then the user should be warned of any inconsistency.

Screen design

Maintain logical and functional relationships between items on any given screen.

There is more chance of the user remembering the last few items on a list, so place important information towards the bottom of any list.

Give each type of information in a dialogue a consistent screen position.

Organization

Keep the number of items subsumed under a single name or prompt as small as possible.

Generate categories and rules for categorizing items and provide information about the essential features of a category. Apply these rules consistently to items that the user should see as related.

Encourage users to categorize information, and to structure their directories such that the number of files in a single directory does not exceed the limits of human memory.

Allow users to name their files and avoid default filing.

Multimodal and multimedia interaction

Use speech synthesis and voice annotation to reinforce items that have to be remembered.

Navigation

Place orienting information at the top and bottom of a screen relating to the screen preceding and following it respectively.

Orienting information at the bottom of the screen should relate to the choice and consequences of actions available in the following screen.

Adaptation

Allow users to express the same message in more than one way.

Program for partial recall of key identifying information.

Error management

Novice users need most information about errors, frequent system users may need to be reminded of the correct syntax, while expert users need only be told where an error has occurred.

It is important that critical tasks do not become automatic.

Locus of control

Consider allowing the interface to take the initiative in guiding the user through an explicit task structure.

When information has to be remembered allow the user to control the rate at which information is displayed.

The list of guidelines presented here is only an edited selection from the 162 guidelines that Marshall et al. (1987b) present (interested readers are advised to consult the original paper). While this substantial list is un-doubtedly useful from both a research and a design point of view, there is doubt as to whether guidelines will really influence the design and development process. In other words, it appears unlikely that a design team, in the rush of trying to meet deadlines, will consult a long list of guidelines. Even if such a list were consulted, there may still be doubt as to whether the designers would work through their design considering every guideline in turn. It appears as though our knowledge of the cognitive issues in HCI must be incorporated into the process of design and development itself, if it is to have any lasting and significant effect.

Cognitive Techniques

One possible solution to the difficulty that has just been raised is to have design tools or techniques (other than grammars and formal descriptions) that concentrate upon the cognitive issues of HCI. While few such cognitive techniques exist, one such example has been provided by McDonald et al. (1986).

The technique they suggest consists of obtaining distance estimates for objects or commands within the system, and using these distance estimates to organize the interface. McDonald et al. (1986) describe how they used this method to reorganize the online documentation for a UNIX™ system. Users were presented with 219 cards, one for each of the commands of the system. Each card had the name of the command on one side and a short definition of the command on the other. Users were asked to "place commands [cards] that you believe go together on the same pile." In other words, each user had to arrange the commands into piles according to their function. If a user believed that a command belonged on more than one pile then the name of the command was written on a blank card, and this card was placed on one of the piles. In other words, users could place a command on as many piles as they thought appropriate.

Users were also asked to place commands they did not recognize on a separate pile. A further pile was created for those commands users thought that they recognized, but were not completely confident about. After subjects had placed all of the commands that they recognized into piles, they were asked to take the pile of commands they were unsure about and to place these on their piles using the definitions written on the back of each card. Commands subjects did not recognize remained unplaced.

After the subject had finished placing the commands on the various piles, the experimenter then noted down the cards in each pile and used this to construct a co-occurrence matrix. In other words, a matrix, similar to the one in Fig. 6.5, was constructed with all of the commands. If command 1, for example, had been put in the same pile as command 2 and 4, then a "1" was placed in the matrix. If the two commands in the matrix had not been placed in any of the same piles then a "0" was placed in the matrix. This process was performed for each user, and from these matrices a total co-occurrence matrix was constructed.

As a result of this process distance scores between commands were produced. In crude terms, this may have meant, for example, that 15 users placed commands 1 and 2 together in the same pile, while only 3 subjects placed commands 1 and 4 together. Therefore, commands 1 and 2 were closer than commands 1 and 4, because a larger number of users had placed commands 1 and 2 in the same pile than had placed commands 1 and 4 in the same pile.

However, this sort of technique has certain limitations. Firstly, the method relies on having users who already have experience of a system. It is possible that this approach could be used with people who did not have

	Command 1	Command 2	Command 3	Command 4
Command 1	✕	1	0	1
Command 2	1	✕	0	1
Command 3	0	0	✕	0
Command 4	1	1	0	✕

FIG. 6.5.   An example of what a co-occurrence matrix might look like for a small number of commands.

experience of a system, but who used the terms that were to be employed in the system in their everyday work. This, however, limits the use of the methodology to applications where existing tasks are being automated. In other words, it would be difficult to use this technique for novel applications.

A second factor constraining the application of the method is that it only provides a limited type of information, and can only be used for tasks such as organizing commands into menus. While such techniques are undoubtedly needed within HCI, there are many other cognitive considerations within human-computer interaction that need to be incorporated into the design and development process. This sort of technique can only be considered as a start.

Finally, there is the question of whether we need techniques such as this, or rather comprehensive design methodologies. If we consider a design methodology to be a supported process that covers all, or at least a substantial part, of the design and development process, then the technique suggested by McDonald et al. (1986) can only be considered as a potential methodology component. However, it appears as though there are currently no comprehensive design methodologies that are fundamentally cognitive in their approach.

THE USABILITY APPROACH

The ultimate objective of the usability approach is the incorporation of human factors issues into the design and development process. In other words, this means making the user the centre of the design and development process rather than the system. The emphasis is upon creating computer systems that support the user within an organization, rather than the user supporting the system. Yet we would expect this to be the major objective of all of the approaches to HCI. The answer is that this goal is also shared by both cognitive and mathematical approaches to HCI, but that this objective has been most strongly stated by those pursuing a usability approach.

This usability approach begins with the aim of creating *socio-technical systems*. Quite simply, this means creating a technical system and an organizational system (Eason, 1983b). A socio-technical design process is one where it is recognized that design is not just about creating a computer system, but also about engineering a new organizational system. In order to do this, present design and development practice needs to be redirected towards a consideration of the user. That is to say, that we need to engineer a shift from system-centred to user-centred design. Damodaran (1983) has considered these two different types of design and development process, as well as the different stages between these two extremes. Figure 6.6 shows the five types of user involvement in design that Damodaran identifies.

As can be seen from Fig. 6.6, the form of design that is perceived as being closest to *user-centred* is where the users design the system themselves and experts only advise. These experts cannot be called "designers" as they are no longer designing a system. Whether designers might ever accept this radical approach is not an argument that will be fully entered

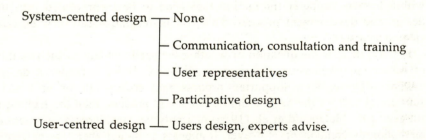

FIG 6.6.   The five types of user involvement in design identified by Damodaran (1983).

into here. Although some might argue that user-centred design and development is a process of partnership between users and designers, rather than a simple handing over of responsibility and control.

Work such as Damodaran (1983), where present design and development practice is considered as well as its alternatives, is central to the usability approach. These alternatives usually involve some form of *iterative design* and prototyping of systems. Iterative design is where a system is built as a prototype and then evaluated, using some of the methods discussed in the last chapter. The results of this evaluation are then fed back into design to produce the next *iteration* of the system. This design philosophy can be seen in the view of the design process that Rubinstein and Hersh (1984) present (see Fig. 6.7).

Prototyping and Iterative Design

The problem with adopting this prototyping approach is that it requires time and effort to produce the prototypes. Many design teams argue that they do not have the time to build a prototype, and that building a system that is ultimately not going to be the final design is a waste of time. In other words, the argument against prototyping is largely an economic one. That is to say, that design teams cannot afford the time to develop and test their system, and then redesign it in the light of what users do and say.

However, usability difficulties often force designers to change their system anyway, albeit late in the development process, after the system has been trailed or released. These changes usually involve *patching* the software. This means, that carefully designed software, with its economical and elegant technical solutions, has to have chunks of programming code crudely inserted. The argument for an iterative approach that involves prototyping is that this sort of software patching could be avoided if systems were tested with users before their design was fully implemented.

In response to the criticism that prototyping is too time consuming, there has been a great deal of effort directed towards the development of prototyping tools and languages (e.g. MacLean, Barnard, & Wilson, 1986; Richards, Boies, & Gould, 1986). The idea behind these prototyping applications (systems that enable prototypes to be built) is that the dialogue for a system can be specified quickly and with the minimum of effort on the part of the engineer. The central goal for these prototyping tools is not that they should be economical with memory space, nor that they should produce programs that are technically elegant, but that they should be quick and easy to use. A more recent emphasis within prototyping tool development,

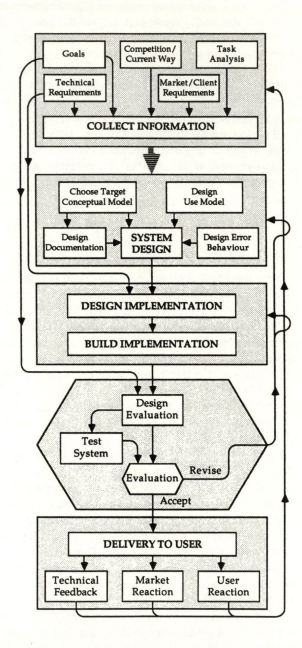

FIG 6.7. The elaborate view of the design and development process presented by Rubenstein and Hersh (1984).

however, is that they should allow the work that has been completed to be directly compiled into programming code.

Iterative prototyping can provide the design team with information on the usability of their proposed design, and the design of the system can be changed accordingly. Clark, Drake, Kapp, & Wong (1984) make just this point, and argue that developing prototypes for iterative design allows users to make a contribution to the design process. They state that prototyping is: "A means for end users to define, refine and re-define their own systems under their own control, within a systematic framework."

This view has been widely supported within HCI (cf. Bury, 1984; Wixon, Whiteside, Good, & Jones, 1983), and it appears as if the arguments for prototyping are gradually being accepted, at least at a corporate level within the large computer manufacturers such as IBM, DEC, Hewlett Packard, etc. However, iterative prototyping is by no means the only answer that the usability approach has to offer.

Design Guidelines and Processes

A general iterative design and development process was outlined by Rubin-stein & Hersh (1984) and can be seen in Fig. 6.7. Nevertheless, this is only a generalized diagram, and while it proscribes a process, it does not bring out the essential characteristics socio-technical design (the idea of designing both a technical and an organizational system). Shackel (1986), however, outlines five fundamental features that he argues the design and development process should possess to produce usable systems (the following has been taken directly from Figure 7 in Shackel's paper):

User-centred design—focused from the start on users and tasks.

Participative design—with users as members of the design team.

Experimental design—with formal user tests of usability in pilot trials, simulations and full prototype evaluations.

Iterative design—design, test and measure, and redesign as a regular cycle until results satisfy the usability specification.

User supportive design—training, selection (when appropriate) manuals, quick reference cards, aid to 'local experts', 'help' systems, e.g. online: context specific, off-line: 'hot-line' phone service.

Shackel (1986) then suggests how these features are incorporated within the process of design and what should be considered during design (the following has been taken directly from Figure 8 in Shackel's paper):

System Design Stage Usability Actions

Feasibility: Define the range of users, tasks and environments to be covered. Do the proposals match the needs? Preliminary functions and operations analyses. Preliminary allocation of functions. Participative design–panel of users in the design team. Create and formalize the usability specification by defining user requirements and setting usability goals.

Research: Studies, often experimental, of human capabilities re system operation concepts. Use pilot studies in the field to explore users' operational needs and to study possible effects upon organizational and social structure.

Development: Detailed analyses of all functions, tasks and operations involving or affecting humans. Design all human factors aspects of equipment and workplaces. Specify all environmental issues. Use guidelines to assist as design ideas are developing. Check design ideas against available human dimension, behaviour and performance data. Test subsystem sections in initial evaluation trials with samples of likely users. Iterative design—use test results as basis for re-design, and test again. Propose selection criteria (if relevant); develop training scheme; provide for other forms of user support needed.

Prototype: Extensive laboratory evaluation with samples of likely users. Full field trials with representative actual users in proper working environment. Iterative design.

Regular operation: Provide for user support—provide training, encourage and aid 'local experts', arrange 'hot-line' for help, et cetera. Gather extensive evaluation data (both objective performance data and subjective attitude data); feed back the evaluation data as check on decisions and predictions made during design; learn from the data—modify the design databases, models and methods for future use.

Shneiderman (1987) goes into more detail about what procedures should be followed during the design process. He suggests that this process should be iterative, where earlier stages are sometimes returned to as the system is refined. The major stages in the process suggested by Shneiderman are: collect information, define requirements and semantics, design syntax and support facilities, specify physical devices, develop software, integrate system and disseminate to users, nurture the user community, and prepare evolution plan. In essence, Shneiderman has suggested a set of activities that might be thought of as an initial outline for a usability action plan.

These sorts of activities, although they are not necessarily the same, have also been suggested by Hewlett Packard. Moreover, not only has the place of such activities within the design and development process been charted (see figure 5.11), but they have been related to the different roles that various departments within an organization might play. That is to say, that there is an implicit link between activities and roles within the corporation or company that is developing the software. The list of human factors activities suggested by Hewlett Packard, together with the related activities of other departments, is as follows:

Needs Analysis

Identify target users and characteristics that will affect product success

Identify and analyse user tasks

Identify physical and organizational environment

Identify usability problems with similar or exisiting products

Develop initial product feature list

Human Factors assists MARKETING in the identification and investigation of users and their needs, and in the analysis of competitor products

Human Factors provides R&D with information on users and tasks and helps to scope the design, development and test process

Requirements specification

Identify ergonomic and market-based requirements

Define and develop product usability and user acceptance goals

Define criteria for measuring usability and acceptance

Develop product localization plan

Develop testing schedule

Human Factors provides MARKETING with information about product requirements that will satisfy user needs

Human Factors and R&D work together to set usability goals and specify requirements for each target group

QUALITY works with Human Factors to help determine usability and quality metrics for the product

LEARNING PRODUCTS works with Human Factors to identify support materials which will facilitate learning and effective use of the product

Conceptual Design

Develop user interface requirements

Define user's model(s) which describes system from user's perspective

Determine allocation of function between user(s) and system

Interpret Human Factors data, principles, and guidelines

Test Concept models with representative users

Human Factors assists R&D in exploring the usability implications of the intended implementation of the design concepts

In this and subsequent phases, QUALITY monitors and documents with Human Factors help, ergonomic requirements and compliance

Human Factors helps LEARNING PRODUCTS to integrate support materials into the development process

Prototype Development and Test

Provide technical support in the development of product prototypes or simulations

Review production prototypes for ergonomic compliance

Test usability of hardware, software, documentation, and training components

Provide feedback to designers on results of usability tests

MARKETING helps Human Factors to identify test subjects and benchmark tasks, and helps to collect usability data

R&D develops hardware and software prototypes for usability and user acceptance testing by Human Factors

LEARNING PRODUCTS submits user documentation, on-line help, classroom and computer-based training for usability testing

Product Evaluation

Review final product specifications to ensure that user interface issues have been addressed satisfactorily

Field test product usability

Provide marketing with data on user interface advantages

Conduct evaluations at customer site to determine how effectively product meets users' needs and necessary improvements

Perform analysis for next generation of products

MARKETING and Human Factors collect field data about usability in order to support the marketing, sale, and support of the product

R&D updates hardware and software as necessary and provides updates for user testing

QUALITY reviews design methods and approach with Human Factors and discusses improvements

LEARNING PRODUCTS updates support materials as necessary and conducts usability testing with Human Factors

The advantage of the processes proposed by Shackel (1986), Shneiderman (1987) and Hewlett Packard is that they set out what needs to be done during design. However, there is still the question of whether designers will really adopt and carefully work through these suggested procedures. In essence, the processes suggested by Shackel and Shneiderman may be susceptible to the same problems that were identified for the cognitive guidelines discussed earlier in this chapter. In other words, because working through the processes requires extra work on the part of the designer, there is a danger that they will not be properly and fully employed.

The answer to this problem may be that we need design and development methodologies that involve the user and designer in a new process of design and development, rather than trying to amend the old process. This does not mean, however, that the processes outlined by Shackel (1986) and Shneiderman (1987) are of no use, only that they may need to be incorporated into methodologies for design and development. As such, they serve as potential blueprints for these methodologies.

DESIGN AND DEVELOPMENT METHODOLOGIES FOR DEVELOPING USABLE SYSTEMS

First, it may be useful to elaborate on the distinction between a design methodology and the prescriptions for design suggested by Shackel and Shneiderman. Here it is suggested that we consider a design methodology to be *a process that is a departure, in some fundamental respect, from present design practice.* This process is usually *supported by manuals, workshops, automated tools, and the like.* It is not simply a list of suggested activities for design, but an *active procedure that is supported and encouraged.*

One methodology, that appears to fit this definition, has been described by Wasserman, Pircher, Shewmake, and Kersten (1985). The development of the User Software Engineering (USE) methodology began in the mid-1970s and has grown into a methodology with four major stages. These stages comprise; identifying the software requirements, designing the user interface, prototyping the user interface, and building a functional prototype. An overview of the methodology including these four stages can be seen in Fig. 6.8.

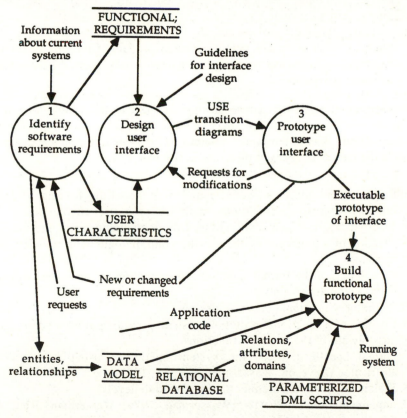

FIG. 6.8. An overview of the User Software Engineering (USE) methodology. Source: Wasserman et al. (1985).

Wasserman et al. (1985) identify seven goals that the USE methodology has been developed to fulfill. These goals are:

Functionality; the methodology should enable the development of systems that achieve predefined requirements.

Reliability; the methodology should support the creation of reliable systems.

Usability; by involving users early and effectively in the design process the methodology should help the developer to assure that the system will be easy to learn and to use.

Evolvability; the methodology should facilitate software and documentation that is easily modified to suit changes in hardware and user needs.

Automated support; the methodology should be supported by automated tools.

Improved developer productivity; the methodology should reduce the time required to create a system.

Reusability; the methodology should be reusable for a large class of products. That is to say, that the design products from one development (e.g. the information on user requests) should be usable for other software developments.

Wasserman et al. (1985) conclude that the USE methodology generally meets these seven goals, and so it may be useful to consider the methodology in more detail. Wasserman and Shewmake (1985) distinguish ten distinct steps in the methodology, and these are as follows:

1. Requirements analyses—activity and data modelling leading to preliminary informal specifications, identification of user characteristics.
2. External design—specification of user/program dialogue and interfaces.
3. Creation of a prototype of the user/program dialogue with revisions as needed.
4. Completion of the formal functional specification of the system operations using narrative text.
5. Preliminary relational database design.
6. Creation of a functional prototype system, providing at least some, and possibly all, of the system's functions.
7. Formal specification of the system operations using behavioural abstraction (Leveson, Wasserman, & Berry, 1983).
8. System design at the architectural and module levels.
9. Implementation in PLAIN (Wasserman, 1979; Wasserman, Riet, & Kerslen, 1981). PLAIN is a programming language.
10. Testing and/or verification.

From this procedure it can be seen that the USE methodology covers almost all of the software developmental life cycle. The strength of this methodology is that it appears to be well supported by an integrated set of automated tools. For example, the specifications for the interface are written using state transition diagrams along with a notation developed as part of the methodology. These diagrams can then be used by the RAPID/USE software tool to produce a prototype of the system. In other words, the specification can be executed; it produces a prototype system when entered into RAPID/USE.

In many respects this is an example of a more mature methodology within HCI. It has been tried and revised where appropriate. It has an integrated set of supporting tools. More importantly, however, it allows and encourages designers to build systems where the user's needs and tasks have been considered. The strength of this sort of approach within design and development is that it allows designers an economical route through the design and development process. However, this economical route takes the designer through many of the human factors considerations that have long been missing from design. This appears to be the fundamental strength of methodologies over simple design guidelines; *good methodologies offer the designer an easy way through design, while at the same time encouraging good design practice. Design prescriptions or guidelines on the other hand offer the designer more work.*

Nevertheless, this is not meant to imply that the USE methodology is a *valuable* methodology that improves design, although this may well be the case. Wasserman et al. (1985) report the advantages of the methodology, and intuitively the approach they describe seems particularly attractive. However, empirical support for Wasserman et al.'s claims has still to be provided.

However, a methodology that is beginning to acquire empirical support for its claimed advantages is the User Skills Task Match (USTM) methodology (Kirby, Fowler, & Macaulay, 1988). The attractive feature of this methodology is that, besides suggesting and supporting a process for the early stages of design, it also suggests a terminology for understanding the user's environment and tasks.

The emphasis within the methodology is upon developing software products for markets, rather than individual organizations. The methodology begins by considering the team that will specify the system. Within ICL, where the methodology has been trialed and used, this team will normally consist of: 1. a marketeer; 2. a chief designer; 3. a back-up designer; 4. a technical author, and 5. a team manager, for the first stage in the methodology. There are three stages to the methodology: 1. Describing a Product Opportunity (DPO); 2. identifying a High Value Solution (HVS); and 3. Delivering the Business Solution (DBS).

Each of the three stages is supported by a workshop that the design team attends. Although it is intended that, after attending the workshop, the designers should be able to use the methodology on their own initiative, it is not clear whether the methodology will be used without workshop support. Therefore, we will discuss the methodology with respect to its constituent workshops. At present, however, only the first stage, DPO, has been fully developed and used in an industrial setting. Consequently, we will concentrate upon this first stage. During the DPO stage the design team consider their proposed product at five levels of abstraction: 1. the market level; 2. the user level; 3. the object level; 4. the task level; and 5. the interactional level.

The Market Level. The workshop (session or phase) begins with a description of the market segment in which a product opportunity is considered to exist. In other words, a gap in the market is identified where present (competing) systems do not adequately fulfill users' needs, or maybe no system exists for a particular set of tasks.

The User Level (Work Groups). Following the market level, user work groups within the organization are identified. Hutt, Donnelly, Macaulay, and Fowler (1987) define a work group as: "...a collection of typical users who share common work goals and objectives." Once work groups have been identified, they are arranged into the sort of table shown in Fig. 6.9. The objective of this stage is to consider the social issues that might affect the products acceptance within a work group and an organization.

Name	Workgroup A	Workgroup B	Other users
Typical users	User X User Y User Z	User P User Q User Y	User R User S
Relationship to product	1	1	2

FIG. 6.9.   A work group table, taken from Hutt et al. (1987). The numbers in the 'relationship to product' row indicate whether the user's relationship to the product is primary (1; direct use of the product), secondary (2; intermittent or infrequent use), or tertiary (3; vested interest in acquiring but not using the product).

The User Level (Generic Users).   Hutt et al. (1987) define a generic user as: "...a typical person identified with a particular occupation or job title." The purpose of this level is to identify those job and user characteristics that might need to be considered with respect to the system's functionality (the functions it provides) and usability. Factors such as the user's attitude and motivation towards work, information technology, etc., are considered here.

The Object Level.   Once the various users of a system have been identified, their environment is described in terms of the objects they use. The objects that form part of the users' jobs are arranged into hierarchies (for a simple example see Fig. 6.10), and objects that are relevant to the product are considered with respect to their flow from one person to another. For example, a file might be passed from one user to the next as its contents are amended. A representation of how a simple object flow is shown in Fig. 6.11.

The Task Level.   Hutt et al. (1987) define a task as a: "...meaningful cluster of actions carried out by a user in order to achieve a work goal." A task hierarchy is constructed at this task level, and tasks are considered with respect to organizational issues, the user's motivation, task fragmentation, etc.

The Interactional Level.   In this case, the interactional level does not necessarily imply a consideration of just the hardware and software of interaction, as was the meaning of the term in Chapter Two. This part of the workshop is concerned with the interaction between the factors identified at earlier levels. These characteristics can be seen in Fig. 6.12.

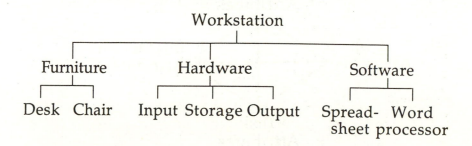

FIG. 6.10.   An object hierarchy, taken from Hutt et al. (1987). This simple hierarchy could be subdivided if necessary.

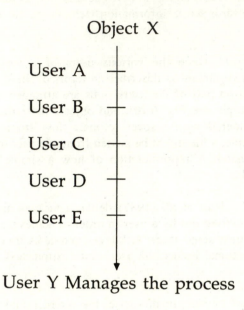

Object X

User A ┼

User B ┼

User C ┼

User D ┼

User E ┼

User Y Manages the process

FIG. 6.11.   A simple object flow.

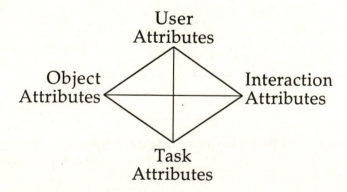

User
Attributes

Object
Attributes

Interaction
Attributes

Task
Attributes

FIG. 6.12.   An interaction diamond, representing the major factors that are considered at the interaction level. Source: Hutt et al. (1987).

Finally, there is a consolidation session, where the design team decide how they can best exploit the results of the workshop. The team plan their actions for the future and decide upon the information that they require to validate some of their decisions.

The following stages of the methodology, as mentioned earlier, are not yet as well developed as the first DPO stage. The second stage, *Identifying a High Value Solution* (HVS), however, is mainly concerned with identifying those product requirements that might be considered to be of high value to various interested parties (stakeholders). In short, this entails a consideration of task allocation issues between man and machine, as well as the acceptability of the product to the different stakeholders.

The final stage of the USTM methodology, *Delivering a Business Solution* (DBS), concentrates upon the non-functional aspects of the proposed product, such as documentation, services and interface requirements. In this stage the design team are encouraged to set usability goals, against which the product will later be measured.

In essence, the methodology works by encouraging a structured and constructive dialogue between the members of the design team. Nevertheless, it can be seen that this methodology only addresses the very first stages of design, from identifying a gap in the market to specifying the product. Furthermore, although this methodology is supported by workshops, there appears to be little encouragement for a design team to continue in the spirit of the methodology once they return to normal work. One answer to this problem is to provide automated tools. However, such tools remain to be developed.

As with the USE methodology, the benefits of the USTM methodology have still to be substantially proven, although there have been positive indications of its worth (Kirby et al., 1988). Furthermore, several products have been abandoned in the early stages of design as a result of considering the product during the first workshop. This, it is argued, demonstrates the strength of the methodology as further effort and money were not invested in a product that would not be used. Moreover, the argument for stopping work on these products was that they would not be usable. In other words, usability is now being seen as a crucial issue in software development.

COMMENTARY

Formal (or analytic) methods appear to offer designers a means by which the logical consistency of an interface can be examined. These methods may appeal to mathematically orientated designers. However, there seems to be an assumption that users are themselves consistent from one task to the next, yet much of the research within cognitive psychology, i.e. work on reasoning and decision making, has shown that human behaviour does not always conform to the rules of formal logic. This does not mean that consistency is an undesirable goal, but that it should not be considered in isolation from the user. In other words, formal methods, if they are of practical use within design and development, should be considered only as one tool that might be used. They cannot be considered as a substitute for involving users in the design and development process, as some researchers have suggested (cf. Polson, 1987). However, even if the advantages of the formal methods approach can be demonstrated empirically, there might still be doubt as to whether they are anything more than research tools (see Chapter Four). The argument is not that they cannot improve design, but that they may not, ultimately, be usable themselves. But what is meant by usable?

Eason (1984) suggests that the user, in deciding whether or not to use a system, performs an implicit cost/benefit analysis. Thus, the ultimate measure of usability is whether a system is used, which will depend upon how a new system fared in this cost/benefit analysis. Yet, while we may agree that systems must be easy to use and easy to learn, as well as serving some useful purpose, we do not appear to have applied these same criteria to the techniques, methods and methodologies that we prescribe for the design and development process. There is no reason to believe that engineers, in evaluating a human factors technique, do not perform a similar cost/benefit analysis.

This analysis, however, is unlikely to be performed in isolation. That is to say, that engineers will not just consider whether a formal method or analytic technique might help them to improve design, but also whether this help might be found in other approaches, such as techniques for involving users in the design and development process. Engineers are likely to evaluate the whole range of possible means for improving the usability of their designs. They may consider, not just what each technique offers, but the effort it requires and the overlaps between techniques. Although Reisner (1987) states that formal methods (or analytic techniques) and usability testing techniques are not in competition, eventually, as the human factors market becomes more sophisticated and competitive, they may well be viewed as alternative rather than complementary approaches. Whether this is desirable, however, is another question.

SUMMARY

The major problems with the design and development process are that the information that is received about an organization does not provide adequate information about users, and designers are unable to properly understand the non-expert user. Current systems analysis techniques are primarily concerned with information flow within a system. Although users are considered to some extent, the central focus is upon the system and the information it must deal with. Consequently, these types of methodologies have been labeled *system-centred*.

The design of a system evolves throughout the design and development process—a system is not simply specified and built. At the beginning of the design and development process some of the low-level goals are known as well as some of the high-level goals. Throughout the design and development process, through compromises and tradeoffs, these goals build into a more complete and coherent picture, as goals are added, changed or discarded. Solutions to design problems often require creativity, and consequently the process of design and development, both in the emergence of goals and the development of solutions, cannot be described as completely rational or logical.

A formal method is a notation for describing some aspect of a system or user behaviour. These notations are used to break down the system's or the user's behaviour into manageable chunks and show where inconsistencies arise, or where the task is too complex. There are two major purposes to which a formal notation can be put; first there are the methods or notations that attempt to cognitively model the user, and second, there are notations that are used to expose logical inconsistencies within a system, and within a system's interfaces.

The aim of the formal mathematical approach is to reduce a system to its basic elements. By exposing the logical relationships between the different elements of a system we provide information that should make it easier for us to reach rational judgements about a system. In essence, mathematical methods allow us to expose the workings of a system, and show a system in a new light that allows direct comparisons to be made between alternative design choices. Formal mathematical notations are used to check a design against various design principles. These principles are often concerned with factors such as the logical consistency of a system and interface.

Formal methods have been criticized with respect to their usefulness in design and development. Few of the proposed modelling techniques or grammars directly involve the user. Therefore, there is a risk that these methods cannot detect when a user's conceptualization of the task is significantly different from that held by the designer or engineer who applies the notation. Moreover, Carroll and Rosson (1985) have argued that current formal methods or modelling techniques do not fit easily into present design practice and do not provide designers with the kind of information that they require.

An alternative approach to using formal methods is to develop *programmable user models*. These are computer programs that can operate the system under development. The advantage of such an approach, according to researchers, is that this would encourage the designer to consider the user in more detail. A more traditional method for incorporating new ideas into the design and development process is to express these ideas as guidelines. However, while such lists are undoubtedly useful from both a research and a design point of view, there is doubt as to whether guidelines are likely to have a lasting effect on the process of design and development.

The ultimate objective of the usability approach is the incorporation of human factors issues into the design and development process. This approach begins with the aim of creating *socio-technical systems*. A socio-technical design process is one where it is recognized that design is not just about creating a computer system, but also about engineering a new organizational system.

The usability approach usually involves some form of *iterative design* and prototyping of systems. Iterative design is where a system is built as a prototype, and then evaluated, using some of the methods discussed in the last chapter. The results of this evaluation are then fed back into design to produce the next *iteration* of the system.

The problem with adopting this prototyping approach is that it requires time and effort to produce the prototypes. However, usability difficulties often force designers to change their system late in the development process after the system has been trialed or released. These changes usually involve *patching* the software. That is to say, that carefully designed software, with its economic and elegant technical solutions, has to have chunks of programming code crudely inserted. The argument for an iterative approach that involves prototyping is that this sort of software patching could be avoided if systems were tested with users before their design was decided.

Several researchers have described procedures for creating usable systems. However, following through this process requires extra work on the part of the designer, and there is a danger that the procedures will not be properly and fully employed. The answer to this problem may be that we need design methodologies that involve the user in a new process of design, rather than trying to amend the old process.

A design methodology is a process that is a departure, in some fundamental respect, from present design practice. This process is usually supported by manuals, workshops, automated tools, and the like. It is not simply a list of suggested activities for design, but an active procedure that is supported and encouraged.

A SELECTIVE ANNOTATED BIBLIOGRAPHY

Anderson, N. S. & Reitman Olson, J. (Eds.) (1985). Methods for designing software to fit human needs and capabilities. Proceedings of the workshop of software human factors, Washington, D.C. Excerpt in R. M. Baecker & W. A. S. Buxton

(1987) *Readings in human-computer interaction: A multidisciplinary approach.* Los Altos, California: Morgan Kaufmann. *This paper suggests that there are three stages within the software development life cycle where human factors issues need to be considered; analysis, design and implementation. The paper then goes on to discuss the various techniques that can be used at these different stages.*

Bannon, L. J. (1986b). Issues in design: Some notes. In D. A. Norman & S. W. Draper (Eds.), *User centred system design: New perspectives on human-computer interaction.* Hillsdale, New Jersey: Lawrence Erlbaum Associates Inc. *The author argues that the organization of work can be a factor that is as important as the fundamental characteristics of the technology itself. Our system designs affect the social organization of those who directly use them, but also affect society in a wider sense. It is suggested that design should be considered in this light.*

Clark, F., Drake, P., Kapp, M., & Wong, P. (1984). User acceptance of information technology through prototyping. In B. Shackel (Ed.), *Human-computer interaction–Interact '84: Proceedings of the first IFIP conference on human-computer interaction, London.* Amsterdam: North-Holland. *The authors argue the need for prototyping and describe two examples of the successful use of prototyping.*

Damodaran, L. (1983). User involvement in system design. *Data Processing, 25 (6),* 6–13. *This paper discusses both the need for effective user involvement in design, and also the means for promoting this involvement. The author directly addresses the question of how to engineer a shift from system-centred to user-centred design. This paper is clear, interesting, and easy-to-read.*

Eason, K. D. (1983b). User-centred design for information technology systems. *Physical Technology, 14,* 219–224. *The author suggests a strategy for design that determines who is involved in various design decisions, and under what conditions. This paper is also concerned with the issue of user involvement and user-centred design. It is concise, well-written and likely to be of interest to both academics and designers alike.*

Gould, J. D. (in press). How to design usable systems. In M. Helander (Ed.), *Handbook of human-computer interaction.* Amsterdam: North-Holland. *The author uses four principles to guide his prescription for design; early focus on users, integrated design (all aspects of usability evolve together from the start), empirical measurement, and iterative design. This paper is written from a practitioners point of view and takes a practical look at usability issues in design. This paper is well-written and worth reading. It is particularly recommended for those who might be developing systems or working in an applied environment.*

Grunenenfelder, T. M. & Whitten, W. B. (1984). Augmenting generic research with prototype evaluation experience in applying generic research to specific products. In B. Shackel (Ed.), *Human-computer interaction–Interact '84: Proceedings of the first IFIP conference on human-computer interaction, London.* Amsterdam: North-Holland. *The authors argue that the results of generic research cannot be applied in all situations, and they go on to identify some of these occasions. They argue that generic research is insensitive to the context of design and suggest guidelines for research into design.*

Hammond, N. V., Jorgensen, A., MacLean, A., Barnard, P. J., & Long, J. (1983a). Design practice and interface usability: Evidence from interviews with designers. In A. Janda (Ed.), *Human factors in computer systems: Proceedings of the CHI '83 conference, Boston.* Amsterdam: North-Holland. *This paper reports the results of interviews with designers, where the designers gave their views of the design process. This research raises many interesting questions and the paper is well worth reading.*

Harker, S. D. P. & Eason, K. D. (1985). Task analysis and definition of user needs. In *IFAC conference proceedings on the Man-Machine Interface, Italy. The authors survey various task analysis methods for the specification of user requirements. They go on to outline a technique for task analysis based upon socio-technical design.*

Hutt, A. F. T., Donnelly, N., Macaulay, L. A., & Fowler, C. J. H. (1987). Describing a product opportunity: A method of understanding the users' environment. In D. Diaper & R. Winder (Eds.), *People & computers III. Proceedings of the Third Conference of the BCS HCI specialist group.* Cambridge: Cambridge University Press. *The authors describe the first of a series of workshops from the User Skills Task Match methodology. This workshop is concerned with identifying a gap in the market for a software product and defining the role of this product within this gap.*

Jacob, R. J. K. (1982). Using formal specifications in the design of a human-computer interface. In *Human factors in computer systems, conference proceedings, Gaithersburg, Maryland.* ACM. *The author provides a list of criteria that a formal specification should meet. This is an interesting and readable paper.*

Marshall, C. J., Nelson, C., & Gardiner, M. M. (1987b). Design guidelines. In M. M. Gardiner & B. Christie (Eds.), *Applying cognitive psychology to user-interface design.* Chichester: Wiley & Sons. *The authors present a comprehensive list of 162 design guidelines based upon the cognitive literature. This impressive collection of research recommendations is easy to read and worth reading.*

Monk, A. F. & Dix, A. (1987). Refining early design decisions with a black-box model. In D. Diaper & R. Winder (Eds.), *People & computers III. Proceedings of the third conference of the BCS HCI specialist group.* Cambridge: Cambridge University Press. *A semi-formal method for describing a system is proposed. A system is considered in terms of its action-effect rules and evaluated against certain design principles such as "predictability" and "consistency." The advantage of this sort of approach is that the semi-formal notation that is suggested appears usable, and is less likely to discourage the non-mathematician, who may have already been confused by some of the existing formal notations.*

Norman, D. A. (1983a). Design principles for human-computer interfaces. In A. Janda (Ed.), *Human factors in computer systems: Proceedings of the CHI '83 conference, Boston.* Amsterdam: North-Holland. *The author suggests four principles for providing design principles. This paper is not directly concerned with providing design principles, but is aimed at guiding others who might wish to provide these principles. Like all of Norman's papers, this is clear and easy to read.*

Pew, D. (1986). Socio-tech: What is it (and why should we care)? The introduction to a panel discussion at the CHI '86 conference. In M. Mantei & P. Orbeton (Eds.), *Human factors in computer systems–III: Proceedings of the CHI '86 conference, Boston.* Amsterdam: Elsevier. *This brief introduction raises some of the interesting questions surrounding the notion of socio-technical design. It is readable and stimulating.*

Runciman, C. & Hammond, N. V. (1986). User programs: a way to match computer systems and human cognition. In M. D. Harrison & A. F. Monk (Eds.), *People & computers: Designing for usability. Proceedings of the Second Conference of the BCS HCI specialist group.* Cambridge: Cambridge University Press. *This paper describes the notion of 'user programs', otherwise called 'programmable user models.' They outline the potential advantages of this approach as well as a possible cognitive architecture upon which these programs might be based.*

Shneiderman, B. (1987). *Designing the user interface: Strategies for effective human-computer interaction.* Reading, Massachusetts: Addison-Wesley. *Chapter Ten in this book deals with iterative design and evaluation. The questions of prototyping, user participation in design, pilot studies, acceptance tests, user surveys and other issues concerned with design are discussed. Furthermore, the author suggests a questionnaire that might be given to users to assess a system.*

Sufrin, B. A. (1986). Formal methods and the design of effective user interfaces. In M. D. Harrison & A. F. Monk (Eds.), *People & computers: Designing for usability. Proceedings of the Second Conference of the BCS HCI specialist group.* Cambridge: Cambridge University Press. *The author advances the arguments for formal mathematical methods. These arguments are illustrated by descriptions of a user interface using Z notation.*

Thimbleby, H. W. (1985). User interface design principles. In A. F. Monk (Ed.), *Fundamentals of human-computer interaction.* London: Academic Press. *The author suggests the notion of "generative user-engineering principles." These principles are assertions about interactive system behaviour and are intended to bridge the gap between the designer and the user.*

Thimbleby, H. W. (1986). User interface design and formal methods. *Computer Bulletin, 2 (3),* 13–15. *This is an easy-to-read introduction to formal methods. While it is brief, it nevertheless provides an interesting flavour of this particular area of work.*

Wasserman, A. I., Pircher, P. A., Shewmake, D. T., & Kersten, M. L. (1985). Developing interactive information systems with the User Software Engineering methodology. *IEEE Transactions on Software Engineering, SE-12 (2),* 326–345. *The major objectives of the USE methodology are outlined, and the stages of the approach are described. This methodology is unusual in that it focuses on the user early in the design process, and covers all of the design and development process. To date, few HCI methodologies have been developed to this extent.*

7 The Organizational Impact of Computer Systems

In collaboration with Gill M. Brown
Department of Psychology, Manchester University

OVERVIEW

In this chapter the impact that computer systems have on individuals, work-groups, and organizations is considered. When a new computer system is introduced into an organization it is expected to produce certain beneficial effects for the organization and for individuals within that organization. These effects are discussed with reference to ideal systems outlined by some researchers. Following this, some of the research that reports the actual effects of implementing computer systems is described. These issues include the impact of a system on the user's tasks, changes in the user's discretion, increases of control over the user, power changes, conflict between groups, and changes in leadership style and organizational structure. Finally, the chapter concludes with a discussion of the approaches to tackling these difficult problems.

INTRODUCTION

In the last chapter we looked at the process of design. It was concluded that the differing approaches to the problems of design all strived for the same goals; those of centring design around the user, and providing the designer with better information about the user and the user's tasks. The success of a system, however, does not just depend upon the system matching user needs and supporting users in their tasks, but also upon the match between the system and the social and political factors within the host organization.

177

Computer systems are often introduced within organizations with the aim of either supporting and improving the existing organizational structure, or changing the organization in some radical manner. These are planned changes for which a computer system is being implemented. For example, a common aim is to reduce the number of staff required within an organization by automating significant aspects of various tasks.

However, systems can change organizations in ways other than simply cutting wage costs. Consequently, several researchers have outlined how systems might be used to enrich the roles of individuals and groups within a business or institution. This sort of approach is based on the idea that, not only is the enriching of an employee's role a desirable objective in itself, but also that people with enriched roles will demonstrate a higher degree of commitment to an organization and, consequently, are likely to produce higher quality work.

When we consider a computer system from this organizational perspective it becomes apparent that its functionality is, to a large extent, determined by its role within an organization. To be of use and of value within an organization a system must play some useful role. This statement of the obvious serves to highlight an important point; *the specification of a system, and the whole of the design and development process, must be placed in the context of organizational considerations.* In other words, the specification and design of a system should be determined, not only by a consideration of the user's tasks, but also by a consideration of the user's role within an organization. Consequently, organizational issues need to be considered throughout the design process, and for this reason, these issues are considered to be an integral part of research into HCI.

Unfortunately, organizational issues are often ignored during the rush of design and development. As a result, systems are frequently targeted at inappropriate and unrelated parts of an organization; they merge incompatible user roles and fail to address the needs of the organization. In short, the role of a computer system within an organization is rarely the subject of much consideration. However, before we consider some of the adverse organizational effects that often result from the introduction of a computer system, it may be useful to outline the positive effects a computer system should have.

WHEN A COMPUTER SYSTEM IS IMPLEMENTED WITHIN AN ORGANIZATION, WHAT EFFECTS SHOULD IT HAVE?

Initially, we can say that a system should support users in their tasks. Systems should be easy to learn, and easy to understand and operate. They should provide users with the information that they require, in an acceptable form, as well as allowing users to perform tasks in way that suits them. A system that fulfills these requirements may appear as though it is all that an organization needs.

Nevertheless, further objectives for computer systems can be identified. These objectives are often related to the social work-life of the user, and the organization within which the user operates. Cypher (1986), for example, argues that computer systems should not only support users in their tasks, but also in their activities. That is to say, that systems should not only help users plan their schedules for the day, week or month ahead, but also support users in their planning so that they can perform more than one task at any one time. At first the idea of performing more than one task at a time may sound rather nonsensical. However, as Miyata and Norman (1986) note, we often perform more than one task at a time. Or to be more precise, we interweave one task with another. For example, in the morning we may make a cup of tea, make the toast, and read the paper. We perform part of one task, before switching to another task, and then another. This way we make the most economical use of our time. In an office we might type part of a report, and then go on to other activities while we wait for information to arrive that is relevant to the report, and that might need to be included.

Miyata and Norman (1986) argue firstly, that performing more than one task at a time is psychologically possible, and secondly, that we should recognize that people are often engaged in more than one task over any given period of time. Cypher (1986) makes the point that we sometimes have problems scheduling these activities. In other words, the person who shouts, "I can only do one thing at once", is often trying to perform several tasks. Furthermore, this person, who shouts that they are being asked to do too much, is usually having problems scheduling these *multiple activities* (as Miyake and Norman call them). Cypher (1986) argues that computer systems need to support users in the scheduling of their activities.

Another aspect of human work behaviour that present system design has tended to ignore, is that people attempt, not only to perform more than one task at once, but often work in groups or as part of a team (Malone, 1985; 1987). Present systems, however, tend to be geared towards users working alone. Bannon (1986a) has criticized this state of affairs, and has argued that effective systems should help to create a sense of community for users in work-groups.

One suggested approach to supporting a sense of community within a work-group is to provide *organizational interfaces* (Malone, 1985; 1987). These are interfaces designed for use by more than one user at a time. The purpose of such interfaces is to allow users, who might normally work together in a non-computerized environment, to work with each other through a computer system. Malone (1985; 1987) has suggested the following distinction between a user interface and an organizational interface: "*user interface*; the parts of a computer program that connect a human user to the capabilities provided by the computer; *organizational interface*; the parts of a computer system that connect human users to each other and to the capabilities provided by computers."

Malone (1987) also suggests several examples of systems with organizational interfaces. These, he proposes, can be classified into three categories: text sharing systems, project management systems, and collaborative authoring systems. Examples of the first category, text sharing systems, are electronic mail systems where messages can be sent from one computer to another, and conferencing systems that allow people to amend topics and subtopics for consideration.

Malone (1987) suggests that an example of a project management system might be a system similar to that described by Sluizer and Cashman (1985). This sort of system is a co-ordinator tool that keeps track of activities and responsibilities. This system should be able to answer questions from the user such as, *what task should I be working on?* or *what point have I reached in this task?* (Malone, 1987). This type of system is exactly what Cypher (1986) was arguing for; a system that supports users in organizing and scheduling their activities. However, the system suggested by Sluizer and Cashman (1985) does not just support one user at a time, but supports several users, scheduling their activities in an attempt to co-ordinate the work-group.

Malone (1987) proposes the PIE system (Goldstein & Bobrow, 1980) as an example of a collaborative writing system. In this system: "...successive versions of a document are constructed from overlays that contain each person's modifications of previous versions." In this sort of system each person makes modifications to a document, while at the same time accepting, rejecting or amending other people's modifications.

Democratic Systems

The view of systems presented so far is one where a system supports a work-group, not just individuals performing particular tasks. This view is based around a consideration of peoples' work patterns, and how computer systems might support these patterns. Nevertheless, although this sort of approach is undoubtedly useful, there have been other approaches that suggest how systems might support organizations in overall terms, besides just considering the social patterns of user activities.

This sort of approach is often called the *Scandinavian* approach or model, after the researchers and the culture from which it originates. The researcher who has been most prominently associated with the Scandinavian approach is Niels Bjørn-Andersen. Bjørn-Andersen (1985) argues that HCI should not just have the aim of reducing the user's resistance to new technology, but should have the clear intention of improving the quality of the user's working life. He asks the question: "...are we just doing our best to adapt the technology to the known so-called 'human weaknesses' to reduce the resistance to using the technology, or are we working on providing a technology that will help to liberate the intellectual capabilities of human beings?" With this aim in mind Bjørn-Andersen goes on to spell out the characteristics of a system according to the Scandinavian model. In many ways these characteristics form the objectives of this Scandinavian approach. Set out below is an edited list of Bjørn-Anderson's (1985) ideal system characteristics, based upon democratic and humanitarian values:

1. No monitoring system: Systems that monitor employees second-by-second will encourage people to use their creative abilities to beat the system rather than perform their job.
2. Assume knowledge: Systems should be developed that assume the user to have substantial functional knowledge (otherwise they tend to treat people like children), but should assume that people know less about the structural aspects of the system.
3. High discretion: Most systems reduce a user's autonomy and discretion. Yet users often know best how to perform a task, and to increase a user's autonomy and discretion would also have the effect of increasing the level of job satisfaction.
4. Possible to modify: No system can be expected to fulfill user needs over a long period of time, and so it should be possible for users to modify the system.
5. Transparency: The method of operation of the system should be transparent to users in order that they can modify the system and deal with unusual situations effectively.
6. Support learning: Systems should lead to a re-qualification of the labour force by stimulating learning about how to take care of one's own situation.
7. Support feelings and intuition: It seems vital that IT should not hamper those cognitive characteristics associated with feelings, emotions, creativity, etc.
8. Social contact: Many systems decrease informal social contact, yet this can alienate users and deprive them of the opportunity to test and modify ideas and values in dialogue with others. New technologies should aim to change the work environment to increase social contact.

Ultimately, the aim of the Scandinavian approach that Bjørn-Andersen (1985) advances, is to improve the quality and productivity of work within organizations and so increase profitability. This is achieved by improving the quality of life for the people within the organization by enriching their jobs. As such, new technology is a means by which this can be achieved; it is not an end in itself, but a means to an end.

Overall, we have developed a picture of an ideal system within an organization. This system should not only support users in their tasks, but also help them to schedule their activities as they perform more than one task at a time. This system should provide organizational interfaces that allow users to work together in groups when required. A system should enrich users' roles within an organization by allowing users the discretion to perform tasks as they choose, by supporting learning as well as feelings and intuition, and by encouraging social contact and a sense of community. In practical terms, the system should take responsibility for the humdrum tasks and allow the user to control the more creative and rewarding aspects of work.

Unfortunately, this is an ideal and not a reality. The question that we need to consider now is, *what really happens when a computer system is implemented within an organization, and how does this reality match up to our ideal?*

IN REALITY, WHAT CAN HAPPEN WHEN WE IMPLEMENT A COMPUTER SYSTEM WITHIN AN ORGANIZATION?

In short, the answer to the question posed in the title of this section is provided by Shneiderman (1987) who suggests that systems can cause or create:

Personal anxiety.
Alienation from other people.
Information-poor minorities.
Feelings of impotence as the individual begins to matter less and the organization becomes more important.
Complexity that bewilders all types of users.
Organizational fragility as system failures halt many users.
Invasions of privacy.
Unemployment and displacement.
Lack of professional responsibility.
A deteriorating image of people as machines are seen to be more important than the people within the organization.

These sort of problems have been best summed up by Eason (1985a) who argues that organizational changes need to be controlled. He suggests that: "If these developments are not monitored, a kind of organizational drift can result with role ambiguity, stress and conflict for staff and probably underutilization for the system."

According to Eason (1985a) the changes that result within an organization generally fall into three categories. The first, are those types of changes that are planned, such as reductions in the total number of staff. The second category of changes are those that are unintended, such as adjustments in job content and increased salaries. The third set of changes are those that are delayed. These sort of developments are where the system gradually becomes integrated within the organizational structure of the business or institution, and users begin to exploit the system's capabilities.

The three categories of change suggested by Eason (1985a) provide an interesting perspective through which the organizational impact of a computer system can be viewed. Having adopted this general structure, we will now consider organizational developments and changes in more detail.

Local Experts

One of the most frequent developments that occurs when a computer system is introduced is that local experts emerge. Local experts are users who tend to find out more about the computer system, or a particular application, than their colleagues, and consequently are used by their colleagues as a source of reference. Generally users prefer to consult local experts to manuals or "professionals" (Damodaran, 1986; Lang, Lang, & Auld, 1981; O'Malley, 1986; Scharer, 1983), and these experts develop because they can provide users with the information they require without the need for the user to consult the documentation (manuals) that usually accompanies a system.

For some time now local experts have been recognized as a positive phenomenon that usually need to be encouraged and supported. Earlier it was mentioned that Bannon (1986a) has argued the need for a sense of community amongst users. At least one of the reasons for this argument is that local experts are more likely to develop and to be used in a community of users than they are when users work in isolation. But what exactly do local experts have to offer users?

O'Malley (1986) suggests that local experts can be characterized, not just by how much they know, but more often by their ability to find information. Many systems are too complex for any one user to understand every aspect and detail. However, a local expert is likely to understand a good deal more of the system than the average user. This knowledge enables the local expert, not only to provide other users with advice and information, but also to locate information that is not known in the system or documentation. In other words, the conceptual model that a local expert possesses not only helps this expert to navigate around the system, but also enables the expert to understand and find information in the system's manuals and other documentation.

However, a local expert is not only someone with knowledge, but a person who is actually consulted by users. That is to say, that systems engineers often possess a great deal of knowledge about a system, but cannot be called local experts because they are not consulted by any significant proportion of the user population. But what factors cause a person to be consulted and to become a local expert? Bannon (1986a) has suggested eight factors that affect whether a person is consulted or not:

Organizational Rank (e.g. sometimes less likely to ask a superior).
Technical Expertise (e.g. the area of concern).

Sociability (e.g. how approachable the person is).
Reciprocity (e.g. the likelihood of being able to return a favour).
Accessibility (e.g. sharing office, same building, remote building).
Availability (e.g. "free," interruptible, busy).
Organizational Role (e.g. official consultant or local expert).
Shared Experiences (e.g. similar backgrounds).

Although Bannon (1986a) is concerned with the factors that might influence any consultation, these factors equally apply in the case of local experts. In some cases local experts are preferred by users to official channels of support such as *hot lines*. These are telephone lines or electronic mail connections to official experts who can advise users on any problems they might have with their system. This may be because the local expert, being a user as well, has a conceptual model of the system that can be more easily be mapped onto other users' models. In more straightforward terms, the local expert is on the same *wavelength* as the user, and experiences the same problems.

This, however, implies that the expert does not just communicate information, but also provides the user with a conceptual model. Indeed, much of the research into how experts advise users shows that this is exactly what happens. For example, Kidd (1985) notes that experts do not always provide straightforward answers to the questions that they are asked, but suggest that the questioner consider the problem in a different light. In other words, experts provide conceptual guidance; they show the inquirer how best to consider the problem. Coombs and Alty (1980), while considering computer user's queries and expert guidance, found similar results.

Consequently, the role of the local expert is not just to provide information, but to help users formulate their problems into more meaningful questions (O'Malley, 1986). In the light of this, it appears as though system documentation will almost always prove to be a second course of action for the bewildered user. Unless system documentation can offer the kind of conceptual guidance that experts provide, and direct the user into asking meaningful questions, then local experts will always have a place within the social structure of an automated organization.

The Impact on Task and Job Satisfaction

When a computer system is introduced within an organization, not only do local experts develop, but the nature and structure of the user's tasks change. With automation certain responsibilities and actions that the user previously performed are taken over by the system, and consequently, there is a change in the overall content of the user's tasks.

Bjørn-Andersen, Eason, and Robey (1986) found that the impact on the user's tasks was greater with more powerful systems. This may be because these system provided new possibilities for users in the way that they worked. On the other hand, powerful systems are often more complex, and it may have been the complexity of the system that forced users to amend their views of the task.

Unfortunately, complex systems are often under-utilized. That is to say, that only a small proportion of the systems functions and capabilities are used on a regular basis. A further problem that Bjørn-Andersen et al., (1986) found was that users of complex systems required more support than users of less complex systems.

The impact that a system has on the user's tasks may be viewed either positively or negatively. By structuring the user's tasks the system can remove the humdrum aspects from the user's job. Consequently, this structuring can enrich the user's work-life. On the other hand, by forcing all users to adopt the same approach to a task this can also be viewed as de-skilling a user's role.

However, there is evidence that structuring the user's tasks can have positive, enriching effects, while at the same time introducing standardization. In a study of managers using a new system Bjørn-Andersen et al. (1986) found that structuring the user's tasks had just this effect. They state that: "More than 60% of all managers had experienced changes in 'intrinsic' job factors (e.g. complexity, feedback) while approximately half of the managers experienced changes in 'structural' (e.g. 'standardization') and 'load' factors (e.g. work pace). Most puzzling perhaps, managers said that while the computer system helped them to develop a more enriched view of their task, they felt that the system was constraining them through more standardization and monitoring of when and how to conduct their task."

Nevertheless, although job enrichment might be seen as a desirable objective in itself, how important is it? In other words, can we manage without an explicit consideration of the job enrichment issue? The evidence that is available suggests not. For example, Straub and Straub (1987) report that the acceptance of information technology into the workplace is related to the user's perceptions of job enhancement and increased self-esteem.

Furthermore, there is evidence that where job enrichment is not taken into account, systems are rejected by their users. Nickerson (1986) reports the attempt by the McGraw-Hill publishing company to centralize its word processing facilities. In 1967 this company opened a word processing centre at its New York headquarters. By the end of 1970 the centre had been discontinued through lack of use. The explanation that Nickerson (1986) offers is that the roles of the employees who were to work in the centre were not properly considered. Indeed, Nickerson suggests that it was not the word processing systems themselves that constituted a "giant step backward for job enrichment", but the way in which the technology was used. That is to say, the roles that were thrust upon the staff were rejected.

People objected to being part of this impersonal monolithic resource, where they had once belonged to a particular section in individual secretarial positions.

Control and Discretion

Changes in organizational structure, such as the introduction of the word processing resource centre at McGraw-Hill, can often reduce the user's discretion over how tasks are performed. They find that they are under greater control, and that the channels by which they could have previously influenced other people within the organization have altered.

Nevertheless, it appears as though these changes cannot be blamed on the technology itself. Above, it was mentioned that Nickerson (1986) suggested that the technology could be used to produce both positive and negative organizational effects. Likewise, Bjørn-Andersen et al. (1986) conclude that it is not the technology itself that induces changes in control or discretion, *but the way in which the technology is used.* Consequently, if we wish to understand why these changes in discretion, control and influence occur when a system is introduced into a business or institution, we need to look more closely at the changes in organization that accompany new technology.

These sorts of changes have been the subject of research for some time now. For example, Pedersen (1986) states that: "Introducing computer systems potentially shifts the patterns of influence and discretion." Indeed, Boddy and Buchanan (1982) found that the two major reasons why managers introduced new technology was to reduce human error and intervention, and to control work flow and operators more closely. It is this increase in control that often leads to a reduction in the degree of discretion that users have over how they perform their tasks. This connection, between increasing control and decreasing discretion, has been supported, to some extent, by Bjørn-Andersen et al. (1986) who found only decreases in discretion when a system was implemented within an organization.

Power Change and Conflict

Bjørn-Andersen et al. found that changes in power or influence within a business or institution were greatest where the various units of the organization were heavily dependent upon one another. Moreover, satellite users (people on the periphery of the organization) experienced the greatest decreases in discretion as others, closer to the centre of the organization, had greater influence over how they worked.

This, however, would appear to be what we might expect. In an organization where one user, or set of users, must wait for the work of another user there is always some degree of power vested in the user whose work is awaited. That is to say, that the user who is first in this chain of work has power over the users that follow (see Fig. 7.1). Consequently, when a new system is introduced within an organization where there is a high degree of interdependence between users and user groups, there is quite simply more power to change, and as a result, more potential for conflict.

As channels of influence and power within an organization change when a computer system is introduced, we might expect those groups of users who experienced increases in the influence over others to welcome the system. On the other hand, those user groups who find that they suffer as a result of the system, and that other groups of workers have gained some control over how they work, are more likely to reject the system, and to avoid working within it. This may partly account for why different professional groups tend to hold differing views about the relative merits of computer systems. For example, Zoltan and Chapanis (1982) found that lawyers held particularly negative views of computer systems while pharmacists expressed positive opinions. This may be because computer systems are better suited to supporting the activities of some professions better than others. However, another explanation is that the present design of computer systems tends to vest power in certain professional groups, while placing other groups at a disadvantage.

Interestingly enough, one of the best known examples of conflict between groups arose in a legal setting. This conflict occurred between a court's

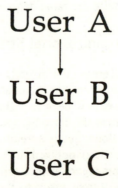

FIG. 7.1.   A diagram of a simple work chain.

legal staff and its probation officers. Kling (1980) describes this conflict in the following way:

> The legal staff members were concerned that cases be processed through the courts in an orderly manner and emphasized due process. In contrast, the probation officers emphasized rehabilitating individuals to become productive and trusted members of the community. When the information system was being designed, each group proposed a reporting structure which minimized its accountability and maximized its visibility and possible control over the other group. An automated system, which included a compromise set of data, was built and operated for four years. During this time it was primarily used as a record-keeping system and rarely used to enhance the control of either group of court administrators. Finally it was removed, and the court reverted to a manual record-keeping system.
>
> Albrecht (1979: who conducted the study into the system and its failure) considered this information system to have been used as an instrument in the power struggle between the legal staff and probation staff. Neither group was able to gain sufficient power to force the other to submit to its form of measurement and management. Since neither group could tightly manage the other and thus provide 'objective' data about the productivity and efficacy of court activities, the automated system was a sterile tool. This case highlights the close coupling of management control systems and the exercise of power in organizations. (Kling, 1980; cited in Baecker & Buxton, 1987).

As Baecker and Buxton (1987) point out, here we have an example of a system failing, not because it was difficult to learn or to use, but because the conflict between the two major groups of users was not properly taken into account. Unfortunately, examples such as this commonly occur, even if they do not always produce quite the same degree of failure.

Leadership Style and Organizational Structure

Not only can a new system decrease the discretion and influence of users at a lower level within an organization, but it can also have similar effects at a managerial level. Indeed, it has now been recognized that the process of de-skilling, that often accompanies the introduction of new technology, is no longer confined to the shop floor, but is spreading to other types of work, such as management, design, etc. (Cooley, 1987).

Reindl (1986) found that managers at different levels in an organization perceived the changes that a system made to their work differently. Some claimed that after the introduction of the new system they had greater contact with their staff, while others claimed that the opposite was true. It appeared as though those with a participative management style were being forced into having less contact with their staff, while those with a non-participative style were finding themselves pushed towards a participative management approach.

Earlier it was noted that Bjørn-Andersen et al. (1986) had found that the introduction of computer systems tended to lead to standardization in the way that managers performed their tasks. According to Reindl (1986) it now appears as though systems can also lead to a standardization in management or leadership style. This standardization, however, does not appear to be limited to the individuals within an organization. There have been suggestions that organizations themselves are becoming more standardized. Indeed, Naisbitt (1984) suggests that organizations that rely upon information technology are gradually moving away from a pyramidal management structure and towards a non-hierarchical or network model.

In summary, within an organization local experts usually emerge. The introduction of this sort of technology often leads to a standardization in tasks and leadership style. Moreover, the increase in control that usually accompanies a new system inevitably leads to a decrease in the discretion that users have over how tasks are performed, and how they fulfill their roles. Furthermore, the power changes that a new system instigates can often lead to conflict between different user groups.

Nevertheless, the message that emerges from the research is that the negative effects of introducing information technology are not inevitable. Indeed, it is generally accepted that all of the changes that have just been outlined are not direct consequences of implementing computer systems, but the product of the purpose to which this technology was put. In other words, if computer systems were not introduced with the primary aims of controlling employees and work flow then the effects of introducing computer systems would be very different. In essence, computers are tools which can be used to produce a variety of effects. The effect that a new computer system might have will be dependent upon its role within the organization.

Why Consider Organizational Issues?

Cynics, however, may argue that the drawbacks of introducing computer systems are not great enough to justify tackling the problems that have been outlined in the last section. In other words, why do we need to bother with these issues?

The answer to this question is, that the magnitude of these sorts of problems is great enough to cause systems to be rejected, even systems that have been well designed in every other respect. For example, consider the case of the legal system described in the last section, where this system failed because the conflict of interests between the two major user groups was not adequately addressed. Usually, however, systems just do not work, or remain underutilized.

A further argument for a consideration of these issues is provided by Bjørn-Andersen (1986). He notes that the costs of hardware have significantly decreased over the past 20 years. However, the organizational costs of implementing computer systems (Bjørn-Andersen calls this *orgware*) have rapidly increased, as businesses and institutions are disrupted as staff roles and duties are changed (see Fig. 7.2). This view is supported by Strassman (1985) who estimates that the organizational costs of introducing a professional workstation are approximately twice the cost of the technology (the hardware and the software).

Perhaps the strongest argument for tackling the problems that were described in the previous section, is that people who have to use systems where these issues have not been thought through, are often unhappy with their jobs. Consequently, they are less likely to produce high quality work. But how can we structure organizations so that jobs are enriched rather than de-skilled?

HOW CAN WE AVOID THE NEGATIVE ASPECTS OF COMPUTER IMPACT?

First, if we are to enrich jobs within an organization, we need to have some understanding of the dimensions along which we can consider the user's role. A framework that allows users to specify organizational requirements

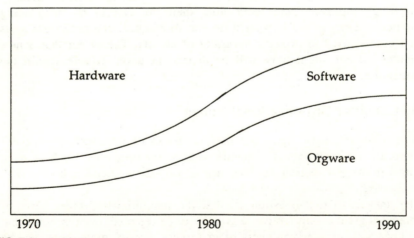

FIG. 7.2.   A distribution of the total costs of an information systems project (Bjørn-Andersen, 1986).

A Job content

Strongly   Varied,
specialized job   enlarged job
└───┘

Polarized division   No division
of work   of work
     └──┘

Structured pre-   Methods and
programmed work   sequence of subtasks is free
     └──┘

Norm or rule-   Consequence-
orientated behaviour   orientated behaviour
     └──┘

B Autonomy and control

Monitoring of   No monitoring
work performance   of performance
     └──┘

Much stress   No stress
     └───────────────────────────────────────┘

No influence   Total
on own job   self-control
└──┘

No influence   Large influence
on company issues   on company issues
     └──┘

C Social relations

No job secutiry   Total
                                                 job security
     └──┘

No possibility of   Great possibility
self-actualization   of self-actualization
     └──┘

                                                 All work done in
Working alone all day   contact with others
└──┘

Alienated   Well integrated
└──┘

D Personal Development

No training demands   Many training
                                                 demands
     └───────────────────────────────────────┘

                                                 High rate of
No personal development   personal development
     └──┘

FIG. 7.3. A framework for the specification of organizational requirements (Bjørn-Andersen, 1984).

such as these has been suggested by Bjørn-Andersen (1984), and this framework can be seen in Fig. 7.3.

As can be seen in Fig. 7.3, Bjørn-Andersen's framework allows users to consider various aspects of their role. These aspects are represented along continui, and the framework appears to provide an excellent means by which users can identify where they would like to be placed upon any of the continui. However, such a framework, while setting out the issues that need to be addressed, does not suggest how a *good* organization might be developed. In this case, a *good* organization is one which creates a user role that scores positively on many of Bjørn-Andersen's dimensions.

The question of designing systems that support *good* organizations has been addressed by Westin, Schweder, Baker, and Lehman (1985). They have proposed a generalized approach to developing systems that support such organizations, and although their approach is aimed primarily at office automation, it can nevertheless be generalized to other areas of information technology. A representation of this approach can be seen in Fig. 7.4. Westin et al. (1985) suggest 12 key people-technology issues that need to be considered:

1. *Strategic planning.* Top management must have a commitment to anticipating people-technology issues associated with new office technologies, and

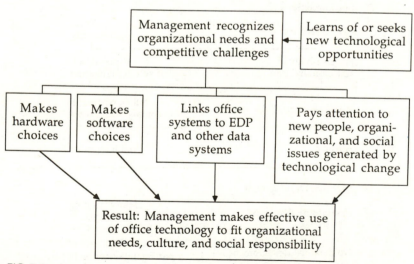

FIG. 7.4.   A socio-technical approach to adopting new office systems technology (Westin et al., 1985).

developing an interdisciplinary approach to translate office automation forces into organizational policies and practices.

2. *Office automation "ownership"*. This entails the identification and involvement of all participants who are affected by, or who might affect the office automation process. This includes functional support groups (e.g. personnel staff, technical staff etc.), and users (e.g. clerical, administrative, professional staff etc.). Effective "ownership" may be facilitated by formal and informal structures that allow interaction and co-ordination among different groups.

3. *Employee involvement and participation*. There needs to be a conscious management decision to actively solicit input and feedback from users on an ongoing basis. This involvement should include decisions and changes that affect users' jobs and work units before, during and after the transition to a computer system-based environment. This involvement not only provides valuable information, but also increases the chances of user acceptance of the new technology. Specific channels for employee involvement include periodic surveys, questionnaires, individual and focus group interviews, quality circles, and formal and informal management/employee discussions.

4. *Communications/problem resolution*. On-going efforts are needed to maintain open management/employee communications, both to inform and to solicit employee complaints. This may include developing in-house brochures, video tapes, newsletters, etc., and providing both formal and informal mechanisms to resolve user problems and complaints.

5. *Training*. New VDT (visual display terminal) users frequently require more training that many managers and vendors think is necessary. Providing both employees and managers with sufficiently broad-based skills and information to integrate the use of new office technologies effectively into their jobs and work units is essential in order to obtain the maximum benefits from office automation. This involves; educating non-technical users to articulate their needs to systems analysts early in the planning stages, tailoring training to suit the needs of different types of user, and following this training with sufficient user support, and training managers and supervisors to oversee the introduction of the new technology (i.e. to have realistic expectations of what users can learn, etc.).

6. *Job redesign*. During and after the transition to a computer system environment it is important to address the impact of the new technology on job satisfaction in order to maintain productivity and quality of work life. This includes; reviewing job tasks with employees to ensure that jobs are not designed around the system, establishing appropriate management practices (e.g. work breaks, social interaction, etc.), evaluating hiring and placement criteria as well as career path opportunities for long-range human resource planning, and restructuring job tasks to maintain sufficient autonomy, variety, etc.

7. *Work monitoring and performance standards.* Developing meaningful and fair qualitative and quantitative measurements of users' performance standards is essential. This involves; incorporating both technical expertise and employee participation during the process of establishing individual and group production standards, openly informing users of work monitoring policies and of their right to contest evaluations, periodically reviewing performance standards for fairness and appropriateness, training supervisors to motivate rather than "police" employees, and emphasizing customer service and quality of work as essential aspects of producing a "whole product".

8. *Health and safety.* Management must assess the overall VDT work environment in terms of health organization and safety practices and determine appropriate organizational policies. This includes; monitoring current scientific research on VDT health and safety issues, as well as general office problems of noise and air quality, communicating this research information with candor to employees, reviewing the scope of employee health-related record-keeping and organizational policies regarding VDTs, providing special channels to solicit employee complaints, questions and experiences with regard to health-related concerns.

9. *Ergonomics.* A sound plan must focus on ergonomic problems affecting user work performance, physical comfort and job satisfaction. This entails; observing work sites and soliciting employee input to evaluate job design, hardware, software, etc., altering and upgrading equipment in the light of the general recognition that there is no "best" solution—flexibility and individual adjustment and the key elements, training employees to recognize ergonomic problems and make maximum available use of workstations, developing and piloting software that responds to the user's needs by involving users in the design and evaluation process, establishing ergonomic standards for work sites, periodically monitoring the ergonomics of current workstations to uncover changes in work conditions and new problems that require adjustments.

10. *Labour relations issues.* Unions have particular interests in how new technology is introduced, work training and re-training programmes, health and safety concerns, ergonomics, VDT work monitoring, job design, and work re-organization. Many unionized firms are pursuing cooperative rather than confrontational approaches to addressing these issues through joint management/union committees.

11. *Women's quality of life and discrimination issues.* Since the great majority of VDT-related jobs are performed by women, and they have a virtual monopoly on clerical and secretarial jobs, it is important that managers pay attention to the growing issues of womens' pay equality and opportunities for promotion. This involves; recognizing that women have unique needs and that labour and economic discrimination issues need to be actively addressed to be overcome, conducting focus group interviews, assessments of hiring and promotion patterns, career path and educational opportunities

for women, making organizational and technological changes with an awareness of the emerging social and legal expectations concerning equality for women and minorities.

12. *Legal/regulatory trends*. Managers need to appreciate that there is a rapidly developing legal milieu and potential regulatory intervention with regard to VDT use which calls for anticipative management in this area.

The list suggested by Westin et al. (1985) is more comprehensive than may be implied from the edited list above, and the original article is recommended to interested readers. This catalogue of issues suggested by Westin et al. is undoubtedly useful to anyone who is involved in designing and implementing a system, although its prescriptions differ in some respects from the ideal system outlined earlier in this chapter (particularly with respect to monitoring the user).

Nevertheless, Westin et al.'s (1985) list of issues does not suggest, in detail, a process by which we might identify the key issues for any particular group (although Westin et al. do provide an interesting discussion of the planning, piloting, implementation and integration into the organization of a system). Eason (1985b), however, suggests just such a procedure.

The essence of Eason's procedure is that each user group is considered in detail. The first stage is to perform a cost/benefit analysis by considering the user group with respect to a series of issues. Each issue is considered in turn, and the costs and benefits for the group are scored on a scale of one to five. Furthermore, the reasons for each score are also recorded. Following this, a second checklist, with the same issues as the first checklist is considered. Here the *desired outcomes* of implementing a system are addressed and scores are dependent upon the conditions that are associated with each issue. The cost-benefit checklist from Eason (1985b) is set out below:

1. Job security

2. Information service from system
a. Financial information processing.
b. Management control.
c. Word processing.
d. Communication.

3. Job content
a. Effort required.
b. New skills/old skills lost.
c. Work pace/deadlines.
d. Work load.
e. Satisfaction.

4. Organizational procedures
a. Standardization.
b. Discretion.
c. Power and influence.
d. Privacy.
e. Communications.
f. Status.

5. Personnel policies
a. Basic pay.
b. Other rewards.
c. Career prospects.
d. Industrial relations.

For example, imagine that our user group (secretaries) had been scored poorly on the issue of career prospects in the first checklist. In the second checklist we might decide to offer all secretaries the opportunity to study for further qualifications that would allow them to progress up the career ladder. Consequently, our rating of this user group with respect to career prospects can be amended to reflect a more positive outcome.

The third stage is to develop these conditions, suggested as part of the second checklist (e.g. offering secretaries opportunities to study for higher qualifications), into a strategy for change. In other words, the collection of conditions suggested as part of the second checklist is used to identify the form a system that the user group would value. Moreover, this list is also used to identify how the user group might best participate in the design of the system Finally, the list of conditions is used to identify the forms of learning that might best suit that particular user group. The three aspects of this third stage from Eason (1985b) (alternative system solutions, user participation, and user learning and adaptation) are shown in more detail below.

Alternative System Solutions

1. Facilities offered: Should the system offer more/less/different facilities to the user?
2. Effort of adaptation: Should the system require more/less effort from the users in terms of data input, time, adaptation, knowledge, etc.?
3. Access to information: Should access to information be greater/more restricted/ different?
4. Allocation of duties: Should the allocation of duties to staff be changed to take advantage of system potential to achieve company goals/overcome organizational problems?
5. Control: Should the procedure for control and responsibility for the system be changed?
6. Introduction schedule: Should system facilities be introduced simultaneously to all users, or in an evolutionary procedure?

User participation

Purposes of participation
1. Influencing overall design decisions.
2. influencing local design decisions.
3. Commitment of staff to system.
4. To identify the indirect consequences of introducing the system.
5. To facilitate organizational change.
6. Staff awareness ad education.
7. Negotiation.

Forms of participation
1. No participation.
2. Inform users of progress.
3. User consulted by designers according to their need.
4. Industrial relations procedures.
5. Steering committee representatives.
6. Main design group representatives.
7. Representatives on working parties.
8. All users on working parties.

Learning and Adaption

Needs
1. To develop general awareness.
2. To reduce anxiety.
3. To educate about the system.
4. To develop specific system skills.
5. To develop ability to participate in design.
6. To educate about organizational change.
7. Point of need participation.

Possible methods
1. Formal training.
2. Appreciation courses.
3. System demonstrations.
4. Visits to similar systems.
5. "Play" opportunities.
6. Pilot system use and evaluation.
7. Provision of manuals.
8. Built-in help and guidance on the system.
9. Displays of procedures, e.g. reference posters.
10. Easy access to a specialist for help.
11. Easy access to a local expert.

The attractive aspect of Eason's (1985b) approach is that its starting point is a consideration of the potential impact of a system on a particular user group. This procedure begins by considering the user's role and needs, and defines both the system and organizational change as a result of this consideration. In other words, *this is user-centred design*, where the user is first and the technology is seen only as a means to an end; that of supporting the user.

COMMENTARY

While the importance of organizational issues is often acknowledged by those who are not directly concerned with these issues, there appears to be a tendency to treat the problems of implementing computer systems within organizations as a separate problem area from the rest of HCI. In other words, it seems sensible to some to imagine that issues such as choosing suitable interactional devices and appropriate metaphors come first in design, and that the problems of introducing a system within an organization come later, once the design has been finalized. This, however, is a fallacy. Of course, a system needs to be designed so that it can be easily understood and used. Nevertheless, the design of a system should be primarily determined by the role it is to play within an organization. Consequently, organizational issues should be paramount in the design and development process. A system may be easy to learn and easy to use, but if it does not have a useful niche within an organization then it will not be used. Indeed, it is this argument, together with the large number of unused systems whose problems can be attributed to a failure to fit into an acceptable and useful organizational role, that has led many of the large IT manufacturers to look towards methodologies for identifying organizational roles for products (e.g. USTM, see Chapter Six).

However, it may not be enough for us to simply identify roles for computer systems within organizations. We may need to define what is, and what is not, an appropriate role for a system. Presently, a major objective in introducing computer systems within organizations is often to monitor and supervise employees on a task-to-task basis. But as Bjørn-Andersen (1985) and others have noted, there are both moral and practical objections to this.

Many of us spend up to half, and sometimes more than half, of our waking lives at work. While some degree of supervision by management of employees may be both inevitable and desirable, the movement towards scrutinizing and regulating employees on a task-to-task basis, and using computers to compile statistics on work rate and performance, seems both morally undesirable and practically inhibiting. The practical argument against this movement is that people, when faced with a system that monitors their performance, use their ingenuity and talents to *beat* the system. Within an organization that monitors its employees, much of the work-force's creativity and talent is directed towards finding means by which they can avoid close supervision. The question seems to be whether we want people to feel as though they work for an organization that attempts to oversee all of their work behaviour, or within an organization where they are an integral but independent part, and where their contribution is both needed and valued.

In essence, we are suggesting, in common with others, that the first stage in design should be to consider organizational issues affecting design. Furthermore, close monitoring and regulation of employees is discouraged. The argument is not just that such computer systems are socially undesirable, but that users will avoid systems that monitor their behaviour. In short, computer systems that monitor users stand less chance of being accepted into the working environment; they are likely to remain both unwanted and unused.

SUMMARY

A system should support users in their tasks. Systems should be easy to learn, and easy to understand and operate. They should provide users with the information that they require, in an acceptable form, as well as allowing users to perform tasks in a variety of ways.

People are often engaged in more than one task over any given period of time. However, we sometimes have problems scheduling tasks in between each other. Computer systems need to support users in scheduling their activities.

Present systems tend to be geared towards users working alone. However, effective systems should help to create a sense of community for users in work-groups. One approach to supporting a sense of community within a work-group is to provide organizational interfaces. These are interfaces designed for use by more than one user at a time. The purpose of such interfaces is to allow users to work with each other through a computer system.

The Scandinavian approach is typified by Bjørn-Andersen (1985), who argues that HCI should not just have the aim of reducing the user's resistance to new technology, but should have the clear intention of improving the quality of the user's working life. Ultimately, the aim of the Scandinavian approach is to improve the quality and productivity of work within organizations and so increase profitability. As such, new technology is a means by which this can be achieved, it is not an end in itself, but a means to an end.

Organizational changes generally fall into three categories. The first, are those types of changes that are planned, such as reductions in the total number of staff, those that are unintended, such as adjustments in job content and increased salaries, and those that are delayed. These last sort of developments are where the system gradually becomes integrated within the organizational structure of the business or institution and users begin to more fully exploit the system's capabilities.

When a computer system is introduced into an organization local experts frequently emerge. Local experts are users who tend to find out more about the computer system than their colleagues, and consequently are used by their colleagues as a source of reference. These experts can be characterized, not just by how much they know, but more often by their ability to find information. However, local experts do not just communicate information, but show the inquirer how best to consider their problem. Bannon (1986a) has suggested eight factors that affect whether a person is consulted or not; organizational rank, technical expertise, sociability, reciprocity, accessibility, availability, organizational role, and shared experiences.

When a system is introduced within an organization the nature and structure of the user's tasks change. The impact on the user's tasks is greater with more powerful systems, and these more complex systems are often under-utilized, possibly because their users require more support than users of less complex systems.

By structuring the user's tasks the system can take the humdrum aspects out of the user's job and enrich the user's work-life. On the other hand, forcing all users to adopt the same approach to a task can also be viewed as deskilling a user's role. However, structuring the user's tasks can have positive, enriching effects, while at the same time introduce standardization.

Acceptance of information technology into the workplace is related to the user's perceptions of job enhancement and increased self-esteem. Furthermore, where job enrichment is not taken into account systems are sometimes rejected by their users.

Changes in organizational structure often reduce the user's discretion over how tasks are performed. Moreover, channels by which users could have previously influenced other people within the organization alter. However, it is not the technology itself that induces changes in control or discretion, but the way in which the technology is used. For example, one of the major reasons why managers introduce new technology is to control work flow and operators more closely. It is this increase in control that often leads to a reduction in the degree of discretion that users have over how they perform their tasks.

Changes in power or influence within a business or institution are greatest where the various units of the organization were heavily dependent upon one another. Moreover, satellite users experience the greatest decreases in discretion, as others, closer to the centre of the organization, have greater influence over how they work. These changes in power can lead to conflict between user groups.

It has been recognized that the process of de-skilling, that often accompanies the introduction of new technology, is no longer confined to the shop floor, but is spreading to other types of work such as management and design. Managers at different levels in an organization often perceive the changes that a system makes to their work differently. Although, overall, a new system can lead to a standardization in management or leadership style.

Organizational issues are important because the magnitude of these sorts of problems is great enough to cause systems to be rejected. There have also been arguments that the organizational costs of introducing computer systems now exceeds the cost of the software and hardware involved.

Bjørn-Andersen (1984) suggests that the user's requirements can be considered along a number of scales relating to job content, autonomy and control, social relations and personal development. This framework provides a means by which we can simply consider the user's role.

Westin et al. (1985) have proposed a generalized approach to developing systems, and suggest 12 key people-technology issues that need to be considered: strategic planning, office automation "ownership", employee involvement and participation, communications/problem resolution, training, job redesign, work monitoring and performance standards, health and safety, ergonomics, labour relations issues, womens' quality of life and discrimination issues, legal/regulatory trends.

Eason (1985b) suggests a procedure in which some of these issues can be taken into account. The essence of this procedure is that each user group is considered in detail. The first stage is to perform a cost/benefit analysis by considering the user group with respect to a series of issues. Following this, the desired outcomes of implementing a system are addressed. In the third stage the collection of conditions suggested as part of the second stage is used to identify the form a system that the user group would value. Moreover, this list is also used to identify how the user group might best participate in the design of the system Finally, the list of conditions is used to identify the forms of learning that might best suit that particular user group.

A SELECTIVE ANNOTATED BIBLIOGRAPHY

Bannon, L. J. (1986a). Helping users help each other. In D. A. Norman & S. W. Draper (Eds.), *User centred system design: New perspectives on human-computer interaction*. Hillsdale, New Jersey: Lawrence Erlbaum Associates Inc. *The author argues that encouraging local experts and a sense of community are important aspects of introducing systems into organizations. By concentrating on the human-computer dyad we are missing out on the social aspects of HCI. This paper concentrates on these social aspects.*

Bjørn-Andersen, N. (1984). Training for subjection or participation. In B. Shackel (Ed.), *Human-computer interaction–Interact '84: Proceedings of the first IFIP conference on human-computer interaction, London*. Amsterdam: North-Holland. *Bjørn-Andersen suggests that most training programmes introduce the user to a system so that the user can be subjected to the system at some later date. An alternative would be to train users to participate in design.*

Bjørn-Andersen, N. (1985). Are 'human factors' human? In N. Bevan & D. Murray (Eds), *Man-machine interaction: State of the art report*. Maidenhead: Pergamon Infotech. *An argument is presented to the effect that many human factors approaches adopt a machine model of man. The author outlines an alternative to this; the Scandinavian approach.*

Bjørn-Andersen, N. (1986). Understanding the nature of the office for the design of third wave office systems. In M. D. Harrison & A. F. Monk (Eds.), *People & computers: Designing for usability. Proceedings of the second conference of the BCS HCI specialist group*. Cambridge: Cambridge University Press. *The author addresses the question, why do office systems fail? He looks at the implementation of systems from an organizational perspective and concludes that computer manufacturers appear to be engaged in a frantic rush to produce new products that are only marginally better than previous systems. The author suggests that manufacturers need to step back and consider some of the organizational issues associated with the third wave of office systems. This is the wave that should concentrate upon supporting user groups rather than just individuals.*

Bjørn-Andersen, N., Eason, K. D., & Robey, D. (Eds.) (1986). *Managing computer impact: An international study of management and organizations*. Norwood, New Jersey: Ablex. *This book reports a number of studies into computer impact, and forms a comprehensive and interesting work. Topics covered include: task fit and ease of use, user support, and the impact of systems upon tasks, leadership style, organizational power systems, organizational structure, and the user's influence and discretion. This book is well written and likely to be of particular interest to academics within business and social sciences.*

Cooley, M. J. E. (1987). Human centred systems: An urgent problem for systems designers. *AI & Society, 1 (2)*, 37–46. *The author argues that the problem of job de-skilling is no longer limited to the shop floor, but is spreading to what the author terms 'intellectual' work. This is a well- written paper that provides a general discussion of some of the social issues.*

Cypher, A. (1986). The structure of users' activities. In D. A. Norman & S. W. Draper (Eds.), *User centred system design: New perspectives on human-computer interaction*. Hillsdale, New Jersey: Lawrence Erlbaum Associates Inc. *The author discusses the issue of people scheduling their time between tasks, i.e. writing a list of foods to buy while waiting for the kettle to boil. Cypher argues that systems need to support users in these activities, and gives the example of windows providing the means by which the user can perform more than one activity on a system at once.*

Eason, K. D. (1985a). Emerging concepts in the implementation of I. T. systems. In N. Bevan & D. Murray (Eds), *Man-machine interaction: State of the art report*. Maidenhead: Pergamon Infotech. *A user centred approach to designing and implementing computer systems is described. The author is concerned that design should take account of the organizational effects of implementing a system, and suggests several methods by which organizational issues might be incorporated into design. This is a well written paper that is recommended to practitioners and academics alike.*

Hirschheim, R. (1985). *Organizational aspects of office automation.* New York: Wiley. *The author provides an interesting overview and critique of organizational issues within the office automation field. This book is well written and likely to be of interest to both academics and practitioners alike.*

Hirschheim, R., Land, F., & Smithson, S. (1984). Implementing computer-based information systems in organizations: Issues and strategies. In B. Shackel (Ed.), *Human-computer interaction–Interact '84: Proceedings of the first IFIP conference on human-computer interaction, London.* Amsterdam: North-Holland. *It is suggested that computer system implementation is based on factors such a human beliefs, emotions and perceptions. The authors discuss human reactions to the types of change that occur when new systems are introduced within an organization. They go on to suggest that the implementation of a computer system can be a threat to both individuals and groups within a business or institution.*

Malone, T. W. (1987). Computer support for organizations: Toward an organizational science. In J. M. Carroll (Ed.), *Interfacing thought: Cognitive aspects of human-computer interaction.* Cambridge, Massachusetts: MIT Press. *It is argued that systems should support groups in their tasks, not just individuals. Malone goes on to define an organizational interface and to give examples of systems that already have this feature. It is suggested that we require an organizational science, and the author considers several perspectives and potential approaches to this science. This paper is interesting and readable.*

Markus, M. L. (1983). Power, politics, and MIS implementation. *Communications of the ACM, 26 (6),* 430–444. *The author considers three theories that attempt to explain why users often resist the introduction of new technology. Markus concludes that interaction theory best explains why systems are resisted. This theory suggests that resistance is produced by a variety of interacting variables.*

O'Malley, C. E. (1986). Helping users help themselves. In D. A. Norman & S. W. Draper (Eds.), *User centred system design: New perspectives on human-computer interaction.* Hillsdale, New Jersey: Lawrence Erlbaum Associates Inc. *The author discusses the question of supporting users at the interface. She suggests that local experts provide conceptual guidance as well as information.*

Rauner, F., Rasmussen, L., & Corbett, J. M. (1988). The social shaping of technology and work: Human centred CIM systems. *AI & Society, 2 (1),* 47–61. *It is suggested that systems should consist of a combination of the technologically possible and the socially desirable. The authors go on to suggest six factors that shape the user's work: time structure, space of movement, social relations, qualification, stress control, and responsibility and control flexibility.*

Straub, J. M. & Straub, J. R. (1987). Comparative factors in user acceptance of office automation. In H. J. Bullinger & B. Shackel (Eds.), *Human-computer interaction–Interact '87: Proceedings of the second IFIP conference on human-computer interaction, Stuttgart.* Amsterdam: North-Holland. *A study is reported, as a follow up to a much earlier study, where user acceptance of new technology* was found to be strongly related to perceptions of job satisfaction and increased self-esteem. The authors also suggest that the problems of alienation and resistance may have been overstated in the literature.

Westin, A. F., Schweder, H. A., Baker, M. A., & Lehman, S. (1985). *The changing workplace: A guide to managing the people, organization, and regulatory aspects of office technology.* White Plains, New York: Knowledge Industry. (A chapter from this book, with the authors major recommendations, is also available in Baecker & Buxton, 1987.) *The authors suggest that managers need to consider 12 key issues when implementing new technology. The authors then go on to discuss how the transition to a computer system environment might be managed.*

Zoltan, E. & Chapanis, A. (1982). What do professional persons think about computers? *Behaviour and Information Technology, 1,* 55–68. *This paper reports the results of a survey that considered attitudes to computers. Differences between professional groups were found. It was also discovered that inexperienced computer users had negative attitudes towards computers while experienced users tended to have more positive attitudes.*

8 The Future of Human-Computer Interaction

In collaboration with Philip H. Marsden
Department of Psychology, Manchester University

OVERVIEW

In this chapter the development and direction of HCI is discussed. First, the research into interactional hardware and software is considered. Following this, the likely changes in the nature of human-computer dialogue are outlined, as well as the roles of intelligent, expert, and adaptive systems within HCI.

Modelling the user, and the user's knowledge of tasks and systems has been one of the major areas of research interest within HCI over recent years. Consequently, the evolution and use of analytic models within design, as well as the development of computational models, is discussed. At the task level, the future of attempts to improve the task match between user and computer is considered, as well as the move towards users programming their own systems.

The changing character of the design process is reviewed, and issues such as the likely adoption of User Interface Management Systems are considered. The increasing recognition of the importance of organizational issues, and the need for interfaces that properly support organizations as well as individuals is discussed. Finally, the likely direction of HCI is considered with respect to some of the emerging trends within research.

INTRODUCTION

In the previous seven chapters we have considered the different areas and aspects of *human-computer interaction*. However, the descriptions provided in these chapters can only be considered as a snapshot of the field as it presently stands. As systems evolve and old problems are solved, new difficulties are likely to emerge, together with new themes and perspectives that suggest where solutions to these difficulties are likely to be found. Nevertheless, the development of HCI is unlikely to be determined only by research perspectives and solutions. Commercial developments are also likely to shape the future of HCI, as past experience has shown.

In the preface to *Interfacing Thought*, Carroll (1987) describes HCI as one of the most active areas of research within cognitive science. Although the origins of HCI can be traced back many years to the early 1960s, it was not until the 1980s that this active interest in the study of human-computer interaction became widespread. One factor that may have contributed towards the realization that the area of HCI required attention, was the recognition of the problems that new computer systems were creating when they were implemented within organizations. Another potent factor may have been the commercial success of those computers where HCI issues had been given serious consideration.

For example, Tognazzini (1986) reports how the Apple Macintosh was developed through a long process of iterative prototyping and user testing. The resulting success of the Macintosh can be seen, not only in its penetration of a highly competitive market, but also in the way that other manufacturers have been forced to follow the Apple Macintosh approach (although the approach can be seen in the earlier Xerox Star system), of using icons coupled with a metaphor that portrayed the system as a desktop, with files, folders and wastepaper baskets. The success of the Macintosh has demonstrated that there are sound commercial reasons for considering the human-computer interface.

Consequently, a number of different factors, from research interests to commercial successes, are shaping the way in which systems are designed and implemented. Although the effects of many of the most significant developments are not foreseen at the time of their inception, we nevertheless have an opportunity to actively steer computer system evolution towards mutually desirable goals. Our ultimate aim must be to improve the quality of life enjoyed by those who work with computer systems or are affected by them. As computer systems increasingly affect almost every aspect of human activity, the importance of HCI continues to grow.

The importance of HCI issues to society as a whole has been most forcefully expressed by Cooley (1987): "We are, I submit, at a unique historical turning point. Decisions we make in respect of technological developments during the next five or ten years will have profound effects upon the way our society develops; the manner in which human beings relate to machines and to each other; and the relationship between human beings, their built environment and nature itself."

Areas of Development Within HCI

Having re-iterated the importance of HCI and its evolution over the coming years, we will now review the different areas of HCI where change and improvement appear likely. These advances will be considered using the simple scheme suggested in Chapter One. This scheme is shown in Fig. 8.1 of this chapter, and shows the different areas of study within HCI. As has been mentioned before, this division of the areas of *human-computer interaction* is artificial, and does not properly reflect the true complexity of the area. Nevertheless, it provides a convenient means by which we can organize how we think about HCI, but its drawbacks need to be borne in mind.

All of the areas shown in Fig. 8.1 will be considered in turn, except for the area of *matching models* at the interface. This particularly large area will be considered in two parts; dialogue and modelling. Dialogue is considered to be the major process by which users construct models of a system, while the section on modelling is devoted to the grammars, methods, and other means by which cognitive models of the user are constructed.

ADVANCES IN INTERACTIONAL HARDWARE AND SOFTWARE

The means by which we communicate with computers has been a source of speculation for many years. However, Marshall et al. (1987a) suggest that the workstation of the future will contain a high resolution display, with

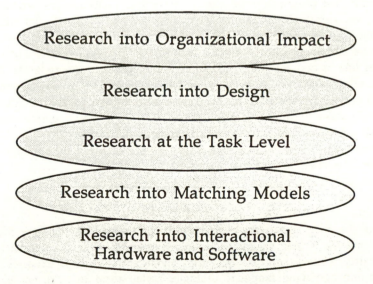

FIG. 8.1.   A representation of the different areas of study within HCI.

mice, icons and windows. Moreover, the operations of the workstation will be accompanied by voice annotation. In other words, verbal commentary or explanation will be available as the system performs its various operations. Most notably, the workstation will be equipped for voice input and output.

Generally, this view of the interactional media through which future human-computer communication will take place is commonly held throughout the research community and industry. The interesting aspect of this perspective is that it sees a general widening of the physical bandwidth (e.g. Thomas, 1986). In other words, the different means of input and output to a computer system are expected to increase.

However, the belief that speech input and output will form the major part of this widening of the physical bandwidth is not shared by all researchers (e.g. Buxton, 1986a; Marshall et al., 1987a). As mentioned in Chapter Two, speech is a form of input and output that may be suitable for some tasks in some situations, but its use may be limited to a small range of tasks, such as those where the operators hands need to be free, etc.

Some attempts to widen the physical bandwidth of human-computer communication were briefly described in Chapter Two. These attempts included using different item selection strategies and pointing devices operated using the feet. This sort of research is only part of a movement to develop better input devices that maximize human physical characteristics to improve both user performance and satisfaction.

However, as the number of input devices increases the difficulties of choosing a device for a particular task are also likely to become worse. Presently, the only means for choosing suitable input devices are common sense and user testing. Unfortunately, the first is renowned for its fallibility and the second noted for its expense (although, as pointed out in earlier chapters, this expense is usually justified). The difficulty may not be in testing one or two devices, but how to test twenty or thirty input devices as the numbers continue to grow. It may be that we require a simple unified theory, possibly drawn from the ergonomics or human factors literature, that will show us how to narrow down our options to a small number of potentially suitable input devices. In essence, *we appear to need theories that will relate tasks and task behaviour to optimal physical actions and the devices that can best match these actions.*

ADVANCES IN DIALOGUE

One of the most significant changes in human-computer dialogue that can be identified is that various dialogue styles appear to be decreasing in popularity while others are becoming more common. For example, form fill-in and command language dialogue styles seem to be used less frequently in systems that are appearing on the software market. While dialogue styles such as command language and form fill-in are always likely to be with us to some extent, their use within everyday systems looks set to decrease in future years. On the other hand, styles such as direct manipulation (see Chapter Three for an explanation), together with various explanatory metaphors and icons are being used on a more widespread basis (for a discussion of icons see Rogers, 1986; Ruge Jervell & Olsen, 1985). Indeed, both Shneiderman (1986) and Buxton (1986a) identify the increasing use of image and direct manipulation as one of the most significant developments in coming years.

Adaptive Dialogues

An area of research interest that has received almost as much attention as direct manipulation is that of adaptive dialogues. These are dialogues that adapt to the user (also called adaptive interfaces and sometimes adaptive systems, although they are not, strictly speaking, the same thing). One example of such a system is reported by Good et al. (1984), who developed a system that adapted to different user derived commands. In other words, the users suggested their own commands and the system was programmed to recognize a high proportion of these different commands. At first, however, the system could only recognize around 7% of all commands, but after development and refinement the system could recognize up to *76%* of all user derived commands.

The system developed by Good et al. (1984) sounds straightforward enough. However, there are a number of important issues associated with adaptive dialogues, such as how to adapt to the user, when to adapt, whether adaption is under system control or the user's, etc. The major concern that is repeatedly raised is the issue of the criteria for adaption. In other words, which groups of users should the system adapt for? The most common distinction is that of novice/expert. That is to say, that novices are provided with one dialogue while experts receive another. This inevitably raises issues of classifying users as to whether they are novices or experts. Commonly, many other means have been used to classify users such as the user's occupation, educational background, or cognitive style (see Kagan, 1966; Richardson, 1977; Witkin, 1976). Some of the issues germane to this question have been raised by Potosnak (1986). Three of the questions she posed were:

What is the purpose of classifying computer users?
Does the design of the best user interface depend on the type of user?
Do different types of users need different interfaces, or is the best interface for a given user the best for everyone?
Can we develop successful adaptive interfaces?

In 1986 these questions were raised at a panel session of the CHI conference, held in Boston, Massachusetts. Rosson (1986) replied by suggesting that any classification of users would fail to adequately account for all of the user variables that affect the usability of a system. Whiteside (1986), however, went further and stated that: "Classification is a cheap solution. Classification arises, not out of inherent characteristics of those things which are classified, but rather out of the need of the classifiers to classify. Once classification is made, it assumes a reality that loses sight of the artificiality of the classification scheme. In this way, classification acts to increase the distance between designer and client, not decrease it."

Despite these criticisms, and the continuing controversy surrounding issues such as user classification and adaption criteria, there is presently a good deal of research into the possible use of adaptive dialogues within HCI (although interest in this subject may be waning). Indeed, as Good et al.'s (1984) system has demonstrated, not all systems that adapt to the user require classifications of their users, and it appears as though significant commercial systems with adaptive dialogues are likely to be developed sometime in the not too distant future.

The Desirable Qualities of Human-computer Dialogue

While a dialogue or script that adapts to suit the needs of the user may be beneficial, such adaption is not the only desirable quality of dialogue. In Chapter Three we considered the features of everyday human dialogue that might be desirable in human-computer dialogue. The conclusion was that all of the features that distinguish human from human-computer dialogue appeared desirable to some extent. These were; the ability to negotiate definitions, natural language, and spoken language. This last feature, spoken language, refers to the kind of language used in normal communication where sentences are not completed as one speaker interrupts, anticipating the other speaker's meaning. This type of communication, where precision is not of paramount importance, is economical and fast, but also open to misinterpretation.

As was mentioned in Chapter Three, the features of human language might be desirable only in certain situations. Indeed, many researchers disagree over the relative merits of natural language and alike. Nevertheless, there is general agreement that "intelligent" systems are required if these features are to become a practical and commercial reality.

Intelligent Systems

It is often argued that intelligent systems are little more than fanciful dreams, and in no way possible to create. Other arguments are that intelligent systems are potentially possible, but we do not presently have the technology or the knowledge to build them (e.g. Kelly, 1987). However, these arguments appear to centre around a definition of *intelligence*. Some might argue that any system that can pass the Turing test (see Chapter One) is, for practical purposes, intelligent, while others would suggest that intelligence implies creativity, the ability to think, and that no computer is ever likely to achieve this.

Regardless of this complex philosophical argument, we have systems that are commonly referred to as *intelligent*, even though many might dispute the use of this term. Thus, the term *intelligent* is often used loosely within computing to mean a sophisticated system, rather than one which attempts to emulate human cognitive abilities in a detailed and deliberate manner.

There are a number of examples of such systems. Jerrams-Smith (1987) describes SUSI, an intelligent help or tutoring system for the UNIX operating system. Elzer et al. (1987) outline a prototype intelligent process monitoring system, and Breuker, Winkels, and Sandberg (1987) discuss an intelligent help system. All of these systems use many of the tools from artificial intelligence (AI). Indeed, Lawrence (1986) suggests that the use of AI tools is likely to become a continuing trend within human-computer interface design.

As the application of AI techniques and tools to interface design becomes more widespread it appears likely that many objectives that previously appeared unobtainable are likely to move within reach. Diaper (1986) for example, has demonstrated that the number of words that users employ when performing a task is limited. In other words, that a natural language system that dealt with one particular task, or set of tasks, might only be required to recognize a limited number of words. That is to say, that although present systems for dealing with natural language can only deal with a limited number of words, this may not be such a large obstacle as was once thought.

In the longer term, systems that can reason and think to some limited extent may not be completely out of reach. Shank (1986) even suggests how computers might be made to work creatively, to produce original solutions to problems. Shank argues that we create new explanations for a sequence of events or a problem by manipulating old *explanation patterns*. Furthermore, he suggests that it is possible to employ this type of process to produce creativity in computers.

However, with respect to HCI, the type of work in which researchers such as Shank are engaged can only be regarded as being of long-term interest. Of more immediate relevance is the proposed role of intelligent systems within HCI. In other words, what are the desirable features of intelligent systems within human-computer interaction? Rissland (1984) suggests that intelligent user interfaces should:

Carry out menial tasks (e.g. set the terminal characteristics and options for the user);

Automate routine tasks (e.g. frequently saving back-ups of files that are being used);

Provide assistance with more complex tasks;

Provide easy access to tools;

Provide status information (e.g. on the progress of tasks like file formatting);

Provide on-line assistance and documentation (e.g. help and manuals);

Allow multi-tasking (e.g. allow the user to perform more than one task at any one time, or perform some aspects of tasks for the user while the user performs other parts).

As can be seen from Rissland's list of desirable features, an intelligent system is likely to take responsibility for a greater number of the more mundane tasks. Consequently, the *power* of the interface is likely to increase (Michaelis, Miller, & Hendler, 1982). That is to say, that instead of having to instruct a system as to how to perform a task in detail, a higher-level command can be used, which implies all of the details of the task. In other words, the level of the dialogue increases and becomes more abstract.

Expert Systems

One particular form of intelligent system that is currently the subject of considerable commercial interest is the expert system (e.g. systems such as MYCIN, Shortliffe, 1976; PROSPECTOR, Duda, Gaschnig, & Hart, 1979; see Nickerson, 1986, for a list and short description of some of the more notable expert systems). The expert system is a relatively new form of computer system that uses techniques developed in the field of artificial intelligence (AI) to solve problems that normally require human expertise. They differ from more traditional data processing (DP) systems insofar as they are said to *deal* with knowledge as opposed to *information*. Moreover, they employ heuristic reasoning mechanisms called *inference engines* rather than the more conventional algorithmic DP techniques.

An algorithm is a mathematical formula or computer program that produces a solution to a problem (a set of procedures for carrying out a task), while a heuristic is a process that produces movement towards a solution, without necessarily producing the solution outright. For example, imagine we are playing chess. Our overall goal is to win the game. If we move a piece because we think that it will help us to attain that goal, but we do not know exactly how the game might finish, then this is a heuristic; a process or rule of thumb that is used to move towards an eventual solution to the problem. However, if we identify two moves that will win the game, then these two moves, or this process, is an algorithm, as it will take us straight to the solution. In systems that deal with complex problems that have certain degrees of uncertainty, heuristics are used, as detailing complex algorithms is often considered impractical.

The two key features of an expert system, the use of inference engines and the use of knowledge rather than information have been used by Goodall (1985) to provide a working definition: "An expert system is a computer system that operates by applying an inference engine to a body of specialist expertise represented in the form of knowledge." In addition to these two components, there exist a number of functional advantages to expert systems. According to Hayes-Roth (1985) their characteristics include the ability to:

Solve complex problems as well as or better than human experts;
Reason heuristically using what experts consider to be effective rules of thumb;
Manipulate and reason about symbolic descriptions;
Function with data that contains errors using judgement rules;
Contemplate multiple, competing hypotheses simultaneously;
Explain why they are asking questions;
Justify their conclusions.

To regard some of these characteristics as achievements may be somewhat premature (see Fox, 1984). However, there is a considerable consensus of opinion that as objectives they describe well the aims of research and development in this area. Moreover, this consensus extends to the view that of those characteristics not yet attained, significant research breakthroughs will occur over the next few years.

In relation to HCI, expert system technology provides some interesting theoretical and practical challenges. The success of the technology in a working environment rests heavily on the appropriateness of the user interface. Young (1984) explains the problem in the following way: "In their home laboratories...[expert systems]...are used primarily by the people who built them, love them, and are tolerant of their idiosyncrasies. Outside the laboratory, these expert systems will be used only if people find that they help them to do a job they have to do more easily and efficiently, and find them easy to work with."

However, as has been mentioned in Chapter Seven, experts do not just provide information, but also conceptual guidance. Yet many expert systems only provide information, and so do not fulfill the role that novices expect from an expert. Furthermore, expert systems often frustrate their users by providing laborious question and answer dialogues (Kidd, 1985; Kidd & Cooper, 1985).

But the major difficulty that has been identified is in the role that an expert system plays with respect to a human expert. The dominant interaction metaphor for expert systems has been that of expert and novice (Hayes-Roth, Waterman, & Lenet, 1983). This is where the system plays the role of the expert and the user is treated as a technician, providing information as it is required. In other words, the user is relegated to the role of an assistant. As we might expect, many experts object to being treated in this fashion, and take exception to the role in which they are placed by the system.

A more profitable interaction metaphor for an expert system has been suggested by Rector, Newton, and Marsden (1985). In this metaphor the human expert is left in the role of expert and the expert system is placed in the role of a helpful and knowledgeable assistant. An example of an expert system in this role is provided by Eason et al. (1987), who report the development of an expert system to help engineers produce switching schedules in electricity grid networks.

When a high-voltage electricity cable needs to be switched off for maintenance, a switching schedule needs to be constructed so that electricity supply is maintained and the various safety rules are not broken. The system described by Eason et al. allows engineers to construct their switching schedules, but provides warnings when various rules have been broken. The role that the system plays, of helpful assistant, together with the warnings that it provides for engineers, appear to have been significant contributing factors in the initial success of the system.

Nevertheless, there are other reasons why expert systems fail. Many expert systems fail because the dialogue they provide is unsuitable and they do not adequately fulfill a role that is acceptable to the expert user. Indeed, Turner (1985) suggests that building cost effective commercial expert systems that are usable is a major problem facing software developers. It has been the problems of designing suitable dialogues for expert systems, together with the difficulties in finding domains where knowledge can be represented within a simple social context (Stamper, 1988), that has prompted Hayes-Roth (1984) to suggest that most commercial expert systems will fail, although a few should prove to be considerable successes.

In summary, expert systems seem to have particular dialogue problems, although intelligent systems as a whole appear to offer new opportunities for more flexible dialogue, where systems can understand natural language and negotiate definitions. Although the relative merits of the human characteristics of dialogue is currently a contentious issue, there is little doubt that development towards robust natural language systems will continue. Overall, it appears as though dialogue between humans and computer should become easier as more intelligent mechanisms become available. That is to say, that, some areas of development within human-computer dialogue are tied closely to developments in artificial intelligence.

ADVANCES IN MODELLING

Development within the field of modelling or analytic techniques is likely to be driven by some of the problems that can be identified with these techniques. One problem we can identify with some of the modelling or analytic techniques, such as TAG (Payne & Green, 1986), is that they deal with only one of the gulfs of HCI identified by Norman (1986; 1987). That is to say, that they only deal with the problems of how we convert our intentions into actions, which Norman calls the gulf of execution. These models do not deal with the problem of how we interpret the systems state (the gulf of evaluation). Thomas Green makes a similar point when he indicates that there has not been enough work on the understanding/ interpreting/perceiving aspect. In future years we might reasonably expect researchers to begin to look at this problem, and to develop notations that attempt to capture its essential cognitive characteristics.

A further area of development for cognitive models has been outlined by Young and Simon (1987). They suggest that we need to consider how users plan their actions, as well as how they convert their intentions into physical action specifications. Young & Simon state that: "...it is beginning to be recognized that an adequate model of planning in the HCI context will have to acknowledge that the very nature of interaction with a computer demands that one conceives of the planning process as being intertwined with the process of execution." In other words, Young & Simon are suggesting that the idea of planning a set of actions for a task and then simply executing these actions does not properly reflect the true nature of planning in HCI. That is to say, that we execute actions, and upon perceiving the new system state we alter our plans accordingly. Planning is an ongoing process driven both by the overall goals and intentions of the user and the interaction between the user and the system.

More general criticisms of present modelling techniques (or analytic grammars) are that they do not fit into the design process (Carroll & Rosson, 1985) and that they are too complex to use and understand on an everyday basis. First, there is likely to be continuing work into the development of grammars that are easier to understand and use. Second, it appears probable that the role of analytic (modelling) techniques within design will become progressively better defined.

This movement towards defining the role of analytic techniques has already begun, with Moran (1986) stating that: "Models [analytic techniques] play a role as elements of the design argument, helping to support certain decisions. Thus, models are best applied locally to small aspects of the design, where they fit the grain size of the design decisions."

Polson (1987) has suggested that modelling techniques might one day replace usability testing. This argument has been rejected by Reisner (1987) however: "Behavioural tests and models are not in competition. They are complementary. Empirical tests are needed to determine whether the predictions of models are correct. Furthermore, when model and experiment do not agree, there is opportunity for further refinement or development of a model." Moreover, Reisner suggests that modelling techniques are unlikely ever to be able to systematically predict some aspects of user behaviour, such as human error. However, one avenue of research that may provide both a theoretical and a practical basis for understanding human error is the development of computational models that simulate human cognitive processes.

Computational Models

In the previous chapters we have considered some of the analytical techniques or grammars for modelling the user. However, development within HCI is unlikely to proceed only along this path. Computational models of human cognitive processes are also likely to play a greater role within HCI, even if their effects might be felt in the longer term rather than in the next two or three years.

First, we ought to make clear what is meant by the term *computational model*. A *computational model* is quite simply a model that can be run as a program on a computer. In other words, at some level of detail, it has been described in programming terms.

It appears as though computational models of human cognitive activity are likely to become more influential in those domains where there is real concern with the nature of human fallibility, such as process control and alike. Furthermore, these models may be of use in situations where generalized knowledge of human cognitive processes is required. The legitimacy of these claims remains, for the moment, the subject of speculation. However, there is growing evidence from AI and cognitive science laboratories that these ambitions may soon be realizable. For example, recent research by McClelland, Rumelhart and the PDP Research Group (1986a; 1986b) has developed a machine that seems to exhibit many of the qualities of human learning (although its slow speed of execution among other things has led some to doubt its practical uses). Clearly, an interface that could learn from experience would be extremely desirable in some situations. However, it must be remembered that systems based upon these sorts of principles remain, for the moment, a long-term research prospect rather than an achievable short-term goal.

Another area of interest is the development of performance models of human cognition. In particular, models that attempt to delineate psychological theories of human error. Contrary to popular opinion, human error is neither as common nor as varied as most people believe (Reason & Mycielska, 1982). One such model has been developed along the lines of certain principles and cognitive process suggested by Reason (1988). While it is not possible to go into great detail here, the overall tenet that Reason employs is that: "When cognitive operations are underspecified, they tend to default to contextually appropriate high frequency responses." In other words, when we retrieve knowledge from memory, and we are not entirely sure what we are looking for, we tend to retrieve items that are *frequently used*. That is to say, we retrieve items or concepts that we frequently encounter and have to often retrieve in a given situation or context.

For example, if we are asked to provide the name for a fruit, we are more likely to pick a high frequency item such as *apple* than an item that is encountered less frequently in social contexts and in speech, such as *yam*. Reason (1988) argues that when we do not have enough information to identify an item in memory we *frequency gamble* and opt for a contextually appropriate high frequency answer.

Reason (1988) suggests that frequency of encounter type information in memory is a major contributing factor to the robust nature of human cognition. That is to say, that much of the time we are given inadequate information, but we still manage to arrive at the correct answer. In short, we *frequency gamble*, but most of the time we guess correctly. Sometimes, however, we arrive at the wrong answer. When this happens the results are usually trivial. For example, we may write the wrong item on a shopping list. Occasionally, however, serious consequences can ensue, and some of the most notable disasters can be traced to human error of some sort.

As a means of supporting the principles and processes suggested by Reason (1988), Marsden (1989) has developed a computational model. This model is a sophisticated instantiation of Reason's proposed processes, and has produced results which correlate highly with human behaviour. The model provides support for the idea that frequency plays a central role both in human knowledge retrieval and in the errors that humans make. Previously, there have been calls for simplifying assumptions to explain human error (Rasmussen, 1985). The notion of frequency of encounter provides just such a simplifying assumption, while the model suggests in more detail how human knowledge retrieval, and human errors, might occur.

From a practical standpoint the model has two potential uses. First, it might be used as the basis for a mechanism that checks users to ensure that they are not making errors. While errors may not be important in office systems and alike, they are of particular concern in nuclear power and chemical process plants. Such a mechanism might be used to warn users when they may be in a situation where error is likely.

Second, the model provides a means by which computer systems might be made to guess. Although the model has been shown to make the same errors as humans, this is not necessarily a disadvantage. We know that humans are particularly good at using small amounts of information to make relatively accurate decisions, and so a mechanism that seems to guess in the same way as humans may prove to be particularly useful in non-risk systems, even if it does make mistakes. From an HCI point of view, Marsden's (1989) model provides a means by which a system might make fairly accurate guesses about a user's intentions, and so reduce the need for absolute precision in the user's input to a system.

ADVANCES IN TASK MATCH ISSUES

To recapitulate; matching tasks means matching the user's needs to the information provision and functionality of the system. Furthermore, the term task match also implies that the user is allowed the freedom to perform tasks in any reasonable way that is preferred. The central question in this area is; how do we ensure that the correct information is presented to the user, in the correct form, on every occasion without a system having so many options and permutations that it is effectively unusable?

It is sometimes suggested that modelling techniques can be used to establish the user's needs. Such techniques, however, only show us what information is required to perform the task in question. The kind of task match issues that researchers such as Eason (1984) address occur at a higher level and relate to the information that the user requires to perform their role within an organization, rather than the detail of a single task. This topic has been considered in Chapter Five, and it was noted then that there are few techniques for eliciting the user's information needs. Consequently, this appears to be one of the areas where more research is required.

One development that seems likely to gain more credence in the coming years is the idea of allowing users to program parts of their own system. An attempt to provide a programming language that might be usable by non-technical people has been described by Eisenstadt (1983). It was intended that this language, called SOLO, should be accessible to the average user.

To be specific, the language was intended for social science students, many of whom had no technical background. The language allowed these students to construct their own programs, and was intended to help students to grasp the principles of artificial intelligence, "...as painlessly as possible." Eisenstadt (1983) reports that the language has been successfully used by over 2,500 students. One drawback of the language, however, was that its limitations tended to frustrate users as they became more experienced. Nevertheless, Eisenstadt's (1983) SOLO demonstrates that programming languages aimed at non-technical users can be successful.

HyperCard™ and Hypertext

A more recent and commercial attempt at a programming package aimed at non-expert users is the HyperCard™ system for the Apple Macintosh (see Fig. 8.2). This system has aroused a great deal of interest for a number of reasons. The first is that it provides a means by which users who lack programming experience can program their own applications. The system is based upon a card metaphor. The user creates cards which define the application. These cards are arranged in stacks. Using the features that are present in existing stacks, supplied with the system, together with the HyperCard™ programming language, HyperTalk™, stacks of cards, which form the application, can be constructed.

The transparency of the system (the extent to which the conceptual model of the system is clearly indicated to the user) is one reason for the interest in this development. Another, equally important, reason is that HyperCard not only employs hypertext to explain itself, but also enables the creation of hypertext documents. But what is hypertext?

A useful way of conceptualizing hypertext is to consider a normal linear document. Here we proceed from beginning to end, with no opportunity to stop at a particular topic and examine it in more detail. In essence, normal text is linear and *passive*. Hypertext, on the other hand, allows the reader to pause at a particular topic and to explore it further. For example, imagine that this book was a hypertext document. We might skim through the topics that do not interest us and then reach a subject that is of concern. Let us suppose that we were interested in Marsden's (1989) computational model

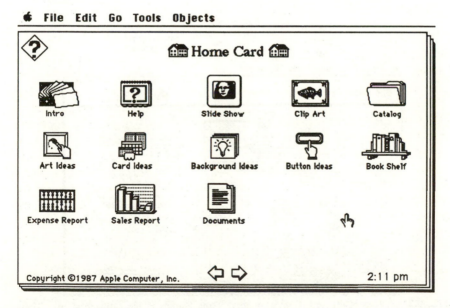

FIG. 8.2. The "Home Card" or beginning screen in HyperCard which shows various icons representing different stacks of cards. By permission of Apple Computer Inc.

mentioned earlier. At this point a hypertext document might allow us to go into this subject further. At the press of a button we might be provided with a more detailed account of the model (see Fig. 8.3). There might then be further options. There might be a button that took us to text that described some of the philosophical issues regarding such a model. Another button might provide text that dealt with the model's implications for human error and human reliability, while a further button might provide details of the programming and mathematics of the model.

In essence, what this illustrates is that, while normal text might be linear and passive (see Fig. 8.4), hypertext is not restricted to this format. Hypertext can adopt a branching structure (see Fig. 8.4), where the reader (user) can pursue those topics that are of interest. Alternatively, hypertext can be arranged in a network structure (see Fig. 8.4) that allows readers to jump immediately from topic to topic, without following any set path. Hypertext is not passive, but interacts with the reader, to provide the information that the reader requires.

However, while there might be justifiable enthusiasm for this new medium, its potential may have been overstated in some quarters. Certain obstacles remain as possible detractors. For example, many people still prefer to read from paper than from screens, and further work into either improving present VDU design or developing new display technology may be required

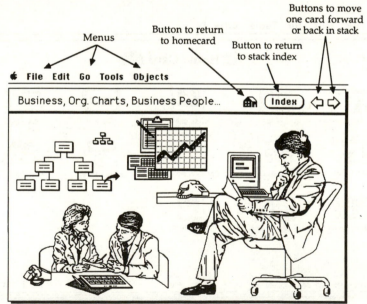

FIG. 8.3. A HyperCard card. Here a number of the buttons in the card are shown. These buttons enable the user to navigate around the system and through stacks of cards. By permission of Apple Computer Inc.

Normal linear text	Branching hypertext	Networked hypertext

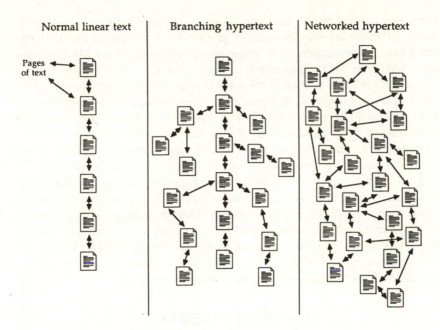

FIG. 8.4.   A representation of a linear text, compared with the structure of a hypertext system where the user can branch to related topics, or a network structure, where no pre-defined linear path exists.

before hypertext can achieve its claimed potential. Furthermore, a new and exciting medium is likely to open the way for better and more useful software documentation (the manuals that arrive with a system and describe its use). However, such a medium will not necessarily solve one of the basic problems with software documentation; it is written from a technical perspective that can bewilder and confuse the user. Hypertext may be of great use in developing on-line documentation for products, but it should not be allowed to distract attention away from the need to improve documentation standards. In other words, hypertext is not a replacement for writing skills, it can only augment well-written documentation, it cannot make bad text easier to understand.

Nevertheless, HyperCard appears to represent a significant step forward. The idea of users creating their own applications is likely to attract further interest, although this too may have its drawbacks.

The Drawbacks of User-Programming Systems

However, the idea of users programming their own systems can, at best, only be seen as a partial solution to the problems of matching a system's

information provision to the user's needs. Although easy-to-use programming languages may be eagerly greeted by many users, not all users
seem likely to appreciate such languages. Furthermore, not all users are
likely to have the time to program their own system.

In some ways the idea of allowing users to program their own system can be
viewed as an easy option. It may prove too tempting for a tired design team to
argue that they do not need to get all of the system to match the user's needs as
the user can program extra sections if they are required.

As an extra option for users, programming languages appear to be
particularly attractive. In an ideal world a system should be designed to
fulfill all of the user's needs, while a programming option should allow
users to customize their system. However, users should not be required to
program major functions into their system. There is a danger that with these
new programming languages users will be expected to do just this, creating
extra work for the user and encouraging non-use of the system. Successful
use of such languages seems more likely where users are encouraged to
program their own system, but are not required to do so.

ADVANCES IN DESIGN

Just as program languages for naïve users need to be easily accessible, then
so the tools and languages that are provided for designers need to help them
to more easily fulfill their role. One tool that has been suggested as an aid
to designing more usable systems is the notion of User Interface Management
Systems (UIMS). The idea behind this approach is that an applications
program can be written that performs all of the functions that might be
required of a system, and a User Interface Management System sits on top
of the application program handling the dialogue with the user.

In essence, a UIMS provides the link between the user and the application
program. This way a large application program can be used with several
different user groups whose needs may differ. For each of these groups,
however, the UIMS differs, providing the dialogue and the functions that
are required in each situation. User Interface Management Systems have
been the focus of research for a number of years now, although they have
yet to be used on a widespread commercial basis (for a discussion of User
Interface Management Systems see Pfaff, 1985).

In the coming years we will not only need to provide tools that help the
designer to build more usable systems, such as User Interface Management
Systems, we will also need to encourage the adoption of user-centred
design practices. In other words, as mentioned in Chapter Six, we appear to
need design methodologies that identify the user as the major focus of
concern within the design process. These methodologies will need to allow

the design team to progress easily through the design process while considering the user. Indeed, the easiest route through the design process should be one which begins with the user's needs, and continually concentrates upon the user.

However, if our methodologies are to fit within the design process we may need to understand, not just the formal technical process of making design decisions, but also the social and political forces that shape design (Whiteside & Wixon, 1987). Furthermore, if we wish to change the design process we may also need to consider how the design process is managed (see Foley, 1986).

It appears probable that methodologies that offer designers an easy route through the design process, and have been developed in the light of what is known about the factors that shape the design and development process, will have the most effect upon the design process. Methodologies that create more work for the design team may lead engineers to use their ingenuity to avoid the steps and stages in the methodology, and hence avoid considering the user. There is little doubt that a great deal of effort is likely to be expended in the coming years developing user-centred design methodologies, but whether these methodologies are adopted and properly used may depend upon what they offer to the designer.

ADVANCES IN ORGANIZATIONAL ISSUES

The problems of implementing computer systems within organizations were considered in the last chapter. The solution that was identified for many of the problems associated with implementation was to involve the user in design. Moreover, it was suggested that organizational issues should be directly considered in design (Eason, 1985a) in order that we might move towards a situation where both technical and social issues are considered together during design and development.

Indeed, during the next few years it seems likely that this socio-technical design philosophy is likely to be adopted within industry, at least within the large IT manufacturers. As part of this movement, it appears probable that users will be involved in design on a more widespread basis. In the more distant future users may be allowed to direct design and make important design decisions. However, the notion of users directing design might be better viewed as a long-term goal, for as Curtis (1986) notes, such changes often take longer to occur than we might initially expect.

The movement towards organizational interfaces and computer support for co-operative work (CSCW, Bannon et al., 1988) seems to be well established within the research literature, although practical examples of such systems or interfaces are uncommon. Malone (1985; 1987) argued the need for such systems, and this was discussed in the last chapter. This argument arises out of the recognition that many users do not work constantly in isolation, but work as part of a group or team. Both Malone (1986) and Shneiderman (1986) have suggested that this is likely to be one of the major developments within HCI in the coming years. However, this development will need theories to guide it, and presently, such theories do not exist (Malone, 1987). Moreover, the development of CSCW is likely to require a cross-disciplinary approach, embracing themes from computer science through to sociology and even anthropology (Bannon et al., 1988).

A further shift of emphasis within HCI is the move towards collaborative systems. The present role of the human and the computer is that of user and tool. However, future systems are expected to be able to play a larger role in the high-level aspects of performing tasks. The idea is that the human-computer role will change, from a user-tool relationship to a user-collaborator relationship, even if the user will still be the dominant influence. This view has been reflected in a number of papers. For example, Kofer (1985) suggests that computers will act as informants and advisors. Turner (1985) suggests that systems, particularly expert systems, will collaborate with the user rather than dominate the interaction which is the present case with some systems. Indeed, it is the work within AI, towards intelligent systems (e.g. McClelland et al., 1986a; 1986b; Shank, 1986) that seems likely to provide this opportunity for systems as collaborators rather than tools.

COMMENTARY

Norman (1987) suggests that HCI is both a research area for cognitive science, as well as being a field for the application of cognitive science, which Norman and others have termed *cognitive engineering*. The purpose of cognitive engineering, according to Norman, is not to replace human factors and ergonomics research, but to combine with them to produce a multi-disciplinary approach to a complex set of problems. Reisner (1987) explains that HCI is not a science, as sciences are the study of natural phenomena, but that the application of a science is called *engineering*. In essence, human-computer interaction is both a field of engineering and a science. Cognitive science is applied to HCI in the form of cognitive engineering, and in turn, the results from HCI feed into cognitive science.

Whiteside and Wixon (1987), however, have questioned this relationship. They question whether the two goals of studying HCI to inform cognitive science and studying human-computer interaction in order to improve interaction are compatible. In essence, Whiteside & Wixon argue that much of *human-computer interaction* research is too theoretical and that it avoids the contextual and practical realities of the process of interaction. They suggest that HCI researchers should be more aggressive in their aims. That is to say, that researchers should state how their research is going to improve some aspect of interaction in concrete terms.

Furthermore, Whiteside and Wixon (1987) suggest that researchers should allow themselves the opportunity to experience the realities of system development:

> To speak effectively to the engineering world, cognitive scientists must develop more sympathy for the engineering perspective...Commit to building a system that will be used in the domain to which your current research project applies. Set definite goals for the usability of such a system in relation to the system that fulfills the same need today. Include in your planning a commitment to a schedule and a development cost. We can guarantee that whether the system developed succeeds or fails, you will come away with a greater appreciation for engineering in the real world and with a more robust model.

One of the major criticisms of a purely theoretical approach, and a criticism that others besides Whiteside and Wixon (1987) have made (e.g. Eason, 1984), is that laboratory evaluations miss out on the social and cognitive context of HCI. The essence of this argument is that in carefully controlling the context in which our experiment takes place we may be separating our experiment from one of the most important variables; context. Indeed, Carroll (1986), while commenting on analytical techniques, although the comment equally applies to over-controlled experiments, has even stated that we should guard against this "...misplaced and superficial scientific rigour".

These criticisms do not necessarily imply that we should totally avoid approaches to HCI such as modelling. Analytic techniques may be used as the basis for developing the first prototype, as part of iterative design (although doubt has been cast upon this in Chapters Four and Six). However, there is a certain scepticism within industry about the value of research papers that report approaches that are heavily theoretically laden, yet where the practical advantages of the approach are added almost as a passing remark. There is certainly nothing wrong with approaches to HCI that are purely theoretical and are not intended to be applied—this is pure research. But maybe researchers need to more clearly distinguish the purpose of their research, and not shy away from stating that it is purely theoretical if this is the case.

In the coming years, if cognitive engineering is to make a practical contribution to *human-computer interaction*, it may need to look further than analytical grammars. Cognitive engineering may need to consider both the cognitive context of HCI and its social and organizational aspects. Indeed, books such as Norman and Draper's (1986) *User Centred System Design* already do this. The critical statements of Carroll and Rosson (1985) and Whiteside and Wixon (1987) do not suggest that there is any general opposition to cognitive science in HCI. Such researchers are best viewed as well-informed critics who are proposing practical goals that should guide the future development of cognitive engineering within human-computer interaction.

SUMMARY

It has been suggested that the workstation of the future will contain a high resolution display, with icons and windows. The operations of the workstation will be accompanied by voice annotation, and most notably, the workstation will be equipped for voice input and output. The interesting aspect of this perspective is that it sees a general widening of the physical bandwidth as the different means of input and output to a computer system are expected to increase.

As the number of input devices increases the difficulties of choosing a device for a particular task are also likely to become worse. It may be that we require a simple unified theory, possibly drawn from the ergonomics or human factors literature, that will show us how to narrow down our options to a small number of potentially suitable input devices. In essence, we appear to need theories that will relate tasks and task behaviour to optimal physical actions and the devices that can best match these actions.

One of the most significant changes in human-computer dialogue that can be identified is that various dialogue styles appear to be decreasing in popularity while others are becoming more common. While dialogue styles such as command language and form fill-in are always likely to be with us to some extent, their use within everyday systems looks set to decrease in future years. On the other hand, styles such as direct manipulation together with various explanatory metaphors and icons are being used on a more widespread basis.

Adaptive dialogues are sometimes also addressed under the titles adaptive interfaces or adaptive systems. There are a number of important issues associated with adaptive dialogues, such as how to adapt to the user, when to adapt, whether adaption is under system control or the user's, etc. The major concern that is repeatedly raised is the issue of the criteria for adaption. In other words, which groups of users should the system adapt for. This inevitably raises issues of classifying users as to whether they are novices or experts. Classification is something of a controversial issue and has been described as a "cheap solution."

Some of the features of human dialogue, such as natural language and the ability to negotiate definitions and repair dialogue failures are sometimes considered to be desirable qualities of future human-computer dialogue. There is general agreement that intelligent systems are required if these features are to become a practical and commercial reality.

The term *intelligent* is often used loosely within computing to mean a sophisticated system, rather than one that necessarily attempts to emulate human cognitive abilities. It has been suggested that intelligent systems should; carry out menial tasks, automate routine tasks, provide assistance with more complex tasks, provide easy access to tools, provide status information, provide on-line assistance and documentation, and allow multi-tasking.

An expert system is (Goodall, 1985): "...a computer system that operates by applying an inference engine to a body of specialist expertise represented in the form of knowledge." In essence, an expert system should be able to make the same sorts of judgements as human experts. Many expert systems have failed as they treat experts as if they were novices, often providing laborious question and answer dialogues. Difficulties with the human-computer dialogue appears to be one of the major causes of the failure of many expert systems.

One problem we can identify with some of the modelling or analytic techniques is that they deal with only one of the gulfs of HCI identified by Norman (1986; 1987). Furthermore, Young and Simon (1987) suggest that we need to consider how users plan their actions. Following criticisms, there is likely to be continuing work into the development of grammars that are easier to understand and use. Moreover, the role of analytic techniques within design will probably become progressively better defined.

A *computational model* is quite simply a model that can be run as a program on a computer. One such model has been developed by Marsden (1989) along the lines of certain principles and cognitive processes suggested by Reason (1988). This model has been shown to accurately simulate human guessing and error-making behaviour. The model has two potential uses. First, it might be used as the basis for a mechanism that checks users to ensure that they are not making errors. Second, the model provides a means by which computer systems might be made to make fairly accurate decisions with incomplete knowledge.

One development that seems likely to gain more credence in the coming years is the idea of allowing users to program parts of their own system. However, not all users seem likely to appreciate such languages. Further-more, not all users are likely to have the time to program their own system.

One tool that has been suggested as an aid to designing more usable systems is the notion of User Interface Management Systems (UIMS). The idea behind this approach is that an applications program can be written that performs all of the functions that might be required of a system, and a User Interface Management System sits on top of the applications program handling the dialogue with the user.

We appear to need design methodologies that identify the user as the major focus of concern within the design process. These methodologies will need to allow the design team to progress easily through the design process while considering the user. Indeed, the easiest route through the design process should be one which begins with the user's needs, and continually concentrates upon the user.

During the next few years it seems likely that this socio-technical design philosophy is likely to be adopted within industry, at least within the large IT manufacturers. As part of this movement, it appears probable that users will be involved in design on a more widespread basis.

The movement towards organizational interfaces seems to be well established within the research literature, although practical examples of such interfaces are uncommon. Both Malone (1986) and Shneiderman (1986) have suggested that this is likely to be one of the major developments within HCI in the coming years. However, theories are required to guide this development.

The present role of humans and computers is that of user and tool (although these tools are certainly not value-free, and some may not be well-designed tools). However, future systems are expected to be able to play a larger role in the high-level aspects of performing tasks. Future systems may perform the role of collaborator rather than tool.

The purpose of cognitive engineering, according to Norman (1987), is not to replace human factors and ergonomics research, but to combine with them. It is argued, however, that much of HCI research is too theoretical and that it avoids the contextual and practical realities of the process of interaction. One of the major criticisms of a purely theoretical approach is that laboratory evaluations miss out on the social and cognitive context of *human-computer interaction*. In the coming years, cognitive engineering may need to consider both the cognitive context of HCI and its social and organizational aspects.

A SELECTIVE ANNOTATED BIBLIOGRAPHY

Bannon, L. J., Bjørn-Andersen, N., & Due-Thomsen, B. (1987). Computer support for co-operative work: An appraisal and critique. In H. J. Bullinger & B. Shackel (Eds.), *Human-computer interaction–Interact '87: Proceedings of the second IFIP conference on human-computer interaction, Stuttgart*. Amsterdam: North-Holland. *The authors discuss the development of computer support for co-operative work (CSCW). CSCW is a recognition that people do not work in isolation, but work together in teams or groups. The authors discuss the need for a cross-disciplinary approach to CSCW and suggest that it is likely to become an increasingly important issue in the next few years. This paper is both easy-to-read and interesting.*

Eisenstadt, M. (1983). A user-friendly software environment for the novice programmer. *Communications of the ACM, 26 (12)*, 1058–1064. *The author describes SOLO, a programming language aimed at novice programmers. This is an example of a usable, if limited programming language. Unlike most papers that describe programming languages, this is readable and interesting.*

Good, M. D., Whiteside, J. A., Wixon, D. R., & Jones, S. J. (1984). Building a user-driven interface. *Communications of the ACM, 27 (10)*, 1032–1043. *The development of an adaptive system is described. This system was designed and iteratively refined to be able to recognize commands that users themselves generated..*

Hayes-Roth, F. (1984). Knowledge-based expert systems–the state of the art in the US. In J. Fox (Ed.), *Expert Systems: State of the art report.* Maidenhead: Pergamon Infotech. *The author outlines the characteristics of expert systems and charts the development of expert systems towards the end of the century. He suggests that many commercial expert systems will fail, but a few will prove to be considerable successes.*

Kidd, A. L. & Cooper, M. B. (1985). Man-machine interface issues in the construction and use of an expert system. *International Journal of Man-Machine Studies, 22,* 91–102. *It is suggested that the human-computer interface is a major determinant of the success of an expert system. Three issues are considered; knowledge acquisition, knowledge representation and the communications interface (the way that knowledge is acquired and represented has implications for how the system will interact with its user). This is an interesting and readable paper.*

Kofer, G. R. (1985). Future uses of future offices. In A. F. Monk (Ed.), *Fundamentals of human-computer interaction.* London: Academic Press. *This unusual paper does not discuss issues in the normal manner, but provides a long example of the experiences of a family buying a house, using the office facilities of the future. The aim of this short paper is to demonstrate how future developments might affect working practices, rather than argue for one approach or another. This is a stimulating and original paper.*

Marshall, C. J., Christie, B., & Gardiner, M. M. (1987a). Assessment of trends in the technology and techniques of human-computer interaction. In M. M. Gardiner & B. Christie, *Applying cognitive psychology to user interface design.* Chichester: Wiley. *The authors consider the trends within HCI, from interactional hardware and software, to natural language, shared-initiative dialogues, and the standards that might be adopted in HCI.*

Reisner, P. (1987). Discussion: HCI, what is it and what research is needed? In J. M. Carroll (Ed.), *Interfacing thought: Cognitive aspects of human-computer interaction.* Cambridge, Massachusetts: MIT Press. *The author discusses the future of human-computer interaction and suggests that HCI is an engineering discipline, where many of the terms and concepts have still to be tightly defined. She considers empirical testing and analytical techniques and their role within HCI, and then goes on to consider some of the research that is required in the area of modelling (analytic) techniques.*

Shackel, B. (1985). Ergonomics in information technology in Europe—a review. *Behaviour & Information Technology, 4 (4),* 263–287. *This paper is the result of a large number of discussions the author had with many researchers throughout Europe. The author outlines 25 areas of research interest where more attention needs to be directed, and finishes by comparing research in Europe to research in the USA.*

Whiteside, J. & Wixon, D. (1987). Discussion: Improving human-computer interaction—a quest for cognitive science. In J. M. Carroll (Ed.), *Interfacing thought: Cognitive aspects of human-computer interaction.* Cambridge, Massachusetts: MIT Press. *The authors question whether the goals of cognitive science and of HCI engineering are compatible. They suggest that many approaches to research miss out on the context of HCI and that approaches that model the user's goals are mistaken, as most users do not have well-defined goals or goal hierarchies. This is an excellent paper that can only be described as essential reading for the academic researcher.*

Exercises

Chapter One

1. Outline the main areas of research within HCI.
2. Describe the main reasons for the growth of research into HCI.
3. Describe two of the major disciplines that contribute towards the study of HCI.
4. Discuss the contributions that the major disciplines offer to the study of HCI.

Chapter Two

1. Choose one task and discuss suitable input and output devices for that task.
2. Contrast three types of input device, stating their major advantages and disadvantages.
3. Critically discuss screen design guidelines.
4. Explain and discuss a novel input device or technology.
5. Outline the major processes involved in automatic speech recognition.
6. Examine the different methods of speech generation.
7. Discuss the physical, health and ergonomic issues associated with using visual display units.

Chapter Three

1. Discuss the advantages and disadvantages of both pragmatic and semantic approaches to studying human-computer dialogue.
2. Study a user (a friend, colleague or fellow student) using an unfamiliar computer or piece of software. Record a short exchange of dialogue and compare semantic interpretations of the dialogue to possible pragmatic analyses.
3. Discuss why dialogue style is an important factor in HCI.
4. Outline the relative merits and drawbacks of direct manipulation interfaces.
5. Compare and contrast dialogue design guidelines.
6. Discuss the critical factors that distinguish human dialogue from human-computer dialogue.
7. Assess the work of Barnard and Hammond and outline their major findings.

Chapter Four

1. Trace the origins of the cognitive approach to HCI.
2. Compare and contrast Norman's (1986) approximate theory of action to Moran's (1981) levels of interaction, used in Command Language Grammar.
3. Outline the major features of a user's mental model.
4. Describe, using examples, how the term *user model* can be used, as well as the purposes that user models can fulfill.
5. Use a modelling (or analytic) technique to describe user interaction with part of a system. Discuss the technique's advantages and assess its shortcomings.
6. Describe two modelling techniques and outline their relative advantages.
7. Discuss the use of metaphors in HCI.

Chapter Five

1. Compare and contrast the cognitive approach to the usability approach within HCI.
2. Discuss the factors that may contribute to the usability of a system.
3. Use Shackel's definition of usability to critically consider a system.
4. Evaluate a system using three measures of usability. Discuss the types of information that these measures produce and suggest how they might be used to contribute towards improving the usability of a system.
5. Outline the major differences between any four methods of evaluation.

6. Describe how different *measures* of evaluation might be used as part of the various *methods* of evaluation.
7. Perform a User Needs Analysis using the checklist provided. Critically consider the use of such checklists.

Chapter Six

1. Describe the major advantages and disadvantages of the mathematical approach to the problems of design.
2. Discuss the role of formal methods in design.
3. Outline the notion of socio-technical design and examine its usefulness.
4. Guidelines are the most useful means by which human factors can be incorporated into design: Discuss critically.
5. Discuss present design practice.
6. Describe a system using a formal specification technique. Comment on the usefulness of the notation.
7. Describe and critically assess one design methodology.

Chapter Seven

1. Contrast Bjørn-Andersen's view of an ideal system with the approach suggested by Westin et al. (1985).
2. Discuss the role of an organizational interface within an office environment.
3. Outline the major changes that can occur when a system is implemented within an organization.
4. Describe the possible advantages and disadvantages of different forms of user support. Pay particular attention to the role of the local expert.
5. Assess the work of Bjørn-Andersen et al. (1986), and outline their major findings.
6. Discuss the impact of computer systems upon the user's tasks.
7. Describe the relationships between control, discretion, power and conflict between user groups.
8. Assess the likely effect of Eason's (1985b) suggested procedure upon the design and implementation of a system.

Chapter Eight

1. Discuss the ways in which the study of HCI is likely to change in the coming years.
2. Outline the probable development of interactional hardware and software for the next 10 years.

3. Critically discuss the role of cognitive science within HCI research.
4. Describe the contribution that artificial intelligence might make to HCI.
5. Programming is one of the most important areas for HCI research to address: Discuss.
6. Contrast current design practice with the design methodologies for the year 2000.

Glossary

Conceptual Model. Norman and Draper (1986) suggest that conceptual models are a form of mental model. They can be of two types; a model of the system formed by the designer (the *Design Model*), or a model of the system constructed by the user (the *User's Model*).

Design Methodology. In Chapter Six it was suggested that a design methodology is a process that is a departure, in some fundamental respect, from present design practice. This process is usually supported by manuals, workshops, automated tools, and alike. It is not simply a list of suggested activities for design, but an active procedure that is supported and encouraged.

Dialogue. Understanding dialogue is not a straightforward case of assigning meanings to the terms and phrases employed by the parties concerned. Meanings depend not only upon the words themselves, but also upon the context in which they are communicated and the recipients knowledge of language and the world generally. Consequently, dialogue might be thought of as the exchange of symbols between two or more parties, as well as being the meanings that the participants in the communicative process assign to these symbols. Human dialogue, however, is richer than this definition might imply. It involves active listening and responding. That is to say, that we search for information in another's speech and look to map this information onto our present knowledge structures.

Expert System.   A working definition has been suggested by Goodall (1985): "An expert system is a computer system that operates by applying an inference engine to a body of specialist expertise represented in the form of knowledge." According to Hayes-Roth (1985), it is ultimately intended that these systems should be able to: solve complex problems as well as or better than human experts, reason heuristically using what experts consider to be effective rules of thumb, manipulate and reason about symbolic descriptions, function with data that contains errors using judgement rules, contemplate multiple, competing hypotheses simultaneously, explain why they are asking questions, justify their conclusions. However, to regard some of these characteristics as achievements maybe somewhat premature.

Formal Method.   A formal method is quite simply a notation for describing some aspect of a system or user behaviour. The idea of such a method is that it breaks down the system's or the user's behaviour into manageable chunks, and shows where inconsistencies arise, or where the task or system is too complex.

HyperCard™.   A commercial programming package aimed at non-expert users. The system is based upon a card metaphor. The user creates cards which define the application. These cards are arranged in stacks. Using the features that are present in existing stacks, supplied with the system, together with the HyperCard programming language, HyperTalk™, stacks of cards, which form the application, can be constructed.

Hypertext.   In a normal document we proceed from beginning to end, with no opportunity to stop at a particular topic and examine it in more detail. In essence, normal text is *linear* and *passive*. Hypertext, on the other hand, allows the reader to pause at a particular topic and to explore it further. That is to say, that texts can be provided to supplement a linear path. Alternatively, hypertext can be arranged in a network fashion that allows the reader to move in any direction, from text to text.

Mental Model.   A mental model is an internal model that is used to guide behaviour at the interface (and in other situations). Norman (1983c) explains this in the following way: "In interacting with the environment, with others, and with the artifacts of technology, people form internal, mental models of themselves and of the things with which they are inter-acting. These models provide predictive and explanatory power for under-standing the interaction."

Organizational Interface.   Malone (1985; 1987) has suggested that a user interface should be considered as those: "...parts of a computer program that connect a human user to the capabilities provided by the computer". While an organizational interface should be considered as those: "parts of a computer system that connect human users to each other and to the capabilities provided by computers."

Programmable User Model.   A programmable user model is, as the term suggests, a model of the user that can operate the system which it has been developed to reflect. In other words, the idea is that designers might, not only write their systems, but also write a program (a programmable user model) that should run the system. Thimbleby (1986) argues that this might help to redress the balance between the system and the user, as the designer has to focus upon the user's immediate needs in performing a task on the system.

System Image.   Norman and Draper (1986) suggest that the system image is the image conveyed to the user via the system (its physical appearance and the nature of its interaction) and its associated documentation. They suggest that one of the primary objectives in design should be to construct a coherent and consistent system image.

Task-action Mapping.   The term *mapping* comes from the discipline of mathematics, where it is used to mean associating one element from one set to another element from another set. In cognitive terms, we say that we *map* our psychological variables to appropriate physical variables, which means almost the same as saying that we *relate* our psychological variables to the physical variables of the task.

User-centred Design.   The term *user-centred* design is a statement of intention; the desire to make the user the central focus of the design and development process. System-centred design approaches are those that concentrate upon the needs of the system (i.e. what information does our system need if it is to operate effectively?) rather than the needs of the user. A user-centred approach is one that begins with the needs of the user and continually focuses upon these needs through each stage of the design and development process.

User Model.   Clowes (1987) suggests that there are four types of user model: the designer's model of the user, the user's model of the task, the user's model of the system, and the system's embedded model of the user. In addition to this, Norman and Draper (1986) suggest that the term *user model* can mean either an individual user's model, or a generalized "typical user" model that a designer might use during the formulation of a design model.

References

Aitkenhead, A. M. & Slack, J. M. (Eds.) (1985). *Issues in Cognitive Modelling.* Hillsdale, New Jersey: Lawrence Erlbaum Associates Inc.

Albert, A. E. (1982). The effect of graphic input devices on performance in a cursor positioning task. *Proceedings of the Human Factors Society,* 54–58.

Albrecht, G. (1979). Defusing technical change in juvenile courts: The probation officer's struggle for professional autonomy. *Sociology of Work and Occupation, 6 (3),* 259–282.

Alexander, H. (1986). ECS–A technique for the formal specification and rapid prototyping of human-computer interaction. In M. D. Harrison & A. F. Monk (Eds.), *People & computers: Designing for usability. Proceedings of the second conference of the BCS HCI specialist group.* Cambridge: Cambridge University Press.

Allen, R. B. (1982). Cognitive factors in human interaction with computers. In A. N. Badre & B. Shneiderman (Eds.), *Directions in human-computer interaction.* Norwood, New Jersey: Ablex Publishing Corporation.

Anderson, J. R. (1983). *The architecture of cognition.* Cambridge, Massachusetts: Harvard University Press.

Anderson, N. S. & Reitman Olson, J. (Eds.) (1985). Methods for designing software to fit human needs and capabilities. Proceedings of the workshop of software human factors, Washington, D.C. Excerpt in R. M. Baecker & W. A. S. Buxton (Eds.), (1987). *Readings in human-computer interaction: A multidisciplinary approach.* Los Altos, California: Morgan Kaufmann.

Badre, A. N. (1982). Designing chunks for sequentially displayed information. In A. N. Badre & B. Shneiderman (Eds.), *Directions in human-computer interaction.* Norwood, New Jersey: Ablex.

Baecker, R. M. & Buxton, W. A. S. (Eds.) (1987). *Readings in human-computer interaction: A multidisciplinary approach.* Los Altos, California: Morgan Kaufmann.

Bailey, P. (1985). Speech communication: The problem and some solutions. In A. F. Monk (Ed.), *Fundamentals of human-computer interaction*. London: Academic Press.

Baker, C. A. (1977). *An investigation of man-computer interaction in an on-line bibliographic retrieval system*. Unpublished manuscript: Loughborough University of Technology Library.

Bannon, L. J. (1986a). Helping users help each other. In D. A. Norman & S. W. Draper (Eds.), *User centred system design: New perspectives on human-computer interaction*. Hillsdale, New Jersey: Lawrence Erlbaum Associates Inc.

Bannon, L. J. (1986b). Issues in design: Some notes. In D. A. Norman & S. W. Draper (Eds.), *User centred system design: New perspectives on human-computer interaction*. Hillsdale, New Jersey: Lawrence Erlbaum Associates Inc.

Bannon, L. J., Bjørn-Andersen, N., & Due-Thomsen, B. (1988). Computer support for co-operative work: An appraisal and critique. In H. J. Bullinger et al. (Eds.), *Information technology for organizational systems*. Amsterdam: Elsevier.

Bannon, L. J. & O'Malley, C. (1984). Problems in evaluation of human-computer interfaces: a case study. In B. Shackel (Ed.), *Human-computer interaction—Interact '84: Proceedings of the first IFIP conference on human-computer interaction, London*. Amsterdam: Elsevier.

Barker, P. G. & Najah, M. (1985). Implementing pictorial interfaces using a high resolution digitizer. *International Journal of Man-Machine Studies, 23*, 153–173.

Barker, P. G., Najah, M., & Manji, K. (1987). Pictorial communication with computers. In H. J. Bullinger & B. Shackel (Eds.), *Human-computer interaction—Interact '87: Proceedings of the second IFIP conference on human-computer interaction, Stuttgart*. Amsterdam: North-Holland.

Barnard, P. J. (1985). Interacting cognitive subsystems: A psycholinguistic approach to short-term memory. In A. Ellis (Ed.), *Progress in the psychology of language*. Hillsdale, New Jersey: Lawrence Erlbaum Associates Inc.

Barnard, P. J. (1987). Cognitive resources and learning of human-computer dialogues. In J. M. Carroll (Ed.), *Interfacing thought: Cognitive aspects of human-computer interaction*. Cambridge, Massachusetts: MIT Press.

Barnard, P. J. & Hammond, N. V. (1982). Usability and its multiple determination for the occasional user of interactive systems. In Williams (Ed.), *Pathways to the information society: Proceedings of the 6th international conference on computer communication, London*. Amsterdam: North-Holland.

Barnard, P. J. & Hammond, N. V. (1983). *Cognitive contexts and interactive communication*. Unpublished manuscript: IBM Hursley Human Factors Laboratory Report.

Barnard, P. J., Hammond, N. V., Morton, J., Long, J. B., & Clark, I. A. (1981). Consistency and compatibility in human-computer dialogue. *International Journal of Man-Machine Studies, 15*, 87–134.

Benbasat, I. & Wand, Y. (1984). A structured approach to designing human-computer dialogues. *International Journal of Man-Machine Studies, 21 (2)*, 105–126.

Bennett, J. L. (1984). Managing to meet usability requirements: Establishing and meeting software development goals. In J. L. Bennett, D. Case, J. Sandelin, & M.

Smith (Eds.), *Usability issues and health concerns*. Englewood Cliffs, New Jersey: Prentice-Hall.

Bennet, J. L. (1986). Observations on meeting usability goals for software products. *Behaviour & Information Technology, 5*, 183–193.

Bertino, E. (1985). Design issues in interactive user interfaces. *Interfaces in Computing, 3*, 37–53.

Bjørn-Andersen, N. (1984). Training for subjection or participation. In B. Shackel (Ed.), *Human-computer interaction–Interact '84: Proceedings of the first IFIP conference on human-computer interaction, London*. Amsterdam: North-Holland.

Bjørn-Andersen, N. (1985). Are 'human factors' human? In N. Bevan & D. Murray (Eds), *Man-machine interaction: State of the art report*. Maidenhead: Pergamon Infotech.

Bjørn-Andersen, N. (1986). Understanding the nature of the office for the design of third wave office systems. In M. D. Harrison & A. F. Monk (Eds.), *People & computers: Designing for usability. Proceedings of the second conference of the BCS HCI specialist group*. Cambridge: Cambridge University Press.

Bjørn-Andersen, N., Eason, K. D., & Robey, D. (Eds.) (1986). *Managing computer impact: An international study of management and organizations*. Norwood, New Jersey: Ablex.

Black, J. B., Kay, D. S., & Soloway, E. M. (1987). Goal and plan knowledge representations: From stories to text editors and programs. In J. M. Carroll (Ed.), *Interfacing thought: Cognitive aspects of human-computer interaction*. Cambridge, Massachusetts: MIT Press.

Bleser, T. & Foley, J. (1982). Towards specifying and evaluating the human factors of user-computer interfaces. In *Human factors in computer systems, conference proceedings, Gaithersburg, Maryland*. ACM.

Boddy, D. & Buchanan, D. A. (1982). Information technology and the experience of work. In L. J. Bannon, Barry & Holst (Eds.), *Information technology impact on the way of life*. Dublin: Tycooly International.

Bolt, R. A. (1980). Put that there: Voice and gesture at the graphics interface. *Computer Graphics* ACM 0-8971-021-4/40/007-262, 262–270.

Branscomb, L. M. (1983). The computers debt to science. *Perspectives in Computing, 3*, 4–19.

Brauninger, U. & Grandjean, E. L. (1983). Lighting characteristics of visual display terminals from an ergonomic point of view. In A. Janda (Ed.), *Human factors in computer systems: Proceedings of the CHI '83 conference, Boston*. Amsterdam: North-Holland.

Breuker, J., Winkels, R., & Sandberg, J. (1987). Coaching strategies for help systems: EUROHELP. In *ESPRIT 1987, conference proceedings, Milan, Italy*, 963–972.

Brooke, J. B. (1986). Usability engineering in office production development. In M. D. Harrison & A. F. Monk (Eds.), *People & computers: Designing for usability. Proceedings of the second conference of the BCS HCI specialist group*. Cambridge: Cambridge University Press.

Burke, P. (1980). *Sociology and history*. London: George Allen & Unwin.

Bury, K. F. (1984). The iterative development of usable computer interfaces. In B.

Shackel (Ed.), *Human-computer interaction–Interact '84: Proceedings of the first IFIP conference on human-computer interaction, London.* Amsterdam: North-Holland.

Bury, K. F., Boyle, J. M., Evey, R. J., & Neal A. S. (1982). Windowing vs scrolling on a visual display terminal. In *Human factors in computer systems, conference proceedings, Gaithersburg, Maryland.* ACM.

Buxton, W. A. S. (1983). Lexical and pragmatic issues of input structures. *Computer Graphics, 17 (2),* 31–37.

Buxton, W. A. S. (1986a). Human-computer interaction in the year 2000: A contribution to a panel discussion. In M. Mantei & P. Orbeton (Eds.), *Human factors in computer systems–III: Proceedings of the CHI '86 conference, Boston.* Amsterdam: Elsevier.

Buxton, W. A. S. (1986b). There's more to interaction that meets the eye: Some issues in manual input. In D. A. Norman & S. W. Draper (Eds.), *User centred system design: New perspectives on human-computer interaction.* Hillsdale, New Jersey: Lawrence Erlbaum Associates Inc.

Buxton, W. A. S. & Myers, B. A. (1986). A study of two-handed input. In M. Mantei & P. Orbeton (Eds.), *Human factors in computer systems–III: Proceedings of the CHI '86 conference, Boston.* Amsterdam: Elsevier.

Card, S. K. (1982). User perceptual mechanisms in the search of computer command menus. In *Human factors in computer systems, conference proceedings, Gaithersburg, Maryland.* ACM.

Card, S. K., English, W. K., & Burr, B. J. (1978). Evaluation of mouse, rate controlled isometric joystick, step keys, and task keys for text selection on a CRT. *Ergonomics, 21 (8),* 601–613.

Card, S. K., Moran, T. P., & Newell, A. (1980). Computer text-editing: An information-processing analysis of a routine cognitive skill. *Cognitive Psychology, 12,* 32–74.

Card, S. K., Moran, T. P., & Newell, A. (1983). *The psychology of human-computer interaction.* Hillsdale, New Jersey: Lawrence Erlbaum Associates Inc.

Carroll, J. M. (1986). Analytical performance models: A contribution to a panel discussion. In M. Mantei & P. Orbeton (Eds.), *Human factors in computer systems–III: Proceedings of the CHI '86 conference, Boston.* Amsterdam: Elsevier.

Carroll, J. M. (Ed.) (1987). *Interfacing thought: Cognitive aspects of human-computer interaction.* Cambridge, Massachusetts, USA: MIT Press.

Carroll, J. M. & Mack, R. L. (1985). Metaphor, computing systems, and active learning. *International Journal of Man–Machine Studies, 22,* 39–57.

Carroll, J. M. & Rosson, M. B. (1985). Usability specifications as a tool in iterative development. In H. R. Hartson (Ed.), *Advances in human-computer interaction.* Norwood, New Jersey: Ablex.

Carroll, J. M. & Thomas, J. C. (1982). Metaphor and the cognitive representation of computer systems. *IEEE Transactions on Systems, Man, and Cybernetics, SMC-12 (2),* 107–116.

Carroll, J. M., Thomas, J. C., & Malhotra, A. (1980). Presentation and representation in design problem solving. *American Journal of Psychology, 93,* 269–284.

Charniak, E. & McDermott, D. (1985). *Introduction to artificial intelligence.* Wokingham: Addison-Wesley Publishing Company.

Cheng, P. W., Holyoak, K. J., Nisbett, R. E., & Oliver, L. M. (1986). Pragmatic versus syntactic approaches to training deductive reasoning. *Cognitive Psychology, 18,* 293–328.

Chomsky, N. (1957). *Syntactic Structures.* The Hague: Moulton & Co.

Clark, F., Drake, P., Kapp, M., & Wong, P. (1984). User acceptance of information technology through prototyping. In B. Shackel (Ed.), *Human-computer interaction–Interact '84: Proceedings of the first IFIP conference on human-computer interaction, London.* Amsterdam: North-Holland.

Clarke, A. A. (1986). A three-level human-computer interface model. *International Journal of Man-Machine Studies, 24,* 503–547.

Clowes, I. (1987). User models. Talk given at Alvey Human Interface Club meeting, 11th May. Reported by K. Robinson in *Alvey Newsletter.*

Computer-Disability News (1984). Featured product: Eye typer allows eye gaze to run computers. Winter 1984–1985, *1(3).*

Cooley, M. J. E. (1987). Human centred systems: An urgent problem for systems designers. *AI & Society, 1 (2),* 37–46.

Coombs, M. & Alty, J. (1980). Face-to-face guidance of university computer users II: Characterizing advisory interactions. *International Journal of Man-Machine Studies, 12,* 407–429.

Conte, S. D., Dunsmore, H. E., & Shen, V. Y. (1986). *Software engineering metrics and models.* Wokingham: Benjamin/Cummings.

Curtis, W. (1986). Human-computer interaction in the year 2000: A contribution to a panel discussion. In M. Mantei & P. Orbeton (Eds.), *Human factors in computer systems–III: Proceedings of the CHI '86 Conference, Boston.* Amsterdam: Elsevier.

Cypher, A. (1986). The structure of users' activities. In D. A. Norman & S. W. Draper (Eds.), *User centred system design: New perspectives on human-computer interaction.* Hillsdale, New Jersey: Lawrence Erlbaum Associates Inc.

Damodaran, L. (1983). User involvement in system design. *Data Processing, 25 (6),* 6–13.

Damodaran, L. (1986). User support. In N. Bjørn-Andersen, K. D. Eason, & D. Robey (Eds.) (1987). *Managing computer impact: An international study of Management and organizations.* Norwood, New Jersey: Ablex.

Danchak, M. M. (1977). Alphanumeric displays for the man-process interface. *Advances in instrumentation, 32, ISA conference, Niagara Falls, Oct. 1977, 1,* 197–213.

Diaper, D. (1986). Identifying the knowledge requirements of an expert system's natural language processing interface. In M. D. Harrison & A. F. Monk (Eds.), *People & computers: Designing for usability. Proceedings of the second conference of the BCS HCI specialist group.* Cambridge: Cambridge University Press.

Draper, S. W. (1986). Display managers as the basis for user-machine communication. In D. A. Norman & S. W. Draper (Eds.), *User centred system design: New perspectives on human-computer interaction.* Hillsdale, New Jersey: Lawrence Erlbaum Associates Inc.

Duda, R. O., Gaschnig, J., & Hart, P. E. (1979). Model design in the Prospector consultant system for mineral exploration. In D. Michie (Ed.), *Expert systems in the microelectronic age*. Edinburgh: Edinburgh University Press.

Duncan, W. J. (1978). *Organizational behaviour*. Boston: Houghton Mifflin Co.

Durrett, J. & Stimmel, T. (1982). A production system model for human-computer interaction. In *Human factors in computer systems, conference proceedings, Gaithersburg, Maryland*. ACM.

Eason, K. D. (1976). Understanding the naive computer user. *The Computer Journal, 19 (1)*, 3–7.

Eason, K. D. (1983a). Methodological issues in the study of human factors in teleinformatic systems. *Behaviour & Information Technology, 2 (4)*, 357–364.

Eason, K. D. (1983b). User-centred design for information technology systems. *Physical Technology, 14*, 219–224.

Eason, K. D. (1984). Towards the experimental study of usability. *Behaviour & Information Technology, 3 (2)*, 133–143.

Eason, K. D. (1985a). Emerging concepts in the implementation of I. T. systems. In N. Bevan & D. Murray (Eds.), *Man-machine interaction: State of the art report*. Maidenhead: Pergamon Infotech.

Eason K. D. (1985b). *User analysis, user participation and organizational change*. Unpublished notes distributed during workshop given at HCI '85 conference, University of East Anglia, Norwich.

Eason, K. D., Damodaran, L., & Stewart, T. F. M. (1975). Interface problems in man-computer interaction. In E. Mumford & Sackman (Eds.), *Human choice and computers*. Amsterdam: North-Holland.

Eason, K. D., Harker, S. D. P., Raven, P. F., Brailsford, J. R., & Cross, A. D. (1987). A user-centred approach to the design of a knowledge-based system. In H. J. Bullinger & B. Shackel (Eds.), *Human-computer interaction– Interact'87: Proceedings of the second IFIP conference on human-computer interaction, Stuttgart*. Amsterdam: North Holland.

Edmonds, E. A. & Guest, S. (1984). The SYNICS2 user interface manager. In B. Shackel (Ed.), *Human-computer interaction–Interact '84: Proceedings of the first IFIP conference on human-computer interaction, London*. Amsterdam: North-Holland.

Eisenstadt, M. (1983). A user-friendly software environment for the novice programmer. *Communications of the ACM, 26 (12)*, 1058–1064.

Elzer, P., Borchers, H. W., Siebert, H., Weisang, C., & Zinser, K. (1987). MAR-GRET–A pre-prototype of an 'intelligent' process monitoring system. In *ESPRIT 1987, conference proceedings, Milan*, 973–984.

Embley, D. W. (1978). Empirical and formal language design applied to a unified control construct for interactive computing. *International Journal of Man-Machine Studies, 10*, 197–216.

Emmons, W. H. & Hirsch, R. (1982). Thirty millimeter keyboards: How good are they? *Proceedings of the Human Factors Society*, 425–429.

Ericsson, K. A. & Simon, H. A. (1980). Verbal reports as data. *Psychological Review, 87 (3)*, 215–251.

Ewing, J., Mehrabanzad, S., Sheck, S., Ostroff, D., & Shneiderman, B. (1986). An experimental comparison of a mouse and arrow-jump keys for an interactive encyclopedia. *International Journal of Man-Machine Studies, 23*.

Foley, J. D. (1986). Managing the design of user-computer interfaces: A contribution to a panel discussion. In M. Mantei & P. Orbeton (Eds.), *Human factors in computer systems–III: Proceedings of the CHI '86 conference, Boston.* Amsterdam Netherlands: Elsevier.

Foley, J. D. & van Dam, A. (1982). *Fundamentals of interactive computer graphics.* Reading, Massachusetts: Addison-Wesley.

Fox, J. (1984). Aims and objectives. In J. Fox (Ed.), *Expert systems: State of the art report.* Maidenhead: Pergamon Infotech.

Gaines, B. R. & Shaw, M. L. G. (1983). Dialogue engineering. In M. E. Sime & M. J. Coombs (Eds.), *Designing for human-computer communication.* London: Academic Press.

Gaines, B. R. & Shaw, M. L. G. (1984). *The art of computer conversation: A new medium for communication.* Englewood Cliffs, New Jersey: Prentice-Hall.

Gaines, B. R. & Shaw, M. L. G. (1986a). From timesharing to the sixth generation: The development of human computer: Part 1. *International Journal of Man-Machine Studies, 24,* 1–27.

Gaines, B. R. & Shaw, M. L. G. (1986b). Foundations of dialogue engineering: the development of human computer: Part 2. *International Journal of Man-Machine Studies, 24,* 101–123.

Gardiner, M. M. & Christie, B. (1987). Communication failure at the person-machine interface: The human factors aspects. In R. G. Reilly (Ed.), *Communication failure in dialogue and discourse.* Amsterdam: Elsevier.

Gardner, H. (1985). *The minds new science: A history of the cognitive revolution.* New York: Basic Books.

Gentner, D. & Stevens, A. L. (Eds.) (1983). *Mental models.* Hillsdale, New Jersey: Lawrence Erlbaum Associates Inc.

Gergen, K. J. & Gergen, M. M. (1981). *Social psychology.* London: Harcourt Brace Jovanovich.

Gerrig, R. J. (1986). Process models and pragmatics. In N. E. Sharkey (Ed.), *Advances in cognitive science.* New York: Ellis Horwood.

Gilhooly, K. J. (1982). *Thinking; directed, undirected and creative.* London: Academic Press.

Goldstein, I. P. & Bobrow, D. (1980). Descriptions for a programming environment. *Proceedings of the 1st annual national conference on artificial intelligence.* Stanford. CA, USA.

Goldthorpe, J. E. (1974). *An introduction to sociology.* Second edition. Cambridge: Cambridge University Press.

Good, M., Spine, T. M., Whiteside, J., & George, P. (1986). User-derived impact analysis as a tool for usability engineering. In M. Mantei & P. Orbeton (Eds.), *Human factors in computer systems–III: Proceedings of the CHI '86 Conference, Boston.* Amsterdam: Elsevier.

Good, M. J., Whiteside, J. A., Wixon, D. R., & Jones, S. J. (1984). Building a user-driven interface. *Communications of the ACM, 27 (10),* 1032–1043.

Goodall, A. (1985). *A guide to expert systems.* Oxford: Learned Information.

Goodman, B. A. (1987). Repairing reference identification failures by relaxation. In R. G. Reilly (Ed.), *Communication failure in dialogue and discourse.* Amsterdam: Elsevier.

Gould, J. D. (in press). How to design usable systems. In M. Helander (Ed.),

Handbook of human-computer interaction. Amsterdam: North-Holland.

Gould, J. D. & Lewis, C. H. (1985). Designing for usability–key principles and what designers think. *Communications of the ACM, 28,* 300–311.

Graf, W., Elsinger, P., & Krueger, H. (1987). Methods for the ergonomic evaluation of alphanumeric computer-generated displays. In H. J. Bullinger & B. Shackel (Eds.), *Human-computer interaction–Interact '87: Proceedings of the second IFIP conference on human-computer interaction, Stuttgart.* Amsterdam: North-Holland.

Green, T. R. G. (1986). Cognitive aspects of HCI. *Computer Bulletin, September.*

Green, T. R. G. (1987). Limited theories as a framework for human-computer interaction. Invited address to the Austrian Computer Society's 6th annual interdisciplinary workshop. *Mental models and human-computer interaction. Schärding, Austria, 9th–12th June, 1987.*

Grishman, R. (1986). *Computational linguistics: An introduction.* Cambridge: Cambridge University Press.

Grunenenfelder, T. M. & Whitten, W. B. (1984). Augmenting generic research with prototype evaluation experience in applying generic research to specific products. In B. Shackel (Ed.), *Human-computer interaction–Interact '84: Proceedings of the first IFIP conference on human-computer interaction, London.* Amsterdam: North-Holland.

Habermas, J. (1981). *The theory of communicative action: One, reason and the rationalization of society.* English translation 1984. Massachusetts: Beacon Press.

Halasz, F. & Moran, T. P. (1982). Analogy considered harmful. In *Human factors in computer systems, conference proceedings, Gaithersburg, Maryland.* ACM.

Hammond, N. V. & Allinson, L. J. (1987). The travel metaphor as design principle and training aid for navigating around complex systems. In D. Diaper & R. Winder (Eds.), *People and computers III, proceedings of the third conference on human-computer interaction.* Cambridge: Cambridge University Press.

Hammond, N. V. & Barnard, P. J. (1985). Dialogue design: Characteristics of user knowledge. In A. F. Monk (Ed.), *Fundamentals of human-computer interaction.* London: Academic Press.

Hammond, N. V., Barnard, P. J., Clark, I. A., Morton, J., & Long, J. B. (1980). *Structure and content in interactive dialogue.* IBM Hursley Human Factors Report, HF034.

Hammond, N. V., Hinton, G., Barnard, P. J., MacLean, A., Long, J., & Whitefield, A. (1984). Evaluating the interface of document processors: A comparison of expert judgement and user observation. In B. Shackel (Ed.), *Human-computer interaction–Interact '84: Proceedings of the first IFIP conference on human-computer interaction, London* Amsterdam: North-Holland.

Hammond, N. V., Jorgensen, A., MacLean, A., Barnard, P. J., & Long, J. (1983a). Design practice and interface usability: Evidence from interviews with designers. In A. Janda (Ed.), *Human factors in computer systems: Proceedings of the CHI '83 conference, Boston.* Amsterdam: North-Holland.

Hammond, N. V., Morton, J., Barnard, P. J., Long, J. B., & Clark, I. A. (1987). Characterizing user performance in command-driven dialogue. *Behaviour &*

Information Technology, 6.

Hammond, N. V., Morton, J., MacLean, A., & Barnard, P. J. (1983b). Fragments and signposts: User's models of systems, In *Proceedings of the 10th international conference on human factors in telecommunications, Helsinki, June,* 81–88.

Harker, S. D. P. & Eason, K. D. (1985). Task analysis and definition of user needs. In *IFAC conference proceedings on the Man-Machine Interface, Italy.*

Hayes-Roth, F. (1984). Knowledge-based expert systems—the state of the art in the US. In J. Fox (Ed.), *Expert systems: State of the art report.* Maidenhead: Pergamon Infotech.

Hayes-Roth, F. (1985). Knowledge-based expert systems—the state of the art in the US. *The Knowledge Engineering Review, 1 (2),* 18–27.

Hayes-Roth, F., Waterman, D. A., & Lenet, D. B. (1983). *Building expert systems.* Reading, Massachusetts: Addison-Wesley.

Hewett, T. T. (1986). The role of iterative evaluation in designing systems for usability. In M. D. Harrison & A. F. Monk (Eds.), *People & computers: Designing for usability. Proceedings of the second conference of the BCS HCI specialist group* Cambridge: Cambridge University Press.

Hillman, D. J. (1985). Artificial intelligence. *Human Factors, 27 (1),* 21–31.

Hirschheim, R. (1985). *Organizational aspects of office automation.* New York: Wiley.

Hirschheim, R., Land, F., & Smithson, S. (1984). Implementing computer-based information systems in organizations: Issues and strategies. In B. Shackel (Ed.), *Human-computer interaction–Interact '84: Proceedings of the first IFIP conference on human-computer interaction, London.* Amsterdam: North-Holland.

Howard, S. & Murray, D. M. (1987). A taxonomy of evaluation techniques for HCI. In H. J. Bullinger & B. Shackel (Eds.), *Human-computer interaction–Interact '87: Proceedings of the second IFIP conference on human-computer interaction, Stuttgart.* Amsterdam: North-Holland.

Hutchins, E. L., Hollan, J. D., & Norman, D. A. (1986). Direct manipulation interfaces. In D. A. Norman & S. W. Draper (Eds.), *User centred system design: New perspectives on human-computer interaction.* Hillsdale, New Jersey: Lawrence Erlbaum Associates Inc.

Hutt, A. F. T., Donnelly, N., Macaulay, L. A., & Fowler, C. J. H. (1987). Describing a product opportunity: A method of understanding the users' environment. In D. Diaper & R. Winder (Eds.), *People & computers III. Proceedings of the third conference of the BCS HCI specialist group* Cambridge: Cambridge University Press.

Jackson, M. A. (1983). *System development.* London: Prentice Hall.

Jacob, R. J. K. (1982). Using formal specifications in the design of a human-computer interface. In *Human factors in computer systems, conference proceedings, Gaithersburg, Maryland.* ACM.

Jacob, R. J. K. (1985). An executable specification technology for describing human-computer interaction. In H. R. Hartson (Ed.), *Advances in human-computer interaction.* Norwood, New Jersey: Ablex.

James, W. (1890). *The principles of psychology*. New York: Holt, Rinehart & Winston.

Jerrams-Smith, J. (1987). An expert system within a supportive interface for Unix. *Behaviour & Information Technology, 6 (1)*, 37–41.

Johnson, L. & Keranov, E. T. (1984). *Expert systems technology*. Tunbridge Wells: Abacus.

Johnson, P., Diaper, D., & Long, J. (1984). Task, skills and knowledge: Task analysis for knowledge based descriptions. In B. Shackel (Ed.), *Human-computer interaction–Interact '84: Proceedings of the first IFIP conference on human-computer interaction, London*. Amsterdam: North- Holland.

Johnson-Laird, P. N. (1981). Mental models in cognitive science. In D. A. Norman (Ed.), *Perspectives on cognitive science*. Norwood, New Jersey: Ablex.

Johnson-Laird, P. N. (1983). *Mental models: Towards a cognitive science of language, inference, and consciousness*. Cambridge: Cambridge University Press.

Kagan, J. (1966). Reflection-impulsivity: The generability and diagnosis of conceptual tempo. *Journal of Abnormal Psychology, 71*, 17–22.

Kelly, J. (1987). Intelligent machines what chance? In Hallam & Mellish (Eds.), *Advances in artificial intelligence*. New York: Wiley.

Kieras, D. E. & Bovair, S. (1984). The role of a mental model in learning to operate a device. *Cognitive Science, 8*, 255–273.

Kieras, D. E. & Polson, P. G. (1985). An approach to the formal analysis of user complexity. *International Journal of Man-Machine Studies, 22 (4)*, 365–394.

Kidd, A. L. (1985). Human factors in expert systems. *Data Processing, 27 (4)*, 15–17.

Kidd, A.L. (1982). Problems in man-machine dialogue design. *International conference on man-machine systems, 6–9th July 1982, UMIST, Manchester*.

Kidd, A. L. & Cooper, M. B. (1985). Man-machine interface issues in the construction and use of an expert system. *International Journal of Man- Machine Studies, 22*, 91–102.

Kirby, M. A. R., Fowler, C. J. H., & Macaulay, L. A. (1988). Overcoming obstacles to the validation of user requirements. In *People & computers IV. Proceedings of the fourth conference of the BCS HCI specialist group*. Cambridge: Cambridge University Press.

Kling, R. (1980). Social analyses of computing: Theoretical perspectives in empirical research. *Computing Surveys 12 (1)*, 61-110.

Knapp, B. G., Moses, F. L., & Gellman, L. H. (1982). Information highlighting on complex displays. In A. N. Badre & B. Shneiderman (Eds.), *Directions in human-computer interaction* Norwood, New Jersey: Ablex.

Kofer, G. R. (1985). Future uses of future offices. In A. F. Monk (Ed.), *Fundamentals of human-computer interaction*. London: Academic Press.

Kolodner, J. L. & Riesbeck, C. K. (Eds.) (1986). *Experience, memory and reasoning*. Hillsdale, New Jersey: Lawrence Erlbaum Associates Inc.

Kroemer, K. H. E. (1972). Human engineering the keyboard. *Human Factors, 14 (1)*, 51–63.

Lakoff, G. & Johnson, M. (1981). The metaphorical structure of the human-conceptual system. In D. A. Norman (Ed.), *Perspectives on cognitive science*. Norwood, New Jersey: Ablex.

Lakoff, G. & Johnson, M. (1980). *Metaphors we live by*. Chicago: University of Chicago Press.

Lang, T., Lang, K. N., & Auld, L. (1981). Support for users of operating systems and applications software. *International Journal of Man- Machine Studies, 14,* 269–282.

Langacker, R. W. (1986). An introduction to cognitive grammar. *Cognitive Science, 10,* 1–40.

Lawrence, K. (1986). Artificial intelligence in the man/machine interface. *Data Processing, 28 (5),* 244–246.

Ledgard, H. F. & Singer, A. (1978). Formal definition and design. *COINS technical report 78-01,* University of Massachusetts, Amherst.

Leventhal, H. & Scherer, K. R. (1987). The relationship of emotion to cognition: A functional approach to a semantic controversy. *Cognition & Emotion, 1,* 3–28.

Leveson, N. G., Wasserman, A. I., & Berry, D. M. (1983). BASIS: A behavioural approach to the specification of information systems. *Information Systems, 8 (1),* 15–23.

Lewis, C. & Norman, D. A. (1986). Designing for error. In D. A. Norman & S. W. Draper (Eds.), *User centred system design: New perspectives on human-computer interaction*. Hillsdale, New Jersey: Lawrence Erlbaum Associates Inc.

Lund, M. A. (1985). Evaluating the user interface: The candid camera approach. In L. Borman, & W. Curtis (Eds.), *Human factors in computer systems–II: Proceedings of the CHI '85 conference, San Francisco*. Amsterdam: North-Holland.

Macaulay, L. A., Fowler, C. J. H., & Hutt, A. (1986). Human factors in the IT specification process. *Computer Bulletin, 2 (3),* 10–12.

MacLean, A., Barnard, P. J., & Wilson, M. (1986). Rapid prototyping of dialogue for human factors research: the EASIE approach. In M. D. Harrison & A. F. Monk (Eds.), *People & Computers: Designing for Usability. Proceedings of the Second Conference of the BCS HCI specialist group*. Cambridge: Cambridge University Press.

Malone, T. W. (1987). Computer support for organizations: Toward an organizational science. In J. M. Carroll (Ed.), *Interfacing thought: Cognitive aspects of human-computer interaction*. Cambridge, Massachusetts: MIT Press.

Malone, T. W. (1986). Human-computer interaction in the year 2000: A contribution to a panel discussion. In M. Mantei & P. Orbeton (Eds.), *Human factors in computer systems–III: Proceedings of the CHI '86 Conference, Boston*. Amsterdam: Elsevier.

Malone, T. W. (1985). Designing organizational interfaces. In L. Borman, & W. Curtis, *Human factors in computer systems–II: Proceedings of the CHI '85 conference, San Francisco*. Amsterdam, Netherlands: North- Holland.

Manktelow, K. I. & Jones, J. (1987). Principles from the psychology of thinking and mental models. In M. M. Gardiner & B. Christie (Eds.), *Applying cognitive psychology to user interface design*. Chichester: Wiley.

Markus, M. L. (1983). Power, politics, and MIS implementation. *Communications of the ACM, 26 (6),* 430–444.

Marsden, P. H. (1989). *Modelling the retrieval of incomplete knowledge*. PhD Thesis, Department of Psychology, University of Manchester, UK.

Marshall, C. J., Christie, B., & Gardiner, M. M. (1987a). Assessment of trends in the technology and techniques of human-computer interaction. In M. M. Gardiner & B. Christie (Eds.), *Applying cognitive psychology to user interface design.* Chichester: Wiley.

Marshall, C. J., Nelson, C., & Gardiner, M. M. (1987b). Design guidelines. In M. M. Gardiner & B. Christie (Eds.), *Applying cognitive psychology to user-interface design.* Chichester: Wiley.

Martin, A. (1972). A new keyboard layout. *Applied Ergonomics, 3 (1).*

Mayer, R. E. (1981). *The promise of cognitive psychology.* San Francisco: Freeman.

McClelland, J. L., Rumelhart, D. E., & the PDP Research Group, (1986a). *Parallel distributed processing: Explorations in the microstructure of cognition. Volume 1: Foundations.* Cambridge, Massachusetts: MIT Press.

McClelland, J. L., Rumelhart, D. E., & the PDP Research Group, (1986b). *Parallel distributed processing: Explorations in the microstructure of cognition. Volume 2: Psychological and biological models.* Cambridge, Massachusetts: MIT Press.

McDonald, J. E., Dearholt, D. W., Paap, K. R., & Schvaneveldt, R. W. (1986). A formal interface design methodology based on user knowledge. In M. Mantei & P. Orbeton (Eds.), Human factors in computer systems - III: Proceedings of the CHI '86 Conference, Boston. Amsterdam: Elsevier.

McMillan, T. C. & Moran, B. P. (1985). Command line structure and dynamic processing of abbreviations in dialogue management. *Interfaces in Computing, 3,* 249-257.

Michaelis, P. R., Miller, M. L., & Hendler, J. A. (1982). Artificial intelligence and human factors engineering: A necessary synergism in the interface of the future. In A. N. Badre & B. Shneiderman (Eds.), *Directions in human-computer interaction.* Norwood, New Jersey: Ablex.

Michaelis, P. R. & Wiggins, R. H. (1982). A human factors engineers introduction to speech synthesizers. In A. N. Badre & B. Shneiderman (Eds.), *Directions in human-computer interaction.* Norwood, New Jersey: Ablex.

Miller, G. A. (1979). A very personal history. Talk to cognitive science workshop, Massachusetts Institute of Technology, Cambridge, Massachusetts, 1st June 1979. Cited in: Gardner, H. (1985). *The minds new science: A history of the cognitive revolution.* New York: Basic Books.

Miyata, Y. & Norman, D. A. (1986). Psychological issues in support of multiple activities. In D. A. Norman & S. W. Draper (Eds.), *User centred system design: New perspectives on human-computer interaction.* Hillsdale, New Jersey: Lawrence Erlbaum Associates Inc.

Monk, A. F. (1986). Mode errors: a user-centred analysis and some preventative measures using key-contingent sound. *International Journal of Man-Machine Studies, 24,* 313-327.

Monk, A. F. & Dix, A. (1987). Refining early design decisions with a black-box model. In D Diaper & R. Winder (Eds.), *People & Computers III. Proceedings of the Third Conference of the BCS HCI specialist group.* Cambridge: Cambridge University Press.

Moody, T., Joost, M., & Rodman, R. (1987). The effects of various types of speech output on listener comprehension rates. In H. J. Bullinger & B. Shackel (Eds.),

Human-computer interaction–Interact '87: Proceedings of the second IFIP conference on human-computer interaction, Stuttgart. Amsterdam: North-Holland.

Moran, T. P. (1986). Analytical performance models: A contribution to a panel discussion. In M. Mantei & P. Orbeton (Eds.), *Human factors in computer systems–III: Proceedings of the CHI '86 Conference, Boston.* Amsterdam: Elsevier.

Moran, T. P. (1983). Getting into a system: External-internal task mapping analysis. In A. Janda (Ed.), *Human factors in computer systems: Proceedings of the CHI '83 conference, Boston.* Amsterdam: North-Holland.

Moran, T. P. (1981). The command language grammar: A representation for the user interface of interactive computer systems. *International Journal of Man-Machine Systems, 15 (1),* 3–50.

Morgan, C. C. & Sufrin, B. A. (1984). Specification of the Unix filing system. *IEEE Transactions on Software Engineering, SE-10 (2),* 128–142.

Morris, C. (1946). *Signs, language and behaviour.* New York: Prentice-Hall.

Morton, J., Barnard, P. J., Hammond, N. V., & Long, J. B. (1979). Interacting with a computer: A framework. In E. J. Boutmy & A. Danthine (Eds.), *Teleinformatics '79.* Amsterdam: North-Holland.

Naisbitt, J. (1984). *Megatrends.* New York: Warner Brothers.

Newman, W. M. & Sproull, R. F. (1979). *Principles of interactive computer graphics.* Second edition. New York: McGraw-Hill.

Nickerson, R. S. (1986). *Using computers: Human factors in information systems.* Cambridge, Massachusetts: MIT Press.

Nickerson, R. S. (1981). Some characteristics of conversations. In B. Shackel (Ed.), *Man-computer interaction: Human factors aspects of computers and people.* Rockville, Maryland: Sijthoff & Noordhoff.

Nielsen, J. (1986). A virtual protocol model for computer-human interaction. *International Journal for Man-Machine Studies, 24,* 301–312.

Norman, D. A. (1987). Cognitive engineering—cognitive science. In J. M. Carroll (Ed.), *Interfacing thought: Cognitive aspects of human-computer interaction.* Cambridge, Massachusetts: MIT Press.

Norman, D. A. (1986). Cognitive engineering. In D. A. Norman & S. W. Draper (Eds.), *User centred system design: New perspectives on human-computer interaction.* Hillsdale, New Jersey: Lawrence Erlbaum Associates Inc.

Norman, D. A. (1983a). Design principles for human-computer interfaces. In A. Janda (Ed.), *Human factors in computer systems: Proceedings of the CHI '83 conference, Boston.* Amsterdam: North-Holland.

Norman, D. A. (1983b). Design rules based on analyses of human error. *Communications of the ACM, 26 (4),* 254–258.

Norman, D. A. (1983c). Some observations on mental models. In D. Gentner & A. L. Stevens (Eds.), *Mental Models.* Hillsdale, New Jersey: Lawrence Erlbaum Associates Inc.

Norman, D. A. (1981a). A psychologist views human processing: Human errors and other phenomena suggest processing mechanisms. In *Proceedings of the international joint conference on artificial intelligence, Vancouver.*

Norman, D. A. (1981b). Twelve issues for cognitive science. In D. A. Norman (Ed.), *Perspectives on Cognitive Science.* Norwood, New Jersey: Ablex.

Norman, D. A. (1981c). What is cognitive science?. In D. A. Norman (Ed.), *Perspectives on Cognitive Science*. Norwood, New Jersey: Ablex.

Norman, D. A. & Draper, S. W. (Eds.) (1986). *User centred system design: New perspectives on human-computer interaction*. Hillsdale, New Jersey: Lawrence Erlbaum Associates Inc.

Ogozalek, V. Z. & Praag, J. V. (1986). Comparison of elderly and younger users on keyboard and voice input computer-based composition tasks. In M. Mantei & P. Orbeton (Eds.), *Human factors in computer systems– III: Proceedings of the CHI '86 Conference, Boston*. Amsterdam: Elsevier.

O'Malley, C. E. (1986). Helping users help themselves. In D. A. Norman & S. W. Draper (Eds.), *User centred system design: New perspectives on human-computer interaction*. Hillsdale, New Jersey: Lawrence Erlbaum Associates Inc.

Payne, S. J. (1984). Task-action grammars. In B. Shackel (Ed.), *Human- computer interaction–Interact '84: Proceedings of the first IFIP conference on human-computer interaction, London*. Amsterdam: North- Holland.

Payne, S. J. & Green, T. R. G. (1986). Task-action grammars: A model of the mental representation of task languages. *Human-computer interaction, 2*, 93–133.

Pearson, G. & Weiser, M. (1986). Of moles and men: The design of foot controls for workstations. In M. Mantei & P. Orbeton (Eds.), *Human factors in computer systems–III: Proceedings of the CHI '86 conference, Boston*. Amsterdam: Elsevier.

Pedersen, P. H. (1986). Organizational power systems. In N. Bjørn- Andersen, K. D. Eason, & D. Robey (Eds.) (1987). *Managing computer impact: An international study of management and organizations*. Norwood, New Jersey: Ablex.

Pew, D. (1986). Socio-tech: What is it (and why should we care)? The introduction to a panel discussion at the CHI '86 conference. In M. Mantei & P. Orbeton (Eds.), *Human factors in computer systems–III: Proceedings of the CHI '86 conference, Boston*. Amsterdam: Elsevier.

Pfaff, G. E. (Ed.) (1985). *User interface management systems*. London: Springer Verlag.

Polson, P. G. (1987). A quantitative theory of human-computer interaction. In J. M. Carroll (Ed.), *Interfacing thought: Cognitive aspects of human-computer interaction*. Cambridge, Massachusetts: MIT Press.

Potosnak, K. M. (1986). Classifying users: A hard look at some controversial issues: A contribution to a panel discussion. In M. Mantei & P. Orbeton (Eds.), *Human factors in computer systems–III: Proceedings of the CHI '86 conference, Boston*. Amsterdam, Netherlands: Elsevier.

Price, L. A. & Cordova, C. A. (1983). Use of mouse buttons. In A. Janda (Ed.), *Human factors in computer systems: Proceedings of the CHI '83 conference, Boston*. Amsterdam: North-Holland.

Rasmussen, J. (1985). Trends in human reliability analysis. *Ergonomics, 28 (8)*, 1185–1195.

Rauner, F., Rasmussen, L., & Corbett, J. M. (1988). The social shaping of technology and work: Human centred CIM systems. *AI & Society, 2 (1)*, 47–61.

Reason, J. T. (1988). Cognitive underspecification: Its varieties and consequences. In B. Baars (Ed.), *The psychology of error*. London: Plenum.

Reason, J. T. & Mycielska, K. (1982). *Absent-minded? The psychology of mental lapses and everyday errors*. Englewood Cliffs, New Jersey: Prentice-Hall.

Rector, A. L., Newton, P., & Marsden, P. H. (1985). What kind of system does an expert need? In P. Johnson & S. Cook (Eds.), *People and computers: Designing the interface*. Cambridge: Cambridge University Press.

Reid, P. (1985). Work station design, activities and display techniques. In A. F. Monk (Ed.), *Fundamentals of human-computer interaction*. London: Academic Press.

Reindl, E. (1986). Impact on leadership style. In N. Bjørn-Andersen, K. D. Eason, & D. Robey (Eds.), *Managing computer impact: An international study of management and organizations* Norwood, New Jersey: Ablex.

Reisner, P. (1987). Discussion: HCI, what is it and what research is needed? In J. M. Carroll (Ed.), *Interfacing thought: Cognitive aspects of human-computer interaction* Cambridge, Massachusetts: MIT Press.

Reisner, P. (1982). Further developments towards using formal grammar as a design tool. In *Human factors in computer systems, conference proceedings, Gaithersburg, Maryland*. ACM.

Reisner, P. (1981). Formal grammar and human factors design of an interactive graphics system. *IEEE Transactions on Software Engineering, SE7 (2)*, 229–240.

Reisner, P. (1977). The use of psychological experimentation as an aid to development of a query language. *IEEE Transactions on Software Engineering, SE-3*, 218–229.

Richards, J. T., Boies, S. J., & Gould, J. D. (1986). Rapid prototying and system development: Examination of an interface toolkit for voice and telephony applications. In M. Mantei & P. Orbeton (Eds.), *Human factors in computer systems–III: Proceedings of the CHI '86 conference, Boston*. Amsterdam: Elsevier.

Richardson, A. (1977). Verbalisers-visualisers: A cognitive style dimension. *Journal of Mental Imagery, 1*, 109–125.

Riley, M. & O'Malley, C. (1984). Planning nets: A framework for analyzing user-computer interactions. In B. Shackel (Ed.), *Human-computer interaction– Interact '84: Proceedings of the first IFIP conference on human-computer interaction, London*. Amsterdam: North- Holland.

Rissland, E. (1984). Ingred of intelligent user interfaces. *International Journal of Man-Machine Studies, 21*, 377–388.

Roberts, T. L. & Moran, T. P. (1983). The evaluation of text editors: methodology and empirical results. *Communications of the ACM, 26 (4)*, 265–283.

Rogers, Y. (1986). Evaluating the meaningfulness of icon sets to represent command operations. In M. D. Harrison & A. F. Monk (Eds.), *People & computers: Designing for usability. Proceedings of the second conference of the BCS HCI specialist group*. Cambridge: Cambridge University Press.

Rollins, A. (1985). Speech recognition and manner of speaking in noise and in quiet. In L. Borman & W. Curtis (Eds.), *Human factors in computer systems–II: Proceedings of the CHI '85 conference, San Francisco*. Amsterdam: North-Holland.

Rollins, A., Constantine, B., & Baker, S. (1983). Speech recognition at two field sites. In A. Janda (Ed.), *Human factors in computer systems: Proceedings of the CHI '83 conference, Boston.* Amsterdam: North- Holland.

Rosson, M. B. (1986). Classifying users: A hard look at some controversial issues: A contribution to a panel discussion. In M. Mantei & P. Orbeton (Eds.), *Human factors in computer systems–III: Proceedings of the CHI '86 Conference, Boston* Amsterdam: Elsevier.

Rosson, M. B. & Cecala, A. J. (1986). Designing a quality voice: An analysis of listeners' reactions to synthetic voices. In M. Mantei & P. Orbeton (Eds.), *Human factors in computer systems–III: Proceedings of the CHI '86 conference, Boston.* Amsterdam: Elsevier.

Rubinstein, R. & Hersh, H. (1984). *The human factor: Designing computer systems for people.* Burlington, Massachusetts: Digital Press.

Rumelhart, D. E. & Norman, D. A. (1981). Analogical processes in learning. In J. R. Anderson (Ed.), *Cognitive skills and their acquisition.* Hillsdale, New Jersey: Lawrence Erlbaum Associates Inc.

Runciman, C. & Hammond, N. V. (1986). User programs: a way to match computer systems and human cognition. In M. D. Harrison & A. F. Monk (Eds.), *People & computers: Designing for usability. Proceedings of the second conference of the BCS HCI specialist group.* Cambridge: Cambridge University Press.

Ruge Jervell, H. & Olsen, K. A. (1985). Icons in man-machine communication. *Behaviour & Information Technology, 4 (3),* 249–254.

Sauter, S. L., Gottlieb, M. S., & Jones, K. C. (1982). A systems analysis of stress-strain in VDT operation. In *Human factors in computer systems, conference proceedings, Gaithersburg, Maryland.* ACM.

Scane, R. (1987). A historical perspective. In M. M. Gardiner & B. Christie (Eds.), *Applying cognitive psychology to user-interface design.* Chichester: Wiley & Sons.

Scharer, L. L. (1983). User training: Less is more. *Datamation,* 175–182.

Schein, E. H. (1970). *Organizational psychology.* Second edition. Englewood Cliffs, New Jersey: Prentice-Hall.

Shackel, B. (1986). Ergonomics in design for usability. In M. D. Harrison & A. F. Monk (Eds.), *People & computers: Designing for usability. Proceedings of the second conference of the BCS HCI specialist group.* Cambridge: Cambridge University Press.

Shackel, B. (1985). Ergonomics in information technology in Europe—a review. *Behaviour & Information Technology, 4 (4),* 263–287.

Shackel, B. (1984). Information technology—a challenge to ergonomics and design! *Behaviour & Information Technology, 3 (4),* 263–275.

Shackel, B. (1981). The concept of usability. In *Proceedings of the IBM software and information usability symposium.* 1–30. New York: Ploughkeepsie.

Shaklee, H. & Fischhoff, B. (1982). Strategies of information search. *Memory and Cognition, 10,* 520–530.

Shank, R. C. (1986). *Explanation patterns: Understanding mechanically and creatively*. Hillsdale, New Jersey: Lawrence Erlbaum Associates Inc.

Shaver, K. G. (1977). *Principles of social psychology*. Cambridge, Massachusetts: Winthrop.

Sheehy, N. P. (1987). Nonverbal behaviour in dialogue. In R. G. Reilly (Ed.), *Communication failure in dialogue and discourse*. Amsterdam: Elsevier.

Sheehy, N. P. & Chapman, A, J, (1987). Nonverbal behaviour at the human-computer interface. *International Review of Ergonomics, 1*, 159–172.

Shneiderman, B. (1987). *Designing the user interface: Strategies for effective human-computer interaction*. Reading, Massachusetts, USA: AddisonWesley.

Shneiderman, B. (1986). Human-computer interaction in the year 2000: A contribution to a panel discussion. In M. Mantei & P. Orbeton (Eds.), *Human factors in computer system–III: Proceedings of the CHI '86 conference, Boston*. Amsterdam, Netherlands: Elsevier.

Shneiderman, B. (1982). The future of interaction systems and the emergence of direct manipulation. *Behaviour and Information Technology, 1*, 237–256.

Shneiderman, B. (1974). A computer graphics system for polynomials. *The Mathematics Teacher*, February, 111–113.

Short, P. L. (1953). The objective study of mental imagery. *British Journal of Psychology, 44*, 38–51.

Shortliffe, E. H. (1976). *Computer based medical consultations: MYCIN*. New York: American Elsevier.

Sluizer, S. & Cashman, P. (1985). XCP: An experimental tool for managing cooperative activity. *Proceedings of the ACM Computer Science conference, New Orleans, LA*.

Smith, H. T. (1980). Human-computer communication. In H. T. Smith & T. R. G Green (Eds.), *Human-computer interaction*. London: Academic Press.

Stamper, R. (1988). Pathologies of AI: Responsible use of artificial intelligence in professional work. *AI & Society, 2*, 3–16.

Steward, D. V. (1987). *Software engineering with systems analysis and design*. Monterey, California: Brooks/Cole.

Stewart, T. F. M. (1976). Displays and the software interface. *Applied Ergonomics, 7*, 137–146.

Storrs, G., Rivers, R., & Canter, D. (1984). The future of man-machine interface research: A discussion and a framework for research. *Applied Ergonomics, 15 (1)*, 61–63.

Strassman, P. A. (1985). *Information payoff*. New York: The Free Press.

Straub, J. M. & Straub, J. R. (1987). Comparative factors in user acceptance of office automation. In H. J. Bullinger & B. Shackel (Eds.), *Human-computer interaction–Interact '87: Proceedings of the second IFIP conference on human-computer interaction, Stuttgart*. Amsterdam: NorthHolland.

Suchman, L. A. (1988). *Plans and situations: The problems of human-machine communications*. Cambridge: Cambridge University Press.

Sufrin, B. A. (1986). Formal methods and the design of effective user interfaces. In M. D. Harrison & A. F. Monk (Eds.), *People & computers: Designing for usability. Proceedings of the second conference of the BCS HCI specialist group* Cambridge: Cambridge University Press.

Sufrin, B. A., Morgan, C. C., Sørensen, I., & Hayes, I. J. (1985). *Notes for a Z handbook: Part 1, the mathematical language.* Oxford: Programming Research Group.

Thimbleby, H. W. (1986). User interface design and formal methods. *Computer Bulletin, 2 (3)*, 13–15.

Thimbleby, H. W. (1985). User interface design principles. In A. F. Monk (Ed.), *Fundamentals of human-computer interaction.* London: Academic Press.

Thomas, J. (1986). Human-computer interaction in the year 2000: A contribution to a panel discussion. In M. Mantei & P. Orbeton (Eds.), *Human factors in computer systems–III: Proceedings of the CHI '86 Conference, Boston.* Amsterdam: Elsevier.

Tognazzini, B. (1986). Usability testing in the real world: A contribution to a panel discussion. In M. Mantei & P. Orbeton (Eds.), *Human factors in computer systems–III: Proceedings of the CHI '86 Conference, Boston.* Amsterdam: Elsevier.

Twigger, D. (1986). *Usability: definition, operationalization, measurement and impact on software design.* Internal report, HCI Research Unit, Huddersfield Polytechnic, UK.

Turner, M. (1985). A consultant's view of expert systems. *Data Processing, 27 (4)*, 12–14.

Turing, A. M. (1950). Computing machinery and intelligence. *Mind, 59* (236).

Waern, Y. & Rollenhagen, C. (1983). Reading from visual display units (VDUs). *International Journal of Man-Machine Studies 18*, 441–465.

Wason, P. C. (1966). Reasoning. In B. M. Foss (Ed.), *New horizons in psychology.* Harondsworth, Middlesex: Penguin.

Wasserman, A. I. (1979). *The data management facilities of PLAIN. Proceedings of the ACM SIGMOD conference, May.*

Wasserman, A. I. (1985). Extending state transition diagrams for the specification of human-computer interaction. *IEEE Transactions on Software Engineering, SE-11 (8)*, 699–713.

Wasserman, A. I. & Shewmake, D. T. (1985). The role of prototypes in the User Software Engineering (USE) methodology. In H. R. Hartson (Ed.), *Advances in Human-Computer Interaction.* Norwood, New Jersey: Ablex.

Wasserman, A. I., Pircher, P. A., Shewmake, D. T., & Kersten, M. L. (1985). Developing interactive information systems with the User Software Engineering methodology. *IEEE Transactions on Software Engineering, SE-12 (2)*, 326–345.

Wasserman, A. I., Riet, R. P. van de, & Kerslen, M. L. (1981). PLAIN: An algorithmic language for interactive information systems. In J. C. van Vliet & J. W. Bakker (Eds.), *Algorithmic Languages.* Amsterdam: North Holland.

Waterworth, J. A. & Lo, A. (1985). Example of an experiment: Evaluating some speech synthesizers for public announcements. In A. F. Monk (Ed.), *Fundamentals of human-computer interaction.* London: Academic Press.

Westin, A. F., Schweder, H. A., Baker, M. A., & Lehman, S. (1985).*The changing workplace: A guide to managing the people, organization, and regulatory aspects of office technology.* White Plains, New York: Knowledge Industry.

Whiteside, J. (1986). Classifying users: A hard look at some controversial issues: A contribution to a panel discussion. In M. Mantei & P. Orbeton (Eds.), *Human factors in computer systems–III: Proceedings of the CHI '86 Conference, Boston.* Amsterdam, Netherlands: Elsevier.

Whiteside, J., Jones, S., Levy, P. S., & Wixon, D. (1985). User performance with command, menu and iconic interfaces. In L. Borman & W. Curtis (Eds.), *Human factors in computer systems–II: Proceedings of the CHI '85 conference, San Francisco.* Amsterdam: North-Holland.

Whiteside, J. & Wixon, D. (1987). Discussion: Improving human-computer interaction—a quest for cognitive science. In J. M. Carroll (Ed.), *Interfacing thought: Cognitive aspects of human-computer interaction.* Cambridge, Massachusetts: MIT Press.

Winograd, T. & Flores, C. F. (1986).*Understanding computers and cognition: A new foundation for design.* New Jersey: Ablex Publishing Corporation.

Witkin, H. A. (1976). Cognitive styles in learning and teaching. In S. Messick, (Ed.), *Individuality in learning.* San Francisco, USA: Jossey-Bass.

Wixon, D., Whiteside, J., Good, M., & Jones, S. (1983). Building a user defined interface. In A. Janda (Ed.), *Human factors in computer systems: Proceedings of the CHI '83 conference, Boston.* Amsterdam: North-Holland.

Woods, D. D. (1984). Visual momentum: A concept to improve the cognitive coupling of person and computer. *International Journal of Man-Machine Systems, 21,* 229–244.

Wright, P. & Bason, G. (1982). Detour routes to usability: A comparison of alternative approaches to multipurpose software design. *International Journal of Man-Machine Studies, 18,* 391–400.

Wundt, W. (1907). *Outlines of psychology.* Third edition. Leipzig: Engelmann.

Young, R. M. (1985). *User models as design tools for software engineers.* Unpublished paper given at Alvey workshop, September 1985, Loughborough, UK.

Young, R. M. (1984). Human interface aspects of expert sytems. In J. Fox (Ed.), *Expert Systems: State of the art report.* Maidenhead: Pergamon Infotech.

Young, R. M. (1981). The machine inside the machine: Users models of pocket calculators. *International Journal of Man-Machine Studies, 15,* 87–134.

Young, R. M. & Harris, J. E. (1986). A viewdata-structure editor designed around task/action mapping. In M. D. Harrison & A. F. Monk (Eds.), *People & computers: Designing for usability. Proceedings of the second conference of the BCS HCI specialist group.* Cambridge: Cambridge University Press.

Young, R. M. & Simon, T. (1987). Planning in the context of human-computer interaction. In D Diaper & R. Winder (Eds.), *People & computers III. Proceedings of the third conference of the BCS HCI specialist group.* Cambridge: Cambridge University Press.

Zoltan, E. & Chapanis, A. (1982). What do professional persons think about computers?. *Behaviour and Information Technology, 1,* 55–68.

Author Index

Subject Index